The Last Pharaoh: BOOK II

by Jay Penner

Series

Book I: *Regent*

Book II: *Queen*

Book III: *Empress* (final)

Prequel novella: *A Dangerous Daughter*

https://jaypenner.com

To my granduncle. He was an incredible storyteller, hymn singer, and a man who painted a thousand mythical worlds to my kid eyes.

Cover designed by Jay Penner

This book is a work of fiction. Names, characters, places, and incidents either are products of the author's imagination or are used fictitiously. Any resemblance to actual persons, living or dead, events, or locales is entirely coincidental.

Jay Penner https://www.jaypenner.com

Printed in the United States of America

First Printing: December 2020

2.1 2021.11.09.06.19.19
Produced using publishquickly
https://publishquickly.com

JAY PENNER
HISTORY AND FANTASY

Choose your interest! A gritty and treacherous journey with Cleopatra in the Last Pharaoh trilogy, or thrilling stories full of intrigue and conflict in the Whispers of Atlantis anthology set in the ancient world.

THE LAST PHARAOH

WHISPERS OF ATLANTIS

https://jaypenner.com

BEFORE YOU READ

———◇———

This book continues from where Book I ends. For your convenience, the opening chapter offers a recap of the events thus far. It's worth remembering that almost everything we know about the principal characters comes from a stilted *Roman vantage* written **seventy to two-hundred years** *after* the major events in this book. And while the novel aligns to major milestones as mentioned in ancient sources, it is important to recognize that this trilogy is a *novel*, and at its heart, the purpose is to take you to an ancient world and entertain you. This is not an academic paper!

The rest, well, how do you know *it didn't happen?*

ANACHRONISMS

an act of attributing customs, events, or objects to a period to which they do not belong

Writing in the ancient past sometimes makes it difficult to explain everyday terms. Therefore, I have taken certain liberties so that the reader is not burdened by linguistic gymnastics or forced to do mental math (how far is 60 stadia again? What is an Artaba?). My usage is meant to convey the meaning behind the term, rather than striving for historical accuracy. I hope that you will come along for the ride, even as you notice that certain concepts may not have existed during the period of the book. For example:

Directions—North, South, East, West.

Time—Years, Minutes, Hours, Weeks, Months, Years.

Distance—Meters, Miles.

Measures—Gallons, Tons.

DRAMATIS PERSONAE

———◇———

Cleopatra–Queen of Egypt and Pharaoh

Theodotus–former Teacher of rhetoric

Arsinoe–Cleopatra's younger sister

Apollodorus the Sicilian–Commander of Cleopatra's army

Kadmos–Captain in Cleopatra's army

Herod–Idumean Arab appointed as King of Jews, ruler of Judaea

Mark Antony–Roman Consul, General

Caesar Octavian–Nephew/Adoptive son of Julius Caesar

TERMS

Gladius–a 1.5 to 2 ft. long sword, typically used by Roman soldiers

Uraeus Crown–the Pharaonic crown with the upright cobra in the front

Shendyt–Egyptian attire: skirt-like garment worn around the waist, to the ankles.

Chiton, Peplos–Greek gowns

DIVINITIES

Isis was an Egyptian goddess, her husband/brother was Osiris, and their son was Horus (represented as a falcon). Ra was a principal deity represented by the Sun. Cleopatra often presented herself as Isis (or as Aphrodite who was the Greek equivalent of Isis).

REGIONS

Google Maps (c) 2021

Note: The eastern Parthian empire (not shown on this map, but would appear to the right) roughly spanned portions of current Syria, Iraq, and Iran.

PART I

Her Majesty Queen Cleopatra, having graced the people for **twenty-two years** since her arrival on this earth, has ruled her subjects for **five years** after ascending the throne as Regent.

ALEXANDRIA
CLEOPATRA

Cleopatra sat on her gilded throne and gently slid her hands on the armrest. She rubbed the ruby studs and marveled at the craftsmanship. The throne was hers, finally. Her meek younger brother, Ptolemy XIV, Ptolemy Theos Philopater, would be quiet and obedient beside her, and she would rule as an absolute monarch.

What a journey it had been! She sat and remembered the life that got her here. How gladly she had accepted the role of regent, at sixteen years of age, as her father lay dying. Pothinus, the chief advisor, had turned on her fairly quickly, siding with her younger brother Ptolemy XIII. The cabal, consisting of Pothinus, Achillas the general, and Theodotus the teacher, had instigated riots, and she had personally gone to quell them. She had even tried to mend the broken relationship, but her brother and his advisors had tried to ambush and kill her. Apollodorus had saved her. And then, she had endured the shame of being run out of Alexandria, causing her to travel to Syria to build a mercenary army. She fondly remembered Kadmos, that loud-mouthed haggler and his uncouth ways, and smiled at the memories of his clumsy flirtation. She had returned with him and a new army, and held off Ptolemy's forces at Pelusium.

But Pompey Magnus, Consul of Rome and Caesar's rival, why did he come to seek asylum in Egypt after losing to Caesar? Theodotus and Pothinus had conspired to kill Pompey on his boat, a dastardly act carried out by Achillas. Caesar had then landed in Alexandria and asked her and her brother to disband their armies. She remembered the battle with Achillas' forces, and then the dangerous journey through the swamps, with Apollodorus, to seek audience with Caesar. Her cheeks reddened at the times they had made love, knowing the limited future of their relationship. The tension and stress of the final moments before she was unveiled before Caesar caused nightmares even now. But she had succeeded in gaining Caesar's confidence. Pothinus was caught in a treacherous act and executed. Her seditious sister Arsinoe, who had abandoned her in Pelusium and joined the enemy, was exchanged for her brother. Caesar had allowed her brother to leave in the hopes he would stand down the army and reconcile, but he had run away to continue the war on Caesar. Eventually, Caesar prevailed. Her brother drowned in the Nile, or so they said for his body was never found, and her sister was off to Rome as a prisoner. Achillas had died at the instigation of Arsinoe. Theodotus had vanished. Caesar had instated her the Queen, with her remaining younger brother/husband Ptolemy XIV as King. But Ptolemy XIV Theos Philopater was too young, powerless, and weak, and she held all the authority.

Apollodorus, Metjen, Kadmos, and her other loyalists were still out in the country, waiting for her orders to return. They would begin arriving soon to be with her.

Cleopatra looked forward to a new beginning.

CHAPTER 1
ALEXANDRIA
CLEOPATRA

Kadmos walked into the throne room with a huge smile. The big and burly rascal's beard had grown longer, his belly larger, and his eyes twinkled with mischief when he spotted Charmian behind her. Metjen, the diminutive and sharp-minded Egyptian advisor, almost galloped across the room and slid across the floor as he knelt before her.

Kadmos too managed to pay respect to the protocol as he knelt beside Metjen, but neither man could control their glee.

She almost had the urge to rise from her throne and embrace them with happiness but checked herself. It had now been a month since Caesar had departed. Alexandria was calm; Caesar's general, Valentinus, was an exceptional peacekeeper who managed to not just quell unrest, but he had brought order and tranquility to the city that had suffered for over a year. His legions respected him, and she had learned how to deal with the gruff, rule-rigid old soldier. And then, having established security, she had summoned those that had stood by her.

"I have prayed the gods for this day, Your Majesty," Metjen said.

"We all have, Your Majesty," Kadmos said, helpfully, while his eyes darted like a bee towards Charmian.

"You may rise," she said, smiling herself. "The mighty Ra and divine Horus have blessed me, giving loyal men like you, even you Kadmos."

They rose and milled about. Eventually, Apollodorus made his entrance, and he had dressed for the occasion. The handsome officer had found himself an impeccable uniform with a blue-dyed cuirass, green-plumed helmet, a very roman-styled rich leather *pteruges*, and a finely crafted scabbard that held his sword.

Her heart beat harder as he neared, and his eyes were bright with devotion and, perhaps love, she could not say. Apollodorus knelt before her.

"Rise, Apollodorus," she said, controlling her urge to rush to him. There would be time for that later.

Kadmos could not control his tongue. "Inspired by the peacocks in the countryside, eh, general?" he asked, leading Metjen to shake his head and for Apollodorus to give him a dirty look before breaking out into a grin.

"Better than being inspired by pigs, Kadmos," Apollodorus retorted, causing them all to chortle. She laughed along with them, partly with relief knowing that these men were getting along with each other rather than being at each other's throat, needing her to intervene.

Once the pleasantries were over, she turned to Charmian, who stood quietly nearby.

"Well, Charmian, have you made arrangements for Kadmos' quarters?" she asked.

Kadmos danced his bushy eyebrows, and Charmian turned several shades of red. She stammered. "Yes, Your Majesty, and, uh, His Excellency Metjen's as well."

"Excellent. Why don't you show Kadmos his quarters while I confer with Metjen and Apollodorus?" she said, enjoying Charmian's discomfort. "Don't be shy!" she said, further embarrassing the girl.

Charmian looked coyly at Kadmos, and he pretended to walk seriously to her side. "I have waited for this day, I meant, for my quarters, Your Excellency," he said to her, causing everyone to laugh. As she watched them go, Cleopatra was filled with a strange sense of happiness and sadness. How long would this last?

And how would she deal with Apollodorus?

She turned to Metjen and Apollodorus. "Well, unless you wish to retire and rest, we must talk of the affairs of the kingdom."

"We are ready and at your service, Your Majesty," Metjen said. In his crisp white shendyt and carefully drawn eye-lining, Metjen exuded confidence and erudition. She would rely much on him.

They walked to a section of the hall to sit down and converse. "What is the situation in the countryside?"

"An uneasy calm prevails. News of your ascension has traveled wide and far, and people are generally happy that there is peace. There is some murmur about His Majesty Ptolemy's disappearance, and they hope there was an older king, but unless we press hard on taxes or impose new restrictions, we can expect peace," Metjen said, summarizing. Apollodorus nodded solemnly.

"And what of the mercenaries? Where is Fabricius?" She asked, referring to the Roman accountant who came with Kadmos' forces in Syria.

"He has vanished. We think he got tired of waiting, for he complained incessantly. We have paid most of the mercenaries–many have returned to their homes, but the rest are settling in the South, ready to be called if needed."

She was relieved. Everything seemed manageable. "Horus smiles," she said.

"And here, Your Majesty, are you safe and protected?" Apollodorus asked.

Oh, to hold him.

"General Valentinus is exceptional. You will get to meet him. We will have to resolve the question of how to separate the duties of the Roman legions and our own," she said.

They then spoke of administrative priorities and tax relief to the southern nomes, until she could control no more. "Metjen, I look forward to continuing this conversation tomorrow. Pothinus' quarters and estate will be yours."

Metjen bowed and thanked her for the generosity. She was filled with fondness for this gentle, soft-spoken man whose mind shined more brilliantly than most she knew.

"Apollodorus, walk with me to my quarters, for I have a few military matters to discuss."

Metjen said nothing, though she caught him smile just the slightest bit, before he bowed and left. Apollodorus walked next to her, but he said not a word, and her own chest felt like it was being boxed by an unruly and riotous heart. It had been nearly a year since she had inhaled his scent or felt his hair.

And now she was the queen and undisputed power. She could do what she wanted to, as long as she balanced the stakes of her kingdom and ambitions with those of her emotion.

They walked together quietly; the tension palpable and as tight as a rope tied to a cedar tree and pulled by an elephant. When they reached her quarters, she dismissed her slaves and maids. When he walked in, she ordered him to close the door.

And then, seeing his nervousness, she walked boldly to him, rose on her toes, grabbed his thick neck, and pulled his face to hers.

CHAPTER 2

ALEXANDRIA

CLEOPATRA

"As much as it bears heavily on me, Apollodorus, you must find a wife. This cannot continue, for I must show that I am waiting for Caesar," she said, as she lay on his chest.

"I understand, Your Majesty," he said, never once slipping into familiarity in these slippery circumstances. "But it is–"

She put a finger on his lips. "Yes, you've told me before. *How can you be with someone once you've been with me.* Well, I was with a half-bald man over twice my age, and I grew to love and respect him. And you must try as well."

"I have no desire to be with a half-bald man twice my age, Your Majesty," he said, causing her to laugh and slap him.

"Kadmos has influenced you," she said. "But you must take my words seriously, or I shall have to order you and arrange a marriage."

He nodded solemnly. "I will try. I will. I know that the well-being of a nation and the future of kingdoms is at stake."

She sighed. They lay that way quietly, listening to the sounds of the night. Milky light suffused their chamber, coming from a large window that overlooked the magnificent Lighthouse and the dark sea.

"Is he mine?" Apollodorus asked, suddenly.

She was jolted by the question. "What do you mean?"

"Is the boy mine?"

She calmed herself. "No, he is not. He was born weeks after the boundary of doubt. He is Caesar's, Apollodorus, and we must not speak of this again."

He went quiet. She did not have the heart to tell him that Ptolemy Caesar *might have been his* for she was not sure. But even the slightest doubt could cause a dangerous situation. Apollodorus needed to understand that.

They stayed that way until he suddenly turned to her again. "I beg your pardon for asking that question. I just needed to know to put it away. I shall never bring it up again," he said, and squeezed her hand.

"Our world is cruel, Apollodorus, and we make the best of what we can, and bear the responsibilities of what we should," she said, cryptically, and then rolled on top of him.

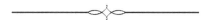

She called council the next morning–Metjen, Apollodorus, Kadmos, Valentinus, and two senior government administrators. Unasankh, a senior administrator in Alexandria, a *Hypodioketes*, the man who had accompanied the delegation to Caesar asking for a cessation of hostilities, and an influential merchant called Galenos. The previous *Dioketes*, the senior official, had died of natural causes, creating a vacuum.

"I laud General Valentinus for bringing peace to Alexandria," Cleopatra began, nodding to the distinguished general who made sure to show off his very Roman attire with reds all around. The general bowed in acknowledgment.

"Trade is picking up. Tax revenues are increasing. Achillas' army has now sworn fealty to me and His Majesty," she said, turning to the quiet younger brother and husband who sat without saying a word. His presence was necessary to send a message: that this was a co-rule (not really), and that she was abiding by the terms (not quite), and that his presence would be calm (as if).

The men all nodded. "But there are malcontents still lurking in the shadows," she said, fixing her eyes on each man, going from one to another. "A new beginning must be cleansing."

They looked at each other but did not respond. She had already announced the roles and made changes. Apollodorus would be commander of the Royal Guard. An experienced soldier trusted by them, a Greek commander called Simonides, would be the general of His and Her Majesty's Egyptian legions. General Valentinus would continue as commander of the Roman legions, exclusively garrisoned in Alexandria, with no jurisdiction outside without express permission from Her Majesty. Kadmos would continue to command the remaining Roman-Trained forces of Egyptian legions, and additionally work towards re-integrating the remaining Gabiniani (a large number had died fighting the Romans in the battle of the Nile) into the Egyptian legions. Metjen was now her Principal advisor for all affairs.

"To the question of reconciliation–" began Unasankh, the Egyptian senior administrator. Unasankh was an impressive looking official who took his heritage very seriously. He was a stocky man with a considerable middle and a finely oiled skull. Two large gold bracelets jingled on his wrists and a threaded, deep-brown leather belt held his shendyt. He looked, sounded, acted, and walked like "government."

"Reconciliation after conspirators pay," she interjected, leaning forward. Unasankh bowed but did not protest.

Unasankh began. "Your Majesty, that would–"

"Quiet!" She hissed at him. "Do you know what I went through, Unasankh?"

"Your Majesty."

"I was ambushed. Then I was hounded from my house. Then I was confronted by an army. Then they tried to prevent me a just audience with Caesar. Then they tried to kill him, with me as their next target. And you think I must send no message? Why?"

Unasankh mustered his courage. His voice had a deep low baritone and it rumbled like distant thunder. "Because people are tired of violence, retributions, and conspiracies, Your Majesty. Whatever they did, they did it under duress and with no direction."

"I am not talking about foot soldiers, door guards, maids and gutter cleaners, *administrator*," she said, icily.

The men kept their head low, and Unasankh, whatever his reservations, said nothing more of the matter.

"I wish to inspect the army. All of it. Egyptian. Roman," she said, looking at Simonides and Valentinus. "Will that be a problem, generals?"

Valentinus, the man she deeply respected, spoke in his halting yet clearly understandable Greek. "To have two different armies together is not advisable, Your Majesty. Chances for mischief."

Simonides took objection to that. "Nonsense. General Valentinus. My men will stay in their lines, and they are disciplined warriors just like yours."

Valentinus took no offense. Instead, the gruff general only smiled and nodded to Simonides. "It is my duty to point out my concern, and as is yours to rebuff, General."

The two men nodded curtly to each other.

"That is settled, then. There should be no question in anyone's mind that it is I who rules Egypt, and it is my will that shall be done. Mine," she said, and then glared at her husband-brother who almost shrank in his seat.

She knew that the next few months would be busy, with her resuming her court, issuing decrees, appointing officials, and opening trade negotiations with eastern partners. Finally, she could live a normal life as a ruler, and then perhaps travel to Rome triumphantly in a year or two. But first, she had to clean house.

"Apollodorus," she said, "I am not yet finished with the subject of the conspirators."

On that hot afternoon, with crowds standing on the broad Canopic way, the procession of traitors began from the palace gates with the announcement of their crimes.

Conspiracy to overthrow Her Majesty's rule.

Conspiracy to harm the great people of Alexandria and Egypt.

Sedition.

Conspiracy to kill Her Majesty.

A wooden board with two lines, one in Egyptian and one in Greek, saying *Traitor*, hung from each of the ninety-two men and eight women. Stripped and beaten, and wearing only the briefest of garments to preserve their modesty, they walked slowly in a long line with a thick rope connecting the neck of one to the other. Their hands were shackled with crude iron cuffs and legs tied with short rope, giving enough length to shuffle along. People jeered them as they walked. Most displayed little emotion for whatever tears they shed had dried long ago. The prisoners, senior and junior administrators, tax and customs officials, officers from the army, granary managers, factory owners, agricultural inspectors, highway and waterway inspectors, bandits, all who had enthusiastically participated in some way against Cleopatra, would pay. Apollodorus and Valentinus had vigorously pursued Pothinus' collaborators and found enough evidence against them.

The announcer walked alongside, shouting the dastardly crimes committed by this treacherous scum, as soldiers who walked by the procession whipped the slower ones. A few of the older prisoners, exhausted and unable to handle the heat, pain, and stress, collapsed, choking themselves and those they were connected to. The prisoners in front and behind these men were forced to lift them up and drag them, adding to the misery. And when that failed, the guards removed the rope and separated them, to be taken away to the side and hacked to death.

The procession arrived at a large clearing by the sea, after turning right from the Canopic way. There, in view of the crowd, were ten heavy wooden posts with nooses hanging from them. And on one side was a podium with a single chair. The lineup was forced to kneel in a line.

And then, gasps and cheers arose as Cleopatra arrived in a chariot, resplendent in a purple chiton, bright white diadem with silver studs, and several gold and silver bracelets. She sat straight, her face stony without emotion, and her eyes looking straight ahead into the unknown. The crowd all knelt as she approached, and soldiers controlled the surge that threatened to break free of the cordons like restless waves against beach barricades.

Cleopatra ignored the loud lamentations of the prisoners and walked up to the podium and took her seat. The announcer, his voice booming like an elephant in a cave, dramatically opened a long scroll and read the charges on each man and woman. A few bold ones shouted recriminations and curses at the queen, and she ignored it all. At the conclusion of the charges, all she gave was the slightest nod, but she spoke not a word nor showed any kind of emotion.

The soldiers began to remove each condemned man and woman in fives and dragged them to the nooses. Some struggled and fought, some spat and shouted, some hung limp on the soldiers' hands, forcing the soldiers to drag them like slugs on the ground, leaving long patterns of their toes in the dirty, gravelly sand. The soldiers simply lifted up the person for the executioner, standing on a tall stool, to place the noose on the neck and tighten it. And then, at his nod, the soldiers dropped the person. Most died quickly, their necks snapped from the force. But some kicked and flailed about, causing the crowd to yell and shout, but their life drained out in a few minutes. And in cases where the kicking continued, soldiers grabbed their legs and pulled the person down forcing death. Nooses snapped twice, and one woman began to bleed heavily from between her thighs, causing the guards to bring her down and severe her neck with a swift blow. And through it all, the Queen sat without expression, and few noticed her flinching once a while.

The soldiers left the final five hanging as a warning to those who would ever attempt such a thing again. The announcer once again described the charges and assured the people that justice had been done and that they should look forward to a prosperous future. Finally, to the cheers and slogans of the crowd, Cleopatra left the scene and the crowd dispersed, with just a few with morbid curiosity spending time near the corpses. Those related to the condemned were allowed to take the bodies, and a few did, while the rest were left on the ground to rot.

After she returned to the palace, Cleopatra spent an hour in the bath, cleansing herself. Her throat was tense with anguish and revulsion at what she had witnessed, no, what she had *wrought*. She discharged the contents of her stomach twice, causing much worry to Charmian and her physicians, but eventually, as the night arrived, Cleopatra went to pray. She stayed at the temple of Isis for an hour, calming her mind. Charmian helped her when she threw up more than once.

Justice could be cruel, but it had to be dispensed, for if she did not wield the sword of law now, far more lives would be lost in a manner far crueler than what she had ordered.

CHAPTER 3
UPPER EGYPT
UNASANKH

Unasankh swung the thin bamboo stick, and it made a sharp *thwack* against the boy's thigh. He yelped and danced about on his feet. "Pay attention, you idiot! How many times does he have to tell you?"

The boy whimpered. His thin lips trembled. The eyes were red from the crying, but no one cared for the orphan and they had no pity for his weak sniveling nonsense.

"You cry again, and I will tie you up and whip you until you bleed," he growled, causing the boy to go silent. "Theodotus, what is your assessment?"

"Almost there. His inflection is good, the gestures are good, but the tone and the posture need work. He cannot be seen as fearful and whiny!" Theodotus said. The former tutor of the royals had found a purpose. And that purpose had little to do with teaching this boy how to act like the now-vanished boy-king Ptolemy XIV but everything to do with destroying that bitch Cleopatra. And what more delicious way than to threaten her crown again using a prop? Unasankh understood this well, and the two men were well aligned. But what would happen if they deposed her? What about the Romans? Well, they'd worry about that later. After all, what Rome cared about was that someone was ruling, and that *someone* would supply grain and war supplies as needed. Caesar was gone, and that womanizer for sure cared little for the hussy here. Unasankh was certain.

Each man there had much to gain. Unasankh's influence was being severely curtailed by the death of his loyalists and recent changes made by Her Majesty. He owed his debtors, cruel and hard men themselves, much from his gambling and profligate habits but now his revenue sources were drying up with Pothinus' death. If he didn't keep up with the repayments, they had warned him, they would smash his balls with a brick, one by one, and then roast him like a pig on a spitfire. Unasankh decided he would want to keep his jewels and life, and go after his debtors with a legion once he put a puppet-king on the top.

Theodotus wanted revenge, and then a chance to elevate himself in the court.

And Fabricius? The wily Roman wanted money. Lots of it. And opportunities to make even more. Of all, he cared the least for anyone. Not the queen. Or the boy-king. Or Unasankh. Or Theodotus. He and the others mattered so long as they paved the path to gold. Unasankh would have to watch out for this slimy bastard. Fabricius sat there, with a stupid grin on his face. And more than once, Theodotus had to stop the man from attempting to molest the boy. Unasankh had observed Fabricius getting visibly excited whenever Unasankh whipped the boy.

"We can't wait too long," said Unasankh. "She lined up a hundred hardworking, good men and women who found themselves on the wrong side. And she had them hung and displayed like worthless garbage. The longer we wait, the worse she gets."

"She's quickly putting her cronies on major posts, dismissing officials who she suspected as with His Late Majesty. That little dwarf Metjen whispers in her ears all the time," said Theodotus. "Metjen is dangerous, Unasankh. I hear you are not on the best of terms with him."

Unasankh glared at Theodotus. "Metjen is a little cockroach I will crush beneath my feet. Let us get back to work!"

Theodotus nodded. Fabricius said nothing—he eyed the boy.

"Back to practice, boy! Let's begin again. Now, the speech!" Unasankh told the fearful boy who hesitatingly stood up to a makeshift podium. His back still had red welts and a new one was developing on the thigh.

Unasankh lifted his bamboo stick again, but Theodotus stopped him. "He cannot focus if you keep hitting him. And if you create more serious injuries, how will we parade him around, you idiot!"

"Watch your mouth, Theodotus, you are no longer with the royals," Unasankh pointed the stick at the Greek.

Fabricius stepped in. "Now, now. Men. Relax. We cannot win this battle with you fighting like dogs. Unasankh, you need to lay off the beating, as much as you enjoy doing it to your slaves and girls. Theodotus is right."

You would love to do some whipping yourself, don't you? Fucking Roman weasel.

Unasankh wiped his bald skull and leaned back on the cushion. A servant began fanning him.

The boy finally composed himself and began. His hands had stopped shivering. He straightened his back, kept his legs slightly separated from each other, lifted his hands up with his elbow forming an angled L, and addressed them. "My people! The gods of this glorious land have brought me back from the depths of the Great River. They have given me life, for they demand justice and deliverance from the wretched woman who has conspired to kill your king and now usurps the throne! What greater shame that your queen sleeping with the Romans to enslave this great land? Will you join me in rising up to this shame and tyranny?"

He stopped and looked around pitifully, hoping that his performance pleased them.

Unasankh grinned. "Now *that* is better. Much better!"

Theodotus smiled. "The boy has improved significantly. Another week or two and we are ready to begin spreading some rumors. Fabricius?"

"Ah, yes. I've got my men nicely positioned in many towns and some important places in Thebes. Also recruited a fine set of bandits to kill some of her tax collectors and generate some unrest. This is about to get really interesting for Her Whore Majesty," Fabricius said, with a glint in his eyes.

"What about an army? Can we create an illusion that an army is being formed to lead His Majesty to the throne?" Theodotus asked.

"Don't worry about that. It is not difficult to find enough actors and stage some marches. I have my men," Fabricius said.

Unasankh was impressed by this genial-looking cunning Roman. He could use him later once all this was over. But one aspect still nagged him. "What about the Romans? How do we dethrone her if they are still guarding Alexandria? We can take care of Simonides' forces and cause defections, but the Romans have no cause to align with us."

Fabricius grinned. "Valentinus may be an honorable man, but I assure you there are plenty of scoundrels in his legions who we can bribe. We just have to find a way to assassinate him, and that won't be too hard in a big and busy city. He is usually out and about on patrols with his men. But we will do that after we weaken other forces under Cleopatra."

And then the conversation turned to the practicality of this whole act. The consensus was that it would be impossible to raise an army that could take on the current ruler's might, and that too with the unpredictability of Roman presence. They may engineer some defections from the Egyptian army, but that would be insufficient. They would have to tear her structures apart limb by limb. But cutting off those who were close to her, by a war of attrition, by unrest and rebellion, by assassinations and ambushes. They would wear her out, make the land question her abilities, and foment enough unrest that either Rome would depose her and accept the boy-king, or she would step down unable to deal with the stress. Whatever the case, they would rise to positions of power with their puppets and rule from behind the throne.

Satisfied with the plan, the men retired for the day. Unasankh could not be spending long periods here in the South, missing from his duties in Alexandria. His proximity to her was of the utmost importance, for that helped him warn his cabal of any danger.

CHAPTER 4
EGYPT

It all began with whispers in the shadows, in little temple gatherings, amongst nosy neighbors, in drunken revelries–that some had seen the King Ptolemy Theos Philopator, arisen from the dead by the grace of gods. Some said they saw him in a resplendent golden vulture dress with a shining gold Uraeus. Others saw him glowing in the darkness, wearing a pristine shendyt, but with water pouring down his hair miraculously. Even more heard him too, late into the night, crying in the wind, lamenting the injustice perpetrated on him by cowards and collaborators with the enemy Romans. They said he floated in the air, ephemeral, forlorn, disappointed at his people for forgetting him so soon. Others said he had returned to bring respect and justice to their land. The whispers made way to real sightings. On one yellow-orange suffused evening, by the spot where they said he went down, throngs of people saw Ptolemy on a litter, carried by weeping slaves, as he stood and looked at them from the other side of the river. This caused such excitement and fear that many fell to their knees, others ran to their homes in the nearby village to call the others. The local government representative was dismissive of this nonsense, but the rumors persisted.

Two days later, a nearby town saw a procession. Hair-rising divine chants came out of a cave, following by incense smoke, and then Ptolemy walked out, holding a gleaming sword, raising it high and asking the people if they would join him. He was protected by heavy security who kept the throngs away, and this time the local representative could not ignore the news. So, he went to see this himself, and there the king was, regal and splendid, standing by the mouth of the cave, like a statue, as copious amounts of water flowed by his feet from the darkness behind him. The representative fell to his knees too, and at once was flummoxed by the requests of the king's priest. They told him that new taxes would go to the king, and not those cowards ruling from Alexandria. As much as he loved the king, the man, desiring to save his own life, quietly sent word through messengers to Alexandria about this sighting. *The rightful king is alive, so who should we follow?*

Then Alexandria dismissed it as nothing short of scaremongering and a ploy to evade taxes, so they sent a strongly worded missive that Queen Cleopatra was the one who ruled Egypt and anyone pretending to be the now supposedly dead king would be arrested and put to death. But with poorly manned garrisons in the southern part of the country, these threats rang hollow. Enraged people, desiring to follow the king, attacked outposts, and ran out tax collectors. The boy-king even made his appearance in the great temple of Re, in Thebes, to adoring masses who were whipped to frenzy. And the few times Her Majesty's forces arrived, somehow the boy-king and his men would know in advance and vanish. This made many people further believe in the boy-king's divinity and his power to foretell the future.

Fabricius had recruited many instigators and actors, drawing them with false promises, but always maintaining that it was really the boy-king.

Unasankh, with his intimate knowledge of local schedules, inspections, military patrols and so on, made sure that each of these sightings and processions went unchallenged. It was all working splendidly.

And that was when they began to instigate riots to demonstrate the people's displeasure with the harlot queen. The whore who slept with Caesar, they said, had also tried to kill Ptolemy three times, including once where she apparently tried to pour poison in the morning water meant for the boy-king's prayer (how *awful!*). It was all her fault, with kind and wise men like Pothinus and Achillas murdered for doing nothing except displaying bravery and loyalty, and all they did was try to protect her and her brothers. And what about the kind and beautiful Arsinoe, her own sister? That brave girl who had risked her life to fight Caesar, noble and honorable? This monstrous bitch had sent Arsinoe away in chains to Rome! And did people know what would happen to her, there? No? Well, she would first be stripped naked, raped by slaves in full view of the public, scourged by whips with nails, and then she would be crucified in this place called the forum. It would take her, their Princess, their beautiful, divine, blameless Princess, three days to die as crows picked on her. How *horrifying!* What a terrible queen Cleopatra was!

Rioting crowds attacked the lightly guarded garrisons, grabbed some of the soldiers, and set fire to them. Some others they beat to death with sticks and rods, breaking every bone and leaving the bodies like they were grotesque dolls. Then they went after government offices and complexes and broke statues of the queen, beat officials, and some went so far as to molest their women. It was first one town, then two more, and then a good portion of the farm producing population along the river was up in arms and unrest. The poison finally reached Alexandria, where many people itched to indulge in mischief. Trouble began to spread in many areas—first just chatter, then tavern-fights and graffiti, and finally infighting within the Egyptian legions, before Alexandria finally realized the seriousness of the situation.

The message was unmistakable: King Ptolemy had returned and sought his rightful place on the throne.

CHAPTER 5
ALEXANDRIA
CLEOPATRA

And it was around this time that Cleopatra decided to have a pet. Something to love unconditionally. Cleopatra had great admiration to many kings of the past, Alexander being the foremost for obvious reasons. But she also revered the Pharaohs. She had learned much about them during her studies, imagining the double-crowned monarchs kneeling in the musky, incense-filled inner sanctums of magnificent temples of Thebes and Memphis. Of the Pharaohs, she admired Ahmose, Hatshepsut, Seti, and the great Ramesses. Her favorite was the second Ramesses who had expanded the Egyptian empire beyond Judaea.

So, Cleopatra adopted a cat, a fluffy orange-furred male, and called him Ramesses. The beast had no respect for her, and endlessly demanded treats. When Ramesses was not lying on her couch or sitting on her throne casting judgment upon her, he climbed every platform and pushed the flower vases and ornaments to the ground. Charmian, Iras, and Cleopatra took turns playing with, or petting the cat, who very much enjoyed all the attention. Iras even devised a little Ramesses court, where the cat would appear wearing a fake double-crown (tied to its head), and the attendants and servants had to kneel before a confused cat. Many attendants loved the amusing routine, and even brought little cups of milk to offer Ramesses. He lapped it all happily.

Now, Kadmos was no fan of cats. And Ramesses was no fan of Kadmos. But Kadmos realized he was no match for the great Ramesses who was backed by considerable forces of a queen and her ladies, and he gave up on antagonizing the cat by nudging him with his feet. And taking unfair advantage of this situation, Ramesses made sure to swipe at Kadmos' legs at every given opportunity and mocked him with hisses.

She woke up to a cloudy morning, with Ramesses cuddled by the side. He had no interest in following her, so she finished her morning ablutions, took a lotus perfumed bath tended to by her attendants, and dressed in a simple white Chiton, helped by Charmian. She walked a few hundred feet to a chapel in the palace, dedicated to three gods. Serapis, the god of the cult founded by Ptolemy Soter, Isis, and Amun. To them she prayed by chanting hymns taught to her by the priests. The ritual in the morning took nearly an hour, needing her to clean the idols, praying before each, and then making offerings of milk, honey, bread, and beer. Once complete, she and Charmian walked to a quadrangle where Ramesses, along with a legion of sacred cats, waited.

"Meow! Meow! Meow!" the chorus filled the space, causing her to smile. She loved this part of the ritual. She filled milk in several bowls and put some meat in others, and they all came running, eager for the morning meal.

"Here! Here!" she said, helping kittens unsure of the ritual, and Iras picked a few to their feeding stations. Ramesses had his own golden bowl from where he drank with arrogance, hissing at any other cat that dared to intrude.

"This one is cute!" Charmian said, picking a healthy little kitten.

Cleopatra petted its head. "He looks scared! Poor little thing."

She watched as they were all fed.

And then it was time to feed the sacred bull. She walked, trailed by the ladies, to a cowshed at the rear end of the complex. The shed held a few cows and a sacred bull representing Apis. The large specimen, muscular and powerful, dark and beautiful with his shining coat and impressive horns, looked at them with casual indifference. But when she neared, he knew what offerings were in tow, so he walked to her imperially, shaking the bronze bells tied to his neck. Cleopatra loved hearing the crystal sounds of those bells, *cling, cling, cling*, as the bull neared. He stuck his snout through the wooden barricades. His handlers stood nearby in attendance.

Cleopatra felt his forehead, rubbing her hands on the smooth, luxurious velvet surface. She scratched his chin and he half-closed his eyes with pleasure. Then she fed him several leaves and fruit. He snorted in happiness. She then walked to another corner where lay many calves. She loved them too—and with some enticement they all trotted to her. She hugged their necks, scratched their necks, kissed their foreheads, and with Charmian and Iras spent many precious moments.

Once done, she knelt before the statue of the Apis bull for blessings, and then headed back to the palace.

General administration would begin in an hour.

Breakfast was light, but sumptuous. Fruit, warm and fresh bread, cheese, beer, and a sweet pastry made of palm dates and honey. After she ate, she usually lounged with Charmian, her nearest, dearest, and the only one who could speak to her with no reservations in private, to chit chat and gossip. A favorite time!

"What is the news of his wife? Is she still with him?" Cleopatra inquired of an official whose adventurous wife was the talk of the court.

"With him for the money, and with the officers for their joy rod," Charmian said, and they began to giggle.

Iras, who was nearby, came running. "What is it?"

"Nothing. You go and find Ramesses and bring him here," Cleopatra said, and sent the eight-year-old running.

She turned to Charmian again. "Really? How is it that he has not separated from her?"

"I think he likes her for her beauty and stature, and the story is he has his own mistresses."

Cleopatra sucked on a honey candy. "Mmm. You know a lot, Charmian."

"My job to bring you interesting news," the girl giggled. "Two women from the kitchen are pregnant, and they are not even married."

Cleopatra shook her head in disapproval. Such was the situation with migrant populations.

"How is Apollodorus' farm?"

"It's fine. Neglected. I tell him to sell it to someone who can care of it, but," Charmian said, and made a gesture of something going in one ear and out the other.

"Men," Cleopatra scoffed. "Stubborn. Who knows what they're thinking, if they think at all. Go bring my baby."

"Yes, Your Majesty," Charmian said, and went to bring Ptolemy Caesar, still only a few months old.

Cleopatra waited, petting Ramesses who was curled up by her on the lounge. "How is my little king today? Is he content?" she murmured to the cat which looked at her lazily with his brilliant green eyes.

Her lady-in-waiting arrived soon, holding the baby. Ptolemy Caesar was a quiet infant, he cried when hungry or needed cleaning, but otherwise was happy where he was. She held him in the crook of her arms and played harp with his lips, singing a little song.

```
Pretty little eyes,

Pretty little nose,

Pretty little lips,

Like the moon is the pose,

Pretty little fingers,

Pretty little toes,

See him giggle when the hurricane blows!
```

She blew a large raspberry on the baby's tummy causing him to giggle. They loved this ritual, and she did it whenever she had him in her arms, which was only rarely on a given day. She wiped the drool off his face.

"Is he fed?"

"Yes, Your Majesty," Charmian said. "Cleaned too."

"Take him to the nursery, let him play there."

With Charmian gone, she turned to Iras.

"Iras, are you going to school every day?"

"Yes, Your Majesty."

"What are they teaching?"

"Some philosophy and mathematics, and a lot about Your Majesty's forefathers."

"Are you doing well?"

"I get beatings only once in two or three days, Your Majesty."

"That is not too bad. You get the best teachers in the world here in Alexandria. Areius and Rhodon are very good."

"Yes, Your Majesty. Areius is scary."

She laughed. The philosopher was known for his temper.

Charmian returned. "They say the clouds should clear soon, if you wish to stroll in the beach this evening, Your Majesty."

"Let us do that. I love playing in the sand."

"Me too!" Iras chimed.

"No one asked you," Charmian said.

"No one asked your opinion," Iras said, sticking her tongue out.

"Iras," Cleopatra said, mock sternly. "Behave yourself."

"Your Majesty. She always–"

"Quiet."

"Yes, Your Majesty."

"I don't feel like going to the court," she said, lazing on the lounge and stretching her back. "It gets so boring. Same petitions. Same arguments. Same quarrels. He took my money. She ran away with my jewelry. He cheated me. He lies. He didn't pay taxes. He's asking for too much in taxes. Drunken soldiers set fire to a shop. This. That. Ugh."

Charmian just grinned.

"Let them know I will be late today. Tell me more about that Enne's mother-in-law!"

They whispered about the really obnoxious mother-in-law of a senior official, and apparently the woman even sometimes beat the poor man. It was all really hilarious, because Enne was the most pretentious Egyptian in the court. The way he puffed up his chest when announcing important matters, the way he rolled his kohl-lined eyes, his facial expressions, the way he even walked, holding his arms wide of his waist and ambling like an elephant, everything screamed drama.

"Have you seen the suspicious bulge in his Shendyt? Some say he stuffs something there," Charmian said, and they sniggered.

Iras, who was nearby, made sure to observe. "You are cackling like old ladies!"

"Iras," Charmian scolded. "How dare you say such a thing to Her Majesty!"

"Yes, Iras! How dare!" Cleopatra said, and they started laughing. "You will understand when you grow up. Now go and find Ramesses. He's gone to destroy some alabaster vases again."

Off Iras went, and the topic turned to fashion and makeup. It was Charmian's duty to ensure Cleopatra had the finest robes in the world, the best wigs (*made of luxurious hair from young girls, and used in ceremonies and court appearances*), and the most beautiful jewelry (*the pearl necklaces, the lapis-lazuli rings, the gold bracelets*). And Cleopatra made sure that her lady-in-waiting got a generous allowance for her own fashion. They both loved talking about the perfumes, the Libyan skin-freshening ointments, the best eyeliners that came from Thebes, the exotic Ethiopian pastes that brought color to the lips and cheeks (*Apollodorus loves it, giggle, giggle, Kadmos too*). They gossiped about the styles of various women in the court (*she paints her face like she is trying to get sold in the market, so much red!* or *she thinks she is the princess of the palace, but she is a good woman though*) and palace, about Romans (*so bland and boring, really*), the Parthians (*so much color, too much actually*), and Greeks (*quite elegant!*).

And so went many mornings, and this day was no different, until Kadmos came rushing, saying the council had something urgent to discuss. It was the same matter about these mysterious sightings in the country.

CHAPTER 6
ΛLEXΛNDRIΛ
CLEOPΛTRΛ

"What do you mean by my brother is alive?" she asked, flabbergasted. The reports were much more urgent, detailed, and left no doubt that it was the king himself, alive, or a masterful impostor seeking to cause unrest.

But by whom? How? Why are my people unable to find the truth behind these claims?

The council had taken up the matter seriously on this day. The topic was a joke not just weeks ago, and now many were dead. And her name was being denigrated in the most unkind ways, so much so that the officials refused to detail the rumors for fear of enraging her. And so they whispered it to Metjen who then made polite translations.

"There are too many reports that speak of sightings and speeches, Your Majesty. We must intervene," Metjen said. "To leave these rumors unattended will cause further unrest, which will lead to tax collection shortfalls and grain shortages. All that will start a new round of rioting here."

Whoever was behind this was clever. They would cause unrest and then blame it all on her. She could wait and let it die, or act on it. Knowing how volatile the countryside was, and how fed-up they were with weakness in Alexandria, a show of force and display of her power were now warranted.

"Valentinus, hold discipline in Alexandria. Simonides, your legions shall travel with me. I intend to hold court in

Thebes and Memphis, and we shall put an end to these conspiracies. Summon the senior officials of the region and question them why they have been unable to apprehend the impostor? What are they waiting for?"

They should earn their denarii instead of sitting behind tables and getting fat.

Unasankh told her that if Her Majesty pleases, he would personally go and quell the trouble. He successfully dissuaded her from sending the troops and causing more violence, imploring that arms in the city would do her no good, and would sully Her Majesty's image. Cleopatra, against Metjen's caution, finally allowed Unasankh to proceed. Unasankh did an exceptional job–he quietened the city with little bloodshed, and his success he attributed to his skills and relations with the many forces within the city. She found him knowledgeable, even if unctuous and sometimes dishonest. But such were the men of administration–they rarely reached those levels by being pious. But they were resourceful, tenacious, loyal, and needed for the functioning of the Royal House.

A few days later, Unasankh came with more news. They convened in the throne room. This time his news was about the unrest in the south. He had his men in the South reporting in great detail. He said that he had personally not been to the South recently, and had never seen this boy-king, but that he understood the pulse of the region for he had spent years there as a governor. The recently appointed governors in the south were inexperienced, terrified, and simply had no network like him, he told her. Cleopatra agreed, for she had seen how well Unasankh had handled Alexandria.

"An armed invasion of the South might send a poor message to the people who are already rioting about the rule," he said, looking concerned.

"Would it not make me look weak and ineffective by sitting on my hands while my men are being dragged out and beaten to death?" she asked, sharply.

"That may be so, Your Majesty. But an army on an inflamed region? If this is an impostor–"

"It is an impostor," Apollodorus warned Unasankh. "Unless you are sowing doubts here, administrator."

"I apologize, Your Majesty. That was not my intention," Unasankh said, bowing his head low. "My point is, we must expose these bastards without setting an army on a population that believes you as gods. They know no better, and must not be punished for it! Have I not silenced Alexandria?"

Unasankh had a point. The people worshipped her as divinity Isis, and so it was no surprise that they had been hoodwinked by this impostor. He was an impostor–she was sure. Almost. But what if?

"What do you suggest then," she said, willing to listen.

"You must send someone closest to the royal throne. Someone who knew the Late boy-king and can positively identify the impostor. Let this person, perhaps it is His Excellency Metjen or General Apollodorus, bring the words of the Queen to the people. Let them show themselves to negotiate."

Unasankh made sense.

"Would they not ask for me?" she asked.

Metjen spoke. "I understand what Unasankh is hinting at, Your Majesty. If you go by yourself, it will appear as if the Queen is afraid and is coming down to negotiate. The first step is to let them know we are listening, but without bringing the full power of the crown."

She understood the reasoning. Project power but hold its full might only for when it is absolutely necessary.

Unasankh continued. His large belly was slick with sweat in the humidity, and his puffy cheeks glistened as he spoke. "General Apollodorus personally leading a delegation and a legion should signal sufficient seriousness. We need to draw them out of the shadows, Your Majesty, for if we move too hard, and too fast, they will vanish and wait for another day. And you will never have peace. How long will you sustain constant disturbances and disruptions?"

She chewed on her lip. "Fine. A full legion will accompany Apollodorus. General Valentinus, will you be able to spare half your legion as backup?"

The Roman General shook his head politely. "Caesar's orders, Your Majesty. My legions are not to be deployed to quell civil unrest outside Alexandria. And this is not yet a military matter that threatens Rome."

Insufferable stickler for rules and orders.

"The General would say no even if I said a hundred beautiful nude women waited for him and his Centurions outside the boundaries of Alexandria," she said, smiling. The stodgy general lowered his eyes and smiled, but he said nothing.

"Apollodorus, plan for departure. Unasankh, use your network in the south to send message that my delegation wishes to speak directly to the king to ascertain his rights. No negotiations without a personal meeting. But how do we know that it is really my brother?"

"Apollodorus could ask him certain details that only he knows," said Unasankh.

"Apollodorus was never close enough to my brother. I can feed some anecdotes. But we need *physical* proof," she finally said.

Metjen agreed.

"My brother had a dark mole patch on the pit of his right elbow. They must allow Apollodorus to inspect and establish its presence," she said. "And Unasankh, you must not reveal this to those men. Let it be a surprise."

Unasankh bowed. "Of course, Your Majesty. That is a clever approach. I will personally leave for Thebes today to deliver and spread the message, Your Majesty. But you must give me a fortnight to confirm if we have audience. Who knows who these people are and what they hold in their dark hearts?"

"It is so ordered then. Report to me when Apollodorus must prepare to leave."

Unasankh smiled at the audience. "I will do my best to bring this unfortunate diversion to closure, Your Majesty," he said, bowing low and rubbing his palms together.

As Unasankh left, Cleopatra sank to her seat, stressed. Would the gods ever give her some respite? She summoned Iras, now eight, to hear stories about falcons. Iras loved falcons. Iras also loved to talk to anyone who would hear about falcons. It was a joke in the palace that to escape Iras' stories, one would need to fly away like a falcon. She could speak eloquently about the live birds, the statues, the paintings, the dramas, and stories of Horus. Cleopatra once told her that a big falcon would swoop down and take her away, but at eight, Iras was smart enough to laugh it off. "I am a grown-up, Your Majesty!" she said, very confidently.

Iras came bouncing and knelt before her. Cleopatra asked the girl to sit by her side. "Iras, now tell me that thrilling story of Horus again!"

As the excited girl started her endless chatter, Cleopatra felt her stress melt slowly, and eventually she drifted to sleep.

CHAPTER 7

ALEXANDRIA

CLEOPATRA

She finally received word, twenty days after the council meeting, that the resurrected boy-king and his senior men were ready to discuss with the Queen's commander of the Royal Guard, though His Majesty was offended that she would not make the trip herself. But that he understood, considering she was the mother of a young child now, and would not want to make the travel south. She bristled at the hint that she was too weak, but ignored it for the sake of the chosen strategy.

What if it was really her brother who had somehow survived?

What if all this was to ensure he was safe and gained enough power with people's backing to avoid being killed by her?

She had to think through what to do if that were the case. General Valentinus would quite likely stick to his orders and begin the same song again–that they must co-rule. She cursed Caesar for not apprehending her brother or finding proof that he was dead. *It's back to the same battles and stress again!*

The meeting venue was a desolate stretch about a day by foot, west of the river. The location, a plateau surrounded by cliffs with a great many hidden paths, had been chosen by the posturers who demanded that any deception or hint of an invasion would cause them to not only call off the parley, but that they would raise a rebellion in large parts of the farm belt. And they were adamant that Apollodorus travel with a guard of five-hundred, and not an entire legion. Frantic messages from the kingdom's spies indicated no large scale "hidden armies." Unasankh's network too reported that there was no imminent threat of an invasion from the South, and that there was no indication of any foreign influence.

While annoyed by the demands and feeling uneasy about the arrangement, Cleopatra decided to proceed with the plan. Ultimately, there could be no negotiations. She would crush them. But she needed to know the enemy first.

"Be careful there," she told Apollodorus. She held him close at a moment of privacy. They had enjoyed their moments together and bursts of intense passion, but she was careful not to get pregnant, for that would create complications with Caesar. She had to be seen as Caesar's wife, even if not officially so. And it was critical for Caesar to acknowledge his son publicly in Rome—and she could not put that to risk.

The next day, Apollodorus left with his legion. He would be there in two days. And hopefully, they could put an end to this nonsense, and she could plan a visit to Rome.

Rome.

Where now her sister Arsinoe was probably executed in the forum. Her heart felt heavy, but what choice did she have? Her temperamental sister had turned on her and worked actively to kill her. She had to be gone. She did feel bad imagining Arsinoe being paraded in a foreign city. Her sister, *family*, a potential queen of Egypt, dragged like a criminal behind Caesar's chariot and strangled. She had tried to convince Caesar to execute Arsinoe quietly and painlessly away from prying eyes, but her laconic lover had only said the people of Rome demanded their trophies and ceremonies, and that they shall have it. That was the only thing that felt terrible.

CHAPTER 8
ROME
CAESAR

Caesar basked in the cheers of the people who lined the streets and crowded the forum as he rode a chariot for the triumph. Flower petals rained on him, trumpets heralded his arrival, drums beat and filled the air with an electric atmosphere. He had returned as a conqueror, and now the undisputed leader, *Dictator*, of Rome.

On that sultry afternoon he walked up on a podium, wearing a resplendent purple toga and gold-leafed laurel wreath. He sat on an exquisite chair to watch the procession of his conquests. First came the bounty–carts of coins, ingots, statuettes, lamps, enamel-studded jewels, ivory boxes, gold leaves, silver votive, blue-glass vessels, amulets, lapis-lazuli plates, marble statues, sphinxes, and polished idols. As the throngs admired these fruits of conquest, came the next exciting parade of caged and free exotic animals. Lions, ox, tigers, colorful parrots, monkeys, baboons, giraffe–all causing much excitement.

Then came the prisoners. First were a smattering hapless officers, disgraced nobles and chieftains of conquered lands in Gaul, Africa, and provinces East. Many of these would be sold off as slaves and others executed in the Mamertine prison.

The procession of the prisoners suddenly stopped as the street cleared. People craned their necks in anticipation of what might come next. It was time for the display of the most prized captives, accompanied by effigies, plays, and paintings. The announcer, a loud tall man, stood on his stepped stool and shouted. "Juba, the son of Juba of Numidia!"

All eyes turned to a woman walking, holding a toddler by his little arms. The child looked around bewildered, and began to cry. The woman was gentle with him, for the boy, Juba, still being a child, would not be treated harshly in front of the people. Thin golden shackles jingled by the little one's feet.

The announcer said more. "Caesar will care for this child, and he shall grow to be a proud citizen of Rome!"

People cheered, the boy cried louder, and the woman finally took him away to caring hands.

Then came drummers, indicating someone even more important. Following them was a cart, on which was a well-crafted mural of a Roman legion fighting Gauls. Excited murmurs began.

"Now, for all Rome to see, the king of the Gauls, Vercingetorix! Defeated by Caesar with utmost bravery in the great battle of Alesia!"

A huge roar rose, and people screamed obscenities at a figure tied to the pole affixed on another wheeled carriage.

Vercingetorix was an emaciated figure. Not yet even forty-years in age, he looked like an old man, with his matted thick brown-black hair falling on his face, and his long dirty beard touching his chest. Naked waist up, his ribs showed prominently, and the torso showed the brutality of the lice and rat-infested dungeons. But his eyes sparkled with defiance, and he held his head high. He never flinched even as a few slippers and balled rags came his way. Once known as a fearsome warrior who tested Caesar's mettle, his body had broken down having spent years in captivity, and yet his demeanor radiated strength.

The carriage came to a halt near an execution platform. The guards held the struggling but dignified king and led him up on a wooden platform erected on the central pathway. An announcer described his crimes. Rebellion. Causing death of Roman soldiers. They tied him to an upright wooden board, with his arms extended. Finally, to the beat of drums, a burly executioner wrapped a knotted rope around his neck from behind, and began to strangle him to the shouts and whoops and cheers of the crowd. Vercingetorix kicked and his eyes bulged, blood vessels in his eyes popped and his tongue protruded. There was some revulsion and much laughter from the crowd. He shuddered one last time and they took him away.

With Vercingetorix dead, the announcer said the people would now witness the extinguishing of the greatest prize of all.

A 20-foot tall effigy of the Lighthouse of Pharos, the spectacular Alexandrian structure many had heard of, was wheeled through for the crowd's admiration. The Lighthouse even had a fire lit on its top. And then, in a dramatic show, several Centurions leaped from the sides and enacted a fight by the structure, and eventually, one of them set fire to the effigy made of hay and wood. The Lighthouse caught fire and burned as they dragged it. But just as the crowd were admiring the sight, their eyes fell on two running figures. One was dressed like an Egyptian, in a Shendyt, but there was a large tear near the crotch, indicating him to be a Eunuch. *Pothinus! The conniving eunuch of Egypt.* He jumped around like a monkey, causing howls of laughter from the crowd. And this man suddenly turned towards a beautiful girl dressed like a Queen–Cleopatra–with her diadem and Greek chiton. He tried grabbing and stabbing her, when a man, dressed like Caesar, leaped from another wheeled carriage behind. He chased Pothinus who hooted and made cartwheels. Finally, the man dressed as Caesar acted as if he stabbed Pothinus, to great applause. This was followed by an enactment of the end of Achillas, the Egyptian general.

With that excitement complete, the crowd finally waited with bated breath for the final captive.

They went silent as a lone figure walked the road, behind the burning effigy and the carts. She was a beautiful girl, wearing a simple, gray Greek gown, shorn of all adornments. But her bearing was regal, her cheeks red and flushed, her straight nose turned up with haughtiness even in the face of death. Her hair was disheveled but fell in cascades over her frail shoulders. They had put golden cuffs on her, and she had to shuffle, for they had also chained her feet with silver shackles.

They waited for the announcer who yelled as loud as he could. "Caesar has conquered Egypt! And here is the woman who saw herself as Queen and plotted to kill Caesar! Princess Arsinoe of the House of Ptolemy, sister of Queen Cleopatra, shall now walk to prepare for her afterlife!"

The crowd that cheered and thirsted for blood was suddenly unsure. They stopped throwing slippers and rotted food. There was a hushed silence as she shuffled slowly. Then the murmurs started and a few sporadic shouts.

"Spare her, Caesar!"

"Why must she die, Caesar?"

"Let her live!"

And suddenly, the smattering protests turned into full-throated bellows from the multitude, all shouting for her to be spared, directed at the great Caesar who was befuddled by the turn of events. Arsinoe walked up to the platform without hesitation and she stood there, staring the hooded executioner in the eyes. This act of courage only emboldened the people to shout more for her cause, directing their pleas and ire and demands at the Dictator. *Spare her!* They shouted in chorus. *The gods will not smile upon us for strangling a brave young princess!*

Caesar rose and raised his hand for the crowd to be silent. He conferred with his trusted lieutenant Mark Antony and nephew Senator Marcus Junius Brutus. Finally, he called the announcer and whispered something in his ears.

As the people watched, the messenger climbed on the platform and announced with his booming voice. "Caesar is merciful and has heard the voice of the people!"

A great cheer arose and the announcer waited for quiet again. "Recognizing the status of the girl, he will spare her life! She shall be banished beyond the boundaries of Cilicia and be allowed to find sanctuary. She shall not step into any land owned by the rulers of Egypt, or anywhere west, including Greece."

Few noticed the single tear fall from Arsinoe's eyes and none knew the rage in her heart.

CHAPTER 9
ALEXANDRIA
APOLLODORUS

Apollodorus squinted in the bright afternoon sun as he walked to the destination, stepping over stones and trudging on fine, hot yellow sand in which his feet sank with each step. A small group of soldiers stood by the entrance of a cave. The location had been expertly identified, he thought, for the cave complex formed the tip of an inverted V with tall sandstone cliffs fanning out from the center. About half-a-mile behind, his Legion waited on open ground, having pitched tents to protect themselves from the searing sun. With him were three senior officers, a messenger, a flag-bearer, a translator, a cavalry officer riding a horse just in case quick messages had to be sent to the waiting legion. He eyed the sides of the bluffs for any sign of ambush, but given his legion waited on a dusty, rock-hewn plain, there was not much chance of a surprise. Nothing hinted at a large army in waiting, though miscreants hiding in any number of crevices along the cliffs was always a possibility. But they would be no match for an armed, trained legion. *What was the strategy?*

Three rough-looking men greeted him near the entrance.

How had they scouted this place?

"Your weapons, general."

Apollodorus looked at the man incredulously. "Are you out of your mind? You expect me to hand over my weapons as I walk into this ridiculous theater? No. If you insist, I return. I and my men, except my cavalry officer, will come in as we are."

They smiled, perhaps knowing of the outcome but having tried nevertheless. The man on the horse drew up a tall green flag and waved it, and whether his Legion saw it or not was unclear, given the distance and the shimmering air between them.

Apollodorus and the others then walked under a makeshift awning and entered the cave. It was suddenly cooler, pleasant, and the immense breadth of the entrance surprised him. Some more men waited in the shadows, and far ahead, he could see a cluster of men around a chair on which a boy sat.

Apollodorus caught his breath. His eyes were still adjusting to the dimmed interior and the surreal nature of this mission. Finally, he saw the big figure of Unasankh walking to him. "We are pleased to see you here, general," he said, grinning.

We? Was he with them all this while?

Apollodorus chose not to litigate Unasankh's loyalty. Instead, he walked forward to the group of men. His heart pounced like a leopard in his chest, when he recognized Theodotus and Fabricius. Apollodorus' blood rushed to his head. *These motherfuckers had formed a new cabal!*

"A new gang of disloyal cowards, I see!" he growled. But they only laughed.

Theodotus, looking leaner with a trimmed beard and having shaved off his head, clapped dramatically. "It is you who abandoned the cause of Egypt, Apollodorus, by siding with a woman who is now nothing more than Rome's whore."

Apollodorus lunged at him, and it took some effort for everyone to separate them and ask for calm. Apollodorus felt sheepish for having lost his temper, and Theodotus, uncharacteristically, apologized for his behavior, which he said came from a place of passion and concern. Unasankh clearly had some sway over these men, for he scolded them for their ways, and they listened.

"I have to see the king, if it is who you say it is, first. There is nothing to parley otherwise."

Fabricius smiled. "Of course. But you may go no further, for His Majesty fears you may assassinate him on the word of his dangerous sister."

Apollodorus stepped forward and stared at the boy, still many feet away, sitting dressed in Pharaonic regalia. With the makeup, lack of bright light, heavy dress, it was difficult to ascertain identity through physical means–but the boy was remarkably similar to the boy he know. Unsure, Apollodorus demanded. "Speak, Your Majesty."

"What do you wish to know, Apollodorus?" came the calm, clear voice. It sounded different, but it had been over a year since he had actually heard the boy's voice, and at his age, physical characteristics changed rapidly.

Apollodorus asked him two questions fed by Cleopatra, for which one answer was correct, and for the other, the boy only said it was long ago and after the traumatic incidents of the past, he could no longer accurately remember. But by then Apollodorus knew that Theodotus was far closer to Ptolemy and knew much about the king's life than either Her Majesty or himself, and this boy had been likely coached heavily.

"One last thing," Apollodorus said. "I wish to ascertain a physical characteristic."

"It depends on how close you must get, Apollodorus. I hope you are not here on a suicidal mission," Theodotus said.

Apollodorus ignored Theodotus. "I can keep my hands behind me and inspect. But His Majesty must extend his left arm and show me the pit of the elbow."

Suddenly, Theodotus protested that this was unnecessary. And oddly, he began to argue with Unasankh and Fabricius that the boy should do no such thing. They pulled him aside and he could see the animated, heated argument and Theodotus was getting frustrated. *Why?* Eventually, they seemed to have shouted him down.

Unasankh walked back looking agitated. But he turned to Fabricius. "That is a reasonable ask, Fabricius, you must allow him to do so. Which arm did you say, Apollodorus?"

"The left."

Theodotus yelled from where he was. "You idiots are denigrating the body of the king!"

The boy looked strangely fearful and unsure, and he looked at Fabricius and Unasankh.

Fabricius turned to the boy. "Extend your left, Your Majesty," he said. And the boy twisted his left arm to expose the elbow. Apollodorus found it odd and theatrical, in spite of the instruction.

"Now the elbow, Your Majesty. The other side. The pit."

The boy turned his arm and extended it.

And there it was, a dark splotch.

CHAPTER 10
ALEXANDRIA – TWO DAYS
BEFORE
CLEOPATRA

She sat quietly, contemplating this insane development. Her brother, alive, really? So, stepping back from the heat of discussions, of high emotions and stress, she sank into the cool, water-lily infused tub as Charmian sat nearby. She tried to tie several facts with two potential outcomes.

If her brother was truly alive, then why was he fomenting all this unrest? Why not simply reveal himself, come with a large group and whatever rag-tag army he had, and present his case? Perhaps they thought any such action would receive an overwhelming response from her, crushing him. By weakening her through all this unrest, perhaps they hoped to bring her to the negotiating table and simply agree to co-rule. But what if this was a pretender? Then it made no sense at all to bring him to her face-to-face, and all the current actions of unrest were strategic to displacing her.

But who was the driving force behind this?

Theodotus had escaped and never been caught. With Pothinus and Achillas dead, who was capable of guiding an impostor to act as a real king?

Fabricius, the duplicitous and clever Roman "accountant" from Syria, had also vanished. He was certainly capable of raising mercenaries and creating mischief. He had fomented rebellions and brought down nobles in Syria.

Could they have gotten together, somehow? And could their strategy be to engulf her in a ruinous civil war until Rome tired of her and brought them on as settlement? It was eerily similar to Pothinus, Achillas, and Theodotus' previous attempt.

But how were they cleverly circumventing administrative protocols and military patrols?

How were they able to impact large populations so easily?

Theodotus knew nothing of the south. Fabricius was a Roman with no knowledge of Egyptian.

She hoped that her little misdirection would help Apollodorus determine if the boy was an impostor or really the boy-king.

CHAPTER II
WEST OF MEMPHIS
APOLLODORUS

Apollodorus stared at the spot on the boy's elbow pit, and without comment stepped back from the podium.

They watched him for a reaction. "Well?" Unasankh asked.

"Why, Unasankh? Why this charade?" Apollodorus said. "And you too, Theodotus? You were her tutor once."

There was silence. And finally Theodotus spoke. "I told you all. She is clever. There was no mole on Ptolemy's elbow pit. You donkey-raping dogs fell for it. She fed this to you, Unasankh, you fat idiot, and you wouldn't listen to me!"

These fools had injected a tattoo to make it look like a mole, to meet Cleopatra's expectations. Except that the presence of it told Apollodorus that this boy was not the boy-king.

Unasankh gnarled. "Watch your mouth, you dramatic bastard. We all have to take our chances!"

Fabricius tried again, for the second time, to bring peace. "Now, once again, warriors. Let us not forget why we are here. Apollodorus, while we argue, these men have nothing but profound respect for you. That is why we wanted you here. To discuss."

"To discuss what, Fabricius? You have an impostor on the throne. What do you hope to get from it?"

Suddenly, the boy, listening to all this, whimpered. "Can I go then?"

Unasankh turned on the boy and slapped him so hard that he fell off the chair and collapsed on the floor. Then Unasankh walked up to him and kicked him in the belly, causing the boy to double up. "Keep your mouth shut!"

Unasankh turned to Apollodorus. "You have a chance of a lifetime, Apollodorus."

"Chance for what?"

Theodotus stepped forward. "Join us. Bring your Legions to us. When we take power, you will not just be a glorified bodyguard but a general of the entire Egyptian army."

Apollodorus spat on the ground. "How shameless you are, Theodotus! You think you can bribe me, because you think I am a weak, hapless coward like you, a dog that looks for the next bone and has not a bit of shame! And that goes to you too, you treasonous crow, Unasankh!"

Theodotus did not take the bait. He only smiled. "Your thinking is shortsighted, Apollodorus. If I am a dog, I could say the same about Her Majesty as well. But we are not here to quarrel. Her Majesty is under Rome's thumb, and it will only get worse. Just think! She says she has Caesar's child. What does that mean to us? Much, much more of Rome down our throat. You have the chance to reshape Egypt. To bring it back to those who care for it. To bring it back to its rightful ruler. To become an independent state in a collaborative alliance with Rome rather than as a subservient client-state."

"You mean a puppet rule with you as the master behind the throne. Who is going to be king? That boy?" he said, looking at the boy lying on his side on the muddy floor, but making no noise.

"How does it matter?" Unasankh said. "People can see the boy as king. But great men, wise men, like you and me, we will guide this kingdom to its glory."

"Glory my arse," Apollodorus scoffed. "You dirty bastards should apply for clemency now and save yourself. There is nothing more to discuss. I am giving you three days to disband and the leaders to surrender."

Unasankh laughed. "Surrender, he says. For what, Apollodorus? So we can spend our lives in a dungeon, or worse, hang on the streets?"

"I will ask Her Majesty–"

"You will ask nothing," said Theodotus, ominously. A few men came out of the shadows.

"You join us. Send us your legions. Or you die," Fabricius said. "There is no other way. You must decide now."

Apollodorus looked at his sides, gauging his situation. He was surrounded by several men. The two men with him pulled out their swords. *Were these swine actually going to attack the Commander of Her Majesty's Royal Guard?*

And then the enemy rushed at them.

Apollodorus, with his two men, created a small protective circle and began to fight. The swords clanged and with his exceptional fighting ability he was able to hack three men in rapid succession, tricking them and cutting off their heads. But more rushed at them, and even as he was tiring, he hoped that his cavalryman had realized what was happening and had rushed to the waiting Legion.

The man to his left let out a scream and a gurgle as an enemy sword went right through him, barely missing Apollodorus' side. In the din he could not hear what was going on, but Apollodorus realized that he would have to break out of the attacking circle and get out. With no idea how many were in the cave or outside, he attempted to push his way out, swinging his sword and killing two more, first chopping their wrists and then hacking at their necks.

And then two things happened simultaneously: he heard someone scream "Kadmos!" and an incredible pain shot up from his torso as an arrow flew in from the darkness.

CHAPTER 12
ALEXANDRIA – TWO DAYS BEFORE
CLEOPATRA

The persistent nag in her head would not go away. Apollodorus had just left, and he was going to parley with these guardians of the resurrected king and verify his authenticity.

She tried to put herself in the minds of the plotters, assuming that this was an impostor. How could they hope to destroy her? It would be near impossible to raise an entire army and march on her–and even if they magically did so, they would be no match to the power of her state and the backing of Roman legions. That would just be a silly idea taking a monumental effort. These cabalists were clever, and therefore such an approach would not muster support.

They could go and get help from the Parthians–but why would Parthia care when they had cordial trade relations with Egypt and had no reason to embark on a ruinous conflict with Egypt and Rome, and that too, on behalf of an illegitimate pretender?

They could go to Rome to ask for intervention. But that would be pointless because Caesar had personally spent so much time with her brother that he would know the plot in an instant and put them all to death.

They could continue the civil unrest. But how long could they sustain it? People would tire of it soon and side with the state to bring order, and start collaborating with her.

But curiously, it seemed for all of the cabal's visibility in the countryside, they were surprisingly elusive to capture. Almost every attempt to find them through military raids had failed, almost as if they knew the plans beforehand.

Was there someone close to her somehow involved in this plot?

She began to feel cold and the it felt like a million little bugs were biting her neck and shoulders. *What was she missing?*

She reoriented herself again, coming back to her hypothesis that this was an impostor-plot, and what if Theodotus and Fabricius had grouped? She remembered something that the wily Roman had told her long ago when on the way from Syria to fight her brother. Fabricius was an expert in fomenting rebellions and dislodging rulers.

There are many ways to kill a man, Your Majesty. You can shoot an arrow through his heart. You can crush him under a boulder. Or you can cut off his limbs one by one, until he bleeds to death.

And then Fabricius had connected allegory to how he operated. *When the enemy is easily accessible and the structures around them are weak, you assassinate them. If they are a military power that is weaker than what you can muster, you fight them in battle. But if neither are options, you create enough disturbance that you break their resolve and destroy those closest to them, one-by-one, until they lose the will to continue. I have never failed, Your Majesty.*

She rubbed her upper arms and hunched in concentration. In this case, it seemed logical that the first two options were not practical, and all signs pointed to the third. It was as if this uprising was a Fabricius planned,

Theodotus supported playbook, for after all, Theodotus, as the rhetorician, had all the tools to make a boy look and talk like her brother. It was all coming together.

How stupid was I? How stupid?

She began to choke with fear. She almost stumbled as she ran out of the chamber, screaming for Kadmos.

She knew what the cabal was trying to do.

CHAPTER 13
WEST OF MEMPHIS
KADMOS

Kadmos charged into the cave, bellowing at the scene far ahead. Even in the dimmed light he could make out the unmistakable figure of Apollodorus, clad in his green and gold-veined breastplate and cloak, collapsing on the ground.

His men rushed at the attackers and hacked them to death as they pursued others who had already vanished into the dark tunnels and the many hidden paths of the complex.

"Care for him!" Kadmos shouted at one of his lieutenants, pointing to Apollodorus on the ground, as he rushed forward. There, lying on the ground right ahead, was Unasankh, with gashes on his thigh and shoulder. But he was alive, and he pointed loosely at the direction of one of the many tunnels. A frantic Kadmos flew into one random.

It was dark there. Kadmos slowed down, steadying his breath. He could hear the loud noises of his men, and in fact most of Apollodorus' legion, now near the cave. Suddenly, from somewhere to his left, he felt the slightest breath and then the sensation of blowing wind. Kadmos ducked instinctively and swung his gladius in an arc, putting all his power into it. The blade impacted what appeared to be a leather corset, but then cut through it into flesh and went deep inside. The man screamed and Kadmos felt his warm blood on his arms. He extracted his gladius and supported himself against the cool sandy wall, breathing hard.

What had happened here?

But he could barely see further.

That was when an arrow whooshed past him and lodged itself in the wall. Kadmos cursed and ran back, making long strides until he exited the passage back into the main cave. His men were already swarming the cave area.

"Take groups and run into these passages!" he ordered. "But stop if it gets too dark. I do not want everyone to get ambushed and murdered—it serves no good."

He also ordered the rest of his forces outside to spread and cover the vast landscape, though he was quite certain they would find little. The ringleaders had most certainly vanished.

Then they split into many groups and ran back into the passages. But after many stumbles, falls, and with many soldiers getting lost inside, Kadmos called off the pursuit. They managed to find a few holdouts and kill them, and captured a few sorry fools for questioning.

And just as Kadmos emerged from the tunnel, one of his lieutenants rushed to him. "We found a boy, sir, unconscious, but wearing a king's gown!"

They brought the boy before him. He was frail, but with remarkable likeness to Ptolemy, who Kadmos had only seen a few times. He was barefoot, but his ripped bleeding feet showed signs of someone running frantically on rough, gravelly ground. "Get him attention! I think this is the impostor!"

Kadmos, exhausted, then ran to where the Legion physician was tending to Apollodorus. The general was unresponsive. Blood caked in his mouth, and the arrows, deeply lodged in his torso, could not be removed without causing heavy bleeding. Apollodorus' body bore many wounds of a brave warrior–gashes on his arms, a cut on his cheek, a deep cut on his thigh. His eyes were unfocused.

The army physician looked at Kadmos and shook his head.

Unasankh sat nearby, getting treated. "They ambushed us all. Bastards," he said, sighing.

CHAPTER 14
ALEXANDRIA
CLEOPATRA

She cradled Apollodorus' head in her lap and wept. The sorrow gushed forth like a flooding river, and every time the crying stopped, a new wave of violent grief exploded deep in her being. They had scented Apollodorus' body to prevent it from bloating in the heat before they brought it to her. He looked serene, his face without a blemish, his beard neat and his eyebrows perfect. They had wiped the blood from his mouth and cleaned his tongue. Her fingers shook each time she ran them through his hair, as she called his name. But those kind eyes had no light in them anymore. His torso was bandaged heavily to hide the gaping holes where the many arrows had struck him. The cowards had rained arrows on a man fighting his attackers bravely.

Cowards!

Cowards who killed a man who had gone to discuss with honorable intentions!

"Apollodorus, Apollodorus, Apollodorus," she called him, as she rocked back and forth.

Her tears wet his face. Metjen and Kadmos watched as Charmian cried quietly. Simonides and Valentinus stood outside the chamber. And with no hesitation that their eyes were upon her, she leaned down and kissed his cold, dead lips.

How did I lose you, my Apollodorus? How foolish was I, my love! How did I send you to a trap?

She held him for a long time (*his body feels so cold even this warm afternoon*), until Charmian gently pried her away. She let the embalmers carry out the body.

Cleopatra ritually beat her own chest until the skin became red and raw. Physicians applied medicinal salve to heal her broken skin. Charmian attended to her and the Royal Physicians kept watch for two days as she starved in grief.

Charmian, grieving herself, stayed by Cleopatra's side every minute, watching her like a hawk, and sometimes scolding Her Majesty to follow rules for recuperation. The palace was drowned in grief, but the steady hands of her senior officials nursed it back.

Cleopatra dispatched orders to prepare a magnificent burial to Apollodorus. He would find his rightful place under the auspices of the gods in her favored Alexandrian temple—the Taposiris Magna.

With the period of grieving over and matters attended to, Cleopatra calmed her grief, now replaced by rage.

She summoned Kadmos to get the report.

"Tell me, Kadmos. Everything."

Kadmos was subdued. He kept a dignified posture and explained that after her orders, he had rushed as fast as he could to Apollodorus' location. He took the cavalry from the waiting legion and charged into the cave, but only made it just in time. The fighting was already on, and by the time Kadmos' men butchered those they could lay their hands on, Apollodorus had been fatally struck by several arrows. Most of the enemy had escaped through the many passages and natural tunnels, and pursuit only netted a few men. It was dark and Kadmos had not recognized anyone in the mayhem, except Unasankh, himself lying injured. They had also found a boy, who was recuperating and ready for questioning when Her Majesty was ready.

She was angry at herself. At Kadmos for not reaching sooner. She yelled at him, and he accepted the verbal lashing without a protest. But soon, she calmed down. Kadmos left the room. Cleopatra then let Charmian hold and allow her to let out all the grief. She loved two men, in very different ways, and now the one she loved with greater passion was gone, felled by treachery and her own inability to have seen the danger.

They stayed that way until evening. She would avenge him. Dark anger rose in her belly, hissing, bubbling, burning. They would feel her wrath.

CHAPTER 15
SOUTH OF MEMPHIS
THEODOTUS

Theodotus held his head in his hands and cursed repeatedly. Fabricius nursed an injured thigh. They had just made it out of the surprise attack. How did Kadmos, the man Fabricius was familiar with, show up just in time? What had happened? Apollodorus' Legion was waiting far away and Theodotus had his plan all laid out. If Apollodorus defected, they would bring in the Centurions and convince them, and then convert the Legion. If Apollodorus died, then they would do the same, telling them that Apollodorus tried to assassinate a king. The worst case, they would vanish in the darkness, but leaving a headless Royal Guard and a further weakened Cleopatra. None of that had happened! Now Apollodorus was dead, Unasankh had vanished, and the boy had not returned with them. Fabricius had sent some men a day after the event, but all they found were corpses in the cave, none of which were Unasankh or the boy.

Had they been taken prisoner?

Theodotus shuddered. This was bad. Very bad. It would be impossible for him and Fabricius to do this all over again, for now Cleopatra would return with a vengeance. The momentum had been lost. How quickly had the entire plan unraveled. All that effort down the sewers in an instant!

But how and why did Kadmos appear? How?!

Had to be that bitch somehow realized what might be happening! First, there was that subtle trickery about the mole, and then sniffing that something else was afoot.

Theodotus raged about as Fabricius sat forlornly. Now, they had payments to make to their co-conspirators, and if they did not fulfill those obligations, their own life would be at risk. He could not have that. And the scarier thing was the unwitting participants in this scheme learning that the king was fake. They would flay and hang him.

Fabricius was leaning against the wall, extending his injured leg and sighing time-to-time.

"What are you thinking?" Theodotus asked.

"What is there to think? By Minerva, how did Kadmos show up? We killed Apollodorus' messenger and cavalryman right at the entrance."

"I don't know, Fabricius! But what do you propose we do?"

"There is nothing more we can do now. We either hide in Egypt somewhere or get out undetected. My men know the ways."

Theodotus stared at the slimy Roman. How much could he trust this man now, considering there was nothing of value left anymore for him, and Theodotus was only a burden. Fabricius was an opportunistic bastard, and he had no loyalty to anyone or anything.

Theodotus shuffled closer to the resting Fabricius and leaned over him. "Your men, Fabricius," he said, softly.

Confused, Fabricius swatted his arm. "What are you talking about? Yes, my men, what about that?"

Theodotus suddenly pulled the knife out of his waistband and drove it into Fabricius' ribs. The Roman's eyes opened wide in surprise and pain, but Theodotus was a comparatively bigger, stronger man. He closed Fabricius' mouth with his palms and twisted the knife deep. Fabricius began to thrash about, and as the knife cut through his lungs and vessels, blood gushed up his throat and mouth, and seeped through Theodotus' fingers.

But Theodotus did not slacken his hold or relinquish the pressure on the knife. Deeper it went, and harder he pressed on the blood-filled mouth. Fabricius thrashed about some more, but it was evident the knife had missed the heart.

Fabricius was choking in his own fluids.

Theodotus let go and Fabricius clutched his throat and flopped about, even as he spit out copious amounts of blood and began thrashing. After several disgusting minutes, with the floor wet and slick, Fabricius' eyes went cold.

"You would sell me out at dawn. I know that," Theodotus whispered. And as the crickets chirped outside and dogs howled, Theodotus quietly left that safehouse and vanished into the darkness.

CHAPTER 16
ALEXANDRIA
CLEOPATRA

The capture had netted a few men, but the most important prize was the boy who postured as the boy-king. The prisoners had little to offer–it became quickly clear, without even much persuasion, that they knew nothing. The cabal was clever enough to control information. These men did not even know the names of those close to the impostor, and the names they had heard were mostly certainly fake. They were spared death but sentenced to slavery.

Cleopatra wanted to take her time to decide how to talk to the boy, when her mind was calm, her grief in control. She wanted to speak with Unasankh first, to understand what had transpired. What had gone wrong?

First, she attended Apollodorus' funeral–a solemn and grand affair with a procession to the temple, and her appearing to bless his tomb. Then, she mourned his death again for three days, lying on her bed, shunning food, and grieving as a widow. She went through waves of doubt, even contemplated abdication, before she returned to her current state–one of resolve and revenge. She would not let these conspirators–now or in the future–to break her spirit, and never again would she let herself be waylaid and fooled.

Kadmos had held the boy in a dungeon near the palace. When Cleopatra first met Unasankh as he was recovering, he had made a big show of relief on seeing her and fell to his knees with great effort, saying loudly how he had been made a fool by dastardly conspirators and how he tried to save Apollodorus and how if it were not for Kadmos' arrival he would be dead as well. Tears had fallen on his flabby cheeks and his belly shook in a display of grief. *Why am I held here, Your Majesty? I should be by your side to help mop up the conspirators!*

Unasankh had been informed that the boy was in custody, and the administrator, still recovering, had been insisting that he be given a chance to question and thrash the child. Cleopatra decided to speak to the impostor first. She decided to take Unasankh along, so that the boy would know that someone from her side had survived and could tell the story, so as to dissuade the boy from attempting to lie.

The chamber was dark and damp, and it smelled of fear. She had the boy brought to her. She was surprised when she saw him, and understood how they could posture him as her brother. He was of the same height and build, and they had even cut his hair to be like the now vanished boy-king.

The boy looked at her, and his eyes darted towards Unasankh standing right next. He was frightened out of his mind. On seeing them, he collapsed and fell to the ground, crying hysterically. The guards roughly pulled him to his feet and forced him down a chair.

She appraised him quietly. The boy had welts all over his body. But they seemed older, some crusted and dried after the skin broke.

Before any talk began, Unasankh leaned towards her. "May I speak to him first, Your Majesty," he whispered, "it was evident to me when I saw him that he had been beaten and tortured already, and such a person will not speak the truth easily."

Cleopatra appraised him. Unasankh had deftly put down violence in Alexandria without inflicting violence himself. Perhaps he knew the right words.

"Go on," she said.

Unasankh walked to the fearful boy and knelt before him. The boy flinched and shrunk into his chair and began to sob.

"Be truthful and everything will be all right. You know the names of the others who were around you. I have seen them all. Tell us the truth and you will be treated well. You have her permission," he said, and then, oddly, added, "and my permission as well. Her Majesty is merciful."

The boy nodded fervently. With that, Unasankh walked back. "He has seen you, he had seen me before, and he will speak the truth, Your Majesty. I have learned much from body language," he said, proudly.

"We will see," she said, and forgot the brief distraction of his words to the boy. "Do you know who I am?" she asked, firmly yet gently.

His chin hit his chest and he heaved, unable to speak. A guard raised his hands to strike, but she gestured for him to stop. The boy finally calmed down.

"Yes, Your Majesty."

"Tell me," she said. And that's all she had to do for him to tell his terrible story amidst the heaves and shuddering shoulders.

His name was Erastos and he was thirteen years old. He came from a farming family south of Memphis by the river. Strange men had first spoken to him on the pretext of purchasing their produce, but after two visits to his house, they had attacked and killed his parents and taken him away. He was beaten and tortured, with the threat that if he did not follow their exact instructions, he would be sold away to be raped by barbarians from the north and then thrown into the mines. A man named Theodotus–

She was right. That bastard was back to plotting, and he had escaped again.

She had to confirm twice that it was Theodotus, and his description of the Rhetorician left no doubt. On the way, she had lightly questioned Unasankh on what had happened. The administrator said he had only connected with intermediaries, and had never met the closest members. And when he had finally gone to the cave, they had blindfolded him, until there was mayhem and he was slashed and left to die. The cabal had been *extraordinarily* careful about exposing its inner circle, he said.

The boy continued. Theodotus and Fabricius were in it together, along with some other Egyptians whose names he could not recollect, for they usually used code words and cryptic terms. Unasankh nodded encouragingly. At one point, Unasankh exclaimed that when the boy described an Egyptian administrator simply called *the loopman*, he was referring to an Alexandrian official called Ankheperre!

Kadmos sent out urgent orders to find and arrest Ankheperre.

Members so high in her administration. Just as she wondered. Perhaps it was Ankheperre who had leaked raid plans and output designs to the cabal.

They had trained him to walk, talk, and behave like the boy-king. Theodotus trained him on the behavior. And from what the boy could gather, Ankheperre helped with local matters. Fabricius was apparently the one who raised mercenaries. He knew nothing else and never wanted to be part of any of this. The boy went back to sobbing.

In him she saw herself, sometimes a puppet of forces beyond control, just as she had been when her father dragged her to Rome.

She turned to Kadmos. "I believe him. Shift him to a safe area for now, for there may be attempts on his life if there are people of the cabal in my administration. Treat him kindly."

Kadmos had the boy released and taken away. Unasankh wished him well.

Cleopatra walked out with Unasankh who shed some more light into the events in the cave, none particularly any more illuminating than what she already knew.

Ankheperre would have much to answer.

CHAPTER 17
ALEXANDRIA
CLEOPATRA

Ankheperre was away to his village near Pelusium, and it took two days for the guards to find the man and bring him to Alexandria. She had instructed them not to harm him and allow her to speak to him first. Meanwhile, Unasankh had gotten busy dismissing officials who he thought had failed in their duties to protect her, and had dispatched raid parties to arrest more in the South. She awarded Unasankh a rich tract of land near the delta with tax exemptions for his bravery. Unasankh had asked that he be allowed to supervise Ankheperre's interrogation and torture. *I know how to beat the truth out of entrenched bastards like him, Your Majesty, I can spare you from the ugliness,* he had said, but Cleopatra decided to speak to Ankheperre alone, without Unasankh's knowledge. For all his work, she found Unasankh to be unctuous and insufferable.

Cleopatra knew Ankheperre somewhat. The official handled tax and granary related duties in an eastern subdivision. He was not part of the senior council, but he had appeared before her several time as part of routine reporting. She remembered him for his honest conduct and knowledge of local affairs. His name had never come up during the retaliation against Ptolemy loyalists, and there had been no doubt about his behavior. So what had happened? Why would such a man turn against her in such an idiotic plot?

Ankheperre was a pudgy old man. He kept his head held high when he was brought before her, and while his face was pale and he perspired copiously, he showed no urgency to grovel before her.

He knelt with considerable effort, and she let him stay that way as punishment.

"Do you know why you are here?"

"They have told me nothing, Your Majesty."

She nodded. Best to surprise him and see his reactions. Kadmos pulled a stool and made Ankheperre sit on it. He held a club in his hand.

"I thought you would always serve me faithfully," she said. Ankheperre looked surprised, and his eyes darted between her and Kadmos.

"And I always have, Your Majesty. What is this about?"

His reaction surprised her, or perhaps Ankheperre was a consummate actor. Cleopatra had eschewed the impulse to put to torture every condemned man. Pothinus had instructed her long ago, and she had seen it in incidents since, that those under pain would say whatever their torturers wanted. And often what they said were lies. Sometimes the perpetrators found too late that the men were innocent. She found such instances distasteful. Pothinus had also said that while the people found a man to be strong if his conduct was harsh, the same could not be said about such a woman. She had realized that careful questioning yielded better results than breaking bones or puncturing eyes without much thought.

"What did you hope to get out of conspiring with the men who attempted to bring an impersonator to the throne?" she said, carefully watching his eyes.

Ankheperre jerked back and his palm shot up to his mouth and tapped his cheeks instinctively as if to ward off evil spirits. "That is a lie, Your Majesty!" he said, loudly, and his crackling voice vibrated with righteous anger rather than fear.

"Your name was mentioned by another senior Alexandrian administrator who knew much about the plot, Ankheperre," she said, to see if the man would change the tune knowing someone else was in on the workings of the plot.

But Ankheperre shook his head. "May Amun cast me to the river, may Horus pick my eyes, and may Serapis trample me, Your Majesty," he said, his voice shaking, "I know nothing about the plot, and I had nothing to do with it. Nothing!" he said. He was *angry*. His black eyes blazed as he stared defiantly at a looming Kadmos.

"Kadmos, step back. Why did your name come up?" she asked.

Ankheperre flapped his arms, a sign of exasperation amongst the Egyptians. "How would I know, Your Divine Majesty? How can I defend myself when I know nothing about this, nor have I even remotely considered anything but your service?"

"So you never traveled South to spend time with the cabal and give them plans of military raids and garrison deployments?"

He shook his head vigorously. "I have been here, in Alexandria, every day of the last two hundred days, Your Majesty. All I have done is try to bring stability to by subdivisions. I have been nowhere, and I have done nothing. Someone is trying to destroy me! I have done nothing, nothing!"

Ankheperre was almost quivering with anger. She was surprised by his conduct–this was not someone who had something to hide. But was she missing something? She conferred with Kadmos.

"A great actor or he is truthful," Kadmos whispered.

Cleopatra stared at the man for a long time. He said nothing except keep his head down, and mutter time-to-time that he was innocent. And then, Ankheperre raised his head and addressed her.

"There is a way to ascertain my truth, Your Majesty. And if you cannot do so, then you may torture me and break my bones, for I have nothing to hide and I shall die with a free conscience," he said, and his voice was firm.

Kadmos and Cleopatra exchanged glances.

"Go on," she said.

When Ankheperre finished explaining a method, Cleopatra could not help but admonish herself for not doing so earlier. Kadmos agreed that it was clever.

"Hold him until we learn," she ordered Kadmos. "Do not harm him."

Kadmos bowed.

"Well, administrator, we will find out if we can find the rat by your method, and whether you are telling the truth."

"The gods know I am, Your Majesty," Ankheperre said, firmly and without hesitation.

CHAPTER 18

ALEXANDRIA

CLEOPATRA

Unasankh, The Alexandrian administrator, walked into the chamber with purpose, his big body and the many golden bracelets and bangles shaking as he huffed and knelt before her. "Her Majesty has summoned me for another task?"

"Indeed, Unasankh. You have been immensely helpful in helping the investigation of the impostor plot," she said. "Now, sit down, and I need some help from you."

He was out of breath by the time he stood and sat on a chair before her. Unasankh took a gulp of water from a cup by his side and wiped his puffy lips with the back of his hand.

"There is a matter that the major conspirators are hiding. Ankheperre has confessed to his role, nothing a few jabs of a needle under his fingernails could not do," she said, smiling wickedly.

Unasankh looked mighty pleased. His stomach jiggled as he laughed. "The scoundrels deserve what they get, Your Majesty. I would have happily executed the unholy job on your behalf."

"I could not wait, Unasankh. For sometimes I have to do what I must to identify the poison in my inner circle."

Unasankh looked around with some concern. He nodded halfheartedly but said nothing.

Cleopatra leaned forward conspiratorially. "I thought you should know that I found something amusing from Ankheperre's interrogation."

Unasankh was suddenly interested. "I regret I could not join you, Your Majesty," he said. She recoiled from his fetid breath which smelled like a dead mouse in a mouth.

As Kadmos watched, she placed a palm beneath her chin. "So, I learned from Ankheperre that any administrator's travel is usually recorded by a separate arm of the government. I summoned Ankheperre's records and it seems he never really went anywhere."

Unasankh squirmed in his seat. "These conspirators can be like puppet masters, Your Majesty!" he said, with outrage in his gruff voice. "I hope he revealed those he worked with!"

"That is a possibility, administrator. But Metjen, Kadmos, and I agree that it would be extraordinarily difficult to conduct such a sophisticated operation in such secrecy by just sitting here. There will be inevitable leaks."

Unasankh nodded. His eyes had lost some of that sparkle. A little sweat drop made its way from behind his ear to his neck.

Cleopatra, clearly enjoying herself, continued. "So, it made me wonder, could there be someone else, high in my administration, who could be traveling South once in a while when they really had no business to do so?"

Unasankh gulped and nodded with some hesitation. "Perhaps going to see their family, or personal business?"

"Of course. That cannot be discounted," she said, encouragingly. "So, I summoned more records, and do you know what I found?"

He eyed her with great discomfort. His large frame shifted again in the chair and he looked at an expressionless Kadmos.

Cleopatra continued. "I found that you have been away many times, making short trips, and were sighted several times in a region south of Memphis. And yet all your family, your farms, your villas, are around Alexandria. Not just that, it seems you are in significant debt, and when drunk you have been making disparaging comments about me."

Unasankh became frantic and protested loudly. "I have always been at your service, Your Majesty! These records are incorrect!"

At her cue, a government inspector walked in, holding many records.

Unasankh eyed the official balefully, his yellow conspiratorial eyes shooting daggers and daring him to speak. Perhaps he had something on the man, for the official seemed frightened, trembling as he stood by her, facing Unasankh.

"This man is a liar! He has a grudge against me for I investigated his indiscretions on behalf of Her Majesty! Do not believe him!" Unasankh shouted, his veins bulging in his neck.

Kadmos stepped forward and two guards held a struggling and protesting Unasankh and tied his hands and feet firmly to the armrests and legs of the sturdy oak chair. "I had nothing to do with this, Your Majesty! I am being framed! Your loyal servant is being framed!"

She waited for him to be quiet. "That is not all," she said, and gestured to a guard.

Erastos, the impostor boy, stepped into the room. Unasankh's head jerked up in surprise, and some saliva dripped from the corner of his lips. His breathing was like a stressed bull.

"Is that the man?" Cleopatra asked the boy. "You have nothing to fear for you are now under my protection."

There was strength in Erastos' eyes. He stood straight and his cheeks had regained color. The days of care had done wonders to his demeanor. She noticed the radiating anger in his face, and the dark hate in Unasankh's.

Erastos nodded. "He was always with them. And he was the one that caused all the welts," the boy said, his voice soft and husky. He strained to control his tears.

Unasankh fought his restraints and bellowed. "He is lying! That little bastard is a conspirator and trying to implicate me!"

Kadmos punched Unasankh in the gut, making him double with pain. Unasankh yelled and complained saying this treatment was unjust, uncalled for, and unbecoming of Her Majesty's stature, and unexplainable for a woman. She ignored it all.

"Do you know why I suspected you?"

He did not answer.

"I remembered the boy's fear when he saw you. I remembered Ankheperre's confidence that he had committed no wrong. I remembered your insistence on being in their interrogations. I learned a lot about you and your activities and interests in the last few days."

"They are all liars and I am innocent," Unasankh shouted. Spit flew across him and landed on her shoulder. She recoiled in disgust and Kadmos quickly wiped it with a cloth.

She nodded at a guard who swung his heavy club and shattered Unasankh's wrist—the sounds of the bone cracking with a heavy *crunch* caused her to flinch.

Unasankh let out a loud howl and thrashed around in agony. His wrist hung limp from the chair. He vomited and dark urine pooled beneath him and dripped to the floor. She crinkled her nose in disgust from the acrid smell.

They let him regain his faculties. Unasankh began to swoon in his chair, mumbling incoherently.

The official, who waited quietly, now feeling bolder and secure that Unasankh had no upper hand, recounted all the official travel records, debt, and accounts of Unasankh's seditious comments.

Finally, Unasankh looked up, his eyelids half-closed, and drool dripping from his mouth onto his vomit-crusted chest.

"You will die slowly over days, or you can die quickly, Unasankh, what is your choice?" she asked, coldly.

Even then, weak with pain, Unasankh begged and protested. She heard him calmly. "It seems you do not want to confess," she finally said, and gestured for a guard again.

This time, two men walked in, and Unasankh almost fell off his chair on seeing them. One of them, a big, hirsute man with many scars on his body, grinned and tapped two heavy red bricks in his hand together. Unasankh found energy from the deep recesses of his being and began to shout, *no, no, Your Majesty! I will tell the truth!*

And then he spilled it all. The birth of the conspiracy months ago when Theodotus reached out to him. The plan to draw her into a civil war and weaken her through continuous attacks, the idea to put up a puppet on the throne, various backup plans, and the fact that Apollodorus' options were either death or desertion—he would never have come back to her in his current role. Spit flew from his mouth fast as he said everything he knew, including names, locations of many of his fellow traitors, and the three hideouts they used during these months. He greedily gulped water given to him in between as he told them more.

When it was all done, and everything noted, Unasankh begged for mercy. Maybe to live as a slave, or even be banished forever, or a few years in a dungeon. *Anything to return to your grace* he implored.

It was now overwhelmingly clear to her that her trusted official had diligently worked to overthrow her, and by his actions had caused the torture and death of so many innocents caught in the uprisings. All for what?

Cleopatra looked at Unasankh who looked at her with hope. He even mustered a pathetic smile. "Unasankh. I said you could die slowly over days, or quickly. I did not say how quickly."

The bricks-man stepped forward with a smile, "you haven't paid your debts," he said. Unasankh began to scream and struggle as they held him down. "No, no, please no, kill me! Kill me!"

She stepped out of the room and heard the sound of bricks smashing together, and the screams continued for long after.

CHAPTER 19
ALEXANDRIA
CLEOPATRA

Retribution was swift and violent. With the names and clues given to her by Unasankh and Erastos, Valentinus began round-up operations in Alexandria. Simonides and Kadmos swept the South. Tax collectors, administrators, captains, traders, merchants, farmers, and soldiers, all were rounded up in the hundreds. In large operations, they took the boy with them, dressed plainly but wearing a board around his neck, that he was the impostor. They spread word quickly everywhere that this was all a conspiracy.

Of those captured, many she put to death, and the remaining were sold to a life of servitude. Only a small number were pardoned, for they were truly pawns of the process. She spared villages and towns from mass punishment but made sure to spread the word of their shame, and imposed higher taxes for three years. Then she purged the garrisons of suspected disloyal elements.

The corpses piled up, and she drove herself to exhaustion, often supervising punishments herself, or visiting towns to show her divine presence. It took three months, and by then, she had ruthlessly crushed the conspiracy and even the slightest whisper of it. She had cast aside Pothinus' advice, that a woman must rule with a soft hand, and that ruthlessness would be seen as unbecoming. And it was that soft hand that had caused her travails.

She wanted her people to see her as a benevolent goddess, and yet ruthless when needed. But even after all this, Theodotus was gone.

She put a bounty on his head but recognized the reality that he may have long left Egypt and vanished in the vast spaces of the East. The poisonous snake would rear its head again, she was sure. And the next time, she would not be taken for a fool.

With her son needing her attention, and incessant pressure from Charmian to rest, she finally settled to normal royal duties. Entertaining distinguished visitors, auditing tax, distributing budget, issuing rewards and patronages, running her court, issuing decrees, touring troubled regions, attending priestly duties, blessing applicants, re-engaging in education covering mathematics, economics, trade, medicine, the study of poisons, cosmetics, and anything that caught her interest, to put behind her sadness and stabilize the land.

The smile began to return. The jokes and her wit, her light-hearted arguments with Charmian, Kadmos, Metjen, and even the ever-serious Valentinus, all came back much to their relief. *General Valentinus, would you like to become a priest? You are so serious that even the gods will stop joking with our lives.*

Even the parties became livelier, with lyre players, Nubian dancers, Cymbalists, bull acrobats, sumptuous fifteen-dish dinners served in gold plates, and wine in silver cups.

It was then that the slow burn of longing for Caesar began again.

Did he miss her?

Did he want her by his side?

What had he told the Senate about the liaison?

What was her future with him?

She knew Rome did not recognize marriage between Caesar and a foreigner, so emphasizing that would be futile. But would he recognize his son as heir?

Alexandrians had not only accepted but also appreciated the discipline and presence of Roman troops. They were no longer attacked and harassed on the street, had their food spit on, or their grain mixed with rat droppings. And that meant, in the event of a pan Roman-Egyptian Empire, the volatile Alexandrians would be comfortable with the incorporation of Roman elements into their lives.

She wondered how a Caesar-Cleopatra King-Queen rule would look. Would they rule from Rome? Or Alexandria? Alexandria was, of course, a much greater city, with its pink and green and yellow buildings, the magnificent library, the Lighthouse, the Soma, the palace complex, the glorious temples, zoos, parks, tree and statue-lined streets... Rome was a dirty backward city in comparison.

Would Caesar agree to shift? Would Rome allow that? Her daydreams were filled with such thoughts.

And just when she was getting agitated about no news from Caesar, and no invite, a messenger arrived from Rome with a letter from Caesar himself.

She pulled Ramesses to her lap and opened the sealed scroll apprehensively.

Good news? Bad news?

Her heart quickened as the first dark letters, written in Caesar's clean handwriting, became clear.

Highness and Dear Cleopatra,

Rome is empty without you. I seek your presence

at the earliest so I may enjoy your company and
see the boy. Inform your plans to Valentinus so
he may arrange for the appropriate logistics.
The people of Rome are excited to see the
queen, as am I.

Yours truly,

Gaius Julius Caesar

Consul and Dictator of Rome

Ramesses, as if jealous, swiped at the letter and tried to bite
her. "Stop, Ramesses! Don't! Rome we shall visit."

But there were some other pleasant matters to attend
to, first.

CHAPTER 20
ROME
CLEOPATRA

"You want to marry this brute?" she asked, her eyebrows furrowed in mock seriousness. Kadmos and Charmian knelt before her to seek permission and blessing. "I thought you were intelligent, Charmian!"

"We seek divine Isis' blessing, Your Majesty, and I shall be as gentle as a sheep and baa softly each night," Kadmos said.

The rogue!

Charmian struggled to control her laughter but scolded him to be respectful of the occasion, and Cleopatra whacked him on the shoulder with her wooden blessing cane. But this was an occasion of joy and approved (with plenty of mock disapprovals) by Metjen, now her *Dioketes*, Prime Minister, overseer of all affairs of the kingdom, and other senior officers and officials. The fact that her closest confidante was marrying the new Head of The Royal Guard meant the positions were sensitive and needed concurrence at the highest levels. Kadmos had pursued Charmian relentlessly, and it had become clear to Cleopatra that her lady-in-waiting was deeply in love with this loud and boisterous man with his strange ways.

The wedding was a quiet affair, tasteful and grand in a muted way, and graced by her presence. Neither had parents or siblings, and Iras, now old enough to listen to instructions, would go into the household as if she were Charmian's daughter. Cleopatra gifted the couple all of

Apollodorus' estate, an additional piece of fertile land for apricots and figs, several gifts of gold and silver statuettes, rings, chains, and coins, to keep them financially secure, and exempted them from all tax for life.

Cleopatra bathed in the sweetness of peace and happiness. Egypt was now quiet, trade had picked up considerably, her borders were peaceful, and emissaries from various satrapies came to her in cooperation. Metjen was an exceptional administrator (*why had she not elevated him sooner?*) who took the burdens of internal policy largely out of her hand, and he was unwaveringly loyal. Simonides had also proved to be a calming influence; steady, quiet, and inspiring. Her inner circle was finally *hers*. She did not yet know if Arsinoe was dead, and what had happened to Theodotus, but she would handle them as situations arose.

Cleopatra resolved to spend time in Rome, and she made preparations by issuing appropriate decrees and ensuring that her husband-brother would not override any. Metjen would act as Regent in her absence and keep the boy in check. Cleopatra had plainly told her husband-brother to leave the ruling to her until it was time for him to contribute, and he had turned out to be meek and completely happy with his idle state of affairs. He kept himself busy with studies, field trips, hunting sessions, and leisurely holiday trips.

She set sail with her baby Ptolemy Caesar, Ramesses, and Charmian, on a luxurious ship surrounded by ten guard vessels. Her trip took her along the Levantine coast, for she was nervous traveling through the open waters of the Mediterranean, and at this time of the year, such an endeavor was not recommended. Her ships hugged the coast from Judaea, Syria, Lycia, Anatolia, and then along Greece, and finally across to arrive at Brundisium. She then traveled by road from the harbor to Rome.

Cleopatra's arrival in Rome was both a celebrated affair and a measured one. People lined up on the streets outside the city as she traveled on an open carriage, wearing the Egyptian double crown of Upper and Lower Egypt, with its tall cap shining in blue-and-red, and a shimmering silver gown. It was a beautiful spectacle, her gold-lined open carriage preceded by dancers, flutists, and harp players, and on either side a colorful mix of Roman legionnaires with their reds and Egyptian soldiers with their greens, blues, and gold.

Roman law disallowed a foreign ruler from entering the forum, so she stopped outside the city walls to be met by Caesar, along with several members of the Senate.

She stepped down to the humid late afternoon air, and Caesar, looking relaxed and confident, extended a warm welcome to her by holding both her hands and bringing her forward to the members of the Senate. He looked happy. He wore a purple toga with gold borders. His face had thinned somewhat, and his hair had receded further on his head, on which rested a laurel wreath. But Caesar's eyes shone with that intensity as they always had.

Caesar pointed out six men and she eyed them as Caesar spoke their names. She had agreed to the greetings protocol—that they would not kneel to her, but they would bow to her, which she found acceptable given the circumstance.

Then she walked towards the cluster of senior Senators and addressed each man by name, in Latin, remembering all of them much to their surprise.

"Marcus Brutus, I have heard much about you!"

"Mark Antony, you were stationed as a cavalry officer in Alexandria when I was fourteen, you still look the same!"

she said to the chiseled, curly-haired smiling man besides Caesar. *Certainly handsome,* she thought.

Then she walked towards an older, yet attractive and impeccably robed man. "Honorable Marcus Tullius Cicero, they say many things about your exceptional oratory. You must demonstrate to me sometime."

Cicero bowed, "and I wish to know more about the Queen who defeated the undefeated Caesar," he said, his eyes sparkling with mirth.

You will be an important man to coddle.

Cleopatra acknowledged with a smile and moved to the next man. "Esteemed Gaius Cassius Longinus, very pleased to meet you. I apologize if I do not remember you, for when I met you the last time, I was only ten."

They were charmed by her. Some struck a cordial conversation with her in Greek, responding to her courtesy in Latin. Caesar, she noticed, was mighty pleased. He kept smiling. She turned to the large crowd standing along the road, and waved to them, causing a great uproar of cheers. She noticed a few even kneeling, and by their looks, perhaps migrants from Egypt or lands East, and to them, she was a goddess.

Whatever the Roman Senate's reservations were, the people certainly cared little for it.

Once the courtesies were over, she gestured at the carriage, and Charmian stepped out, holding Cleopatra's child. The baby, Ptolemy Caesar, just over a year old, cooed and sucked on his knuckles. She quietly observed the reactions of the Senators—some looked uncomfortable, others hid whatever emotion bubbled within them.

Caesar, on the other hand, welcomed the child with a big smile, much to her relief. He picked the baby up, but made no announcement of a name, and held him high. The startled baby, unfamiliar with this man, began to cry, and Cleopatra took him from Caesar's arms. "It seems you make many cry, Caesar," she said, teasingly.

"Ptolemy Philopator Philometor Caesar," she said, clearly, looking at the Senators, smiling. She received some awkward acknowledgment, a scowl from Cicero, and a few smiles.

I will need to work on them hard, including Caesar himself, to attest to his paternity and recognize the child as his rightful heir.

After the introductions, she was given a Roman musical welcome, which she found surprisingly moving and joyful. The combination of drums, the Roman tuba (like a trumpet), bagpipes, and horns, played by expert performers was enthralling to her entourage and to the people who got a free show. Even Ramesses sat quietly by her side, his ears twitching every which way, and he seemed to have accepted Rome's welcome.

Once the ceremonies were concluded, she and her retinue were taken to Caesar's villa on the far side of the city, away from the grime, dust, and stink.

The villa, on the west bank of the Tiber river away from Rome, was expansive, with many rooms, servants quarters, slave dormitories, and baths. Its defining characteristic was a beautiful garden lined with marble statues.

"This is your home, my dear," Caesar said, as she entered the tastefully appointed hall, with its cushions, lounges, ochre walls with elegant paintings of myrtle, lily, violets, and roses.

Quite comfortable. Nothing like the palace of Alexandria, but will do.

She settled, and her retinue was shown their quarters. Ramesses went strolling, looking for vases to break and feet to swipe, followed by harried attendants tasked with ensuring he would not run away to conquer the Roman countryside.

Caesar was attentive, having put away all his appointments for the day, and spending time with her exclusively and ensuring she was comfortable. She was pleased with him fussing about the arrangements, knowing that he still cared for her.

They made love for the first time in over a year. He was gentle, even if a little tired. And they had their first quarrel two days later—why had he spared Arsinoe? Did he not know she would never stop plotting? He assuaged her worry and anxiety by saying Arsinoe was far away and would never be allowed to leave her sanctuary.

Cleopatra settled down to spend the months in leisure as she worked her messaging with Caesar and the Senators.

CHAPTER 21
ROME

CICERO

Cicero, no doubt the most distinguished statesman of the Republic and highly respected for his wit and wisdom, decided to meet Queen Cleopatra. He was slightly miffed that she had so far not sought his audience. He was nearing sixty, a veteran of the greatest affairs, a consul, and yet this eastern queen somehow thought it fit that he must go see her. But Cicero was curious, for he had heard much about this woman who had ensnared Caesar and said she carried his child. He had even modified the calendar based on Alexandrian systems, and even ventured so far as to create a public library. Cicero had seen Cleopatra when she was ten, and he barely remembered her. But he would be meeting a Queen now, not a nervous child. Now, Cicero loved books. He wrote much and loved reading whatever he could find. And The Queen of Egypt was the custodian of the largest and greatest library in the world.

He was ushered into her presence. Caesar was there too, sitting on a study and going through some documents. He acknowledged Cicero's presence with a wave. "Welcome, Marcus Tullius. I heard you are here to meet Her Majesty and not to berate me for something I did, for a change," he said, smiling.

"I will always find time to admonish you, Gaius, perhaps not today," Cicero said, and turned his attention to Cleopatra.

She was reclined comfortably on a cushioned flat seat, and he stood before her, awkwardly, unsure what to do. And then, after a few torturous moments, he bowed slightly and she smiled, waving a hand for him to take a seat. Cicero felt somewhat slighted already. Why was he, a distinguished citizen of Rome and a Senator, waiting for the ruler of a client-state to give him permission to sit? Anyway, he brushed those thoughts.

"They say many great things about you, Honorable Cicero," she said, in a melodious, impeccable formal Greek. "And that you sway masses with your words and lead them to where you want."

Cicero let himself smile. "They say many things about me, Your Majesty, and not all of it is charitable. And you have made quite an impression on Rome already," he said, happy to demonstrate his mastery of her language as well.

Cleopatra had become somewhat of a celebrity. Women changed the way they wore their gowns. They tied their hair in buns, and many in the high circles even began wearing cloth ribbons around their hair, fashioned like a diadem. Pearl became popular and prices shot up, for she was seen wearing magnificent pearl necklaces and earrings. Some even went so far as to draw small dark spots on their cheek to represent a dimple. She was mobbed by merchants and ladies alike when on her trips to Rome, and she was known to thrill them with her Latin, Greek, and Aramaic, often switching between them flawlessly. She lavished lovely gifts (*That amethyst earring with pearl studs? incredible!*) on important people and entertained Senators to soften them to her ways. She even had the awful habit of hugging men and kissing women in greeting. Cicero found all this very distasteful. His chaste virtues were offended by her free behavior, and now this royal pretense. Why didn't she hug him, he wondered.

"The Romans are easily impressed," she said, grinning. "Yesterday's fashion in Alexandria is not even today's in Rome."

Insufferably haughty!

"And what brings you here today, Honorable Marcus Tullius?" she continued.

Cicero suddenly found himself at a loss of words. Was she not looking forward to a rich exchange of ideas? Did she see this, *him*, as a transactional presence? His cheeks reddened.

"Well, nothing of substance, but I did wish to inquire your wellbeing as the guest of the Republic."

She was quiet as she appraised him, and Cicero felt immensely uncomfortable. She was just over a third of his age, and how dare she? His arm twitched as he wondered what to say. Suddenly, she rose from the recline with a big, ringing laugh and strode towards him. Cicero was almost taken back when she leaned forward, her ample bosom making its presence felt, and hugged Cicero. He hesitantly patted her as she stepped back. Suddenly, he felt very happy, acknowledged! No, wait, manipulated?

"I was only testing the unflappable Cicero," she teased him. "And it seems even the great Cicero can be shaken!"

She turned to her cat and petted him, a very healthy looking orange beast, and he looked at Cicero with the same imperial insolence.

Caesar chuckled from the corner.

He knew his face was a shade redder and gave his embarrassment away, but this woman had her ways. Cicero laughed and graciously accepted his situation, and they settled into a comfortable conversation. They spoke of Rome, weather, Egypt's great monuments, and even the touchy subject of her father's presence in Rome (Cicero thought her father was a failure, a hustler who tried to bribe his way to the throne and utterly incompetent—how he produced this daughter was a mystery of the universe). He found her witty and very learned about Rome, its people, and its history, though it was apparent from some of her remarks that she found Rome and its ways beneath her. *There's more dung on your fashionable street than in all of Alexandria,* or, *for all the gray hairs and crisp togas, your senators are remarkably dull, but of course, not you, Marcus Tullius,* or, *why are your buildings so drab and colorless? Do you not pay your architects enough? Should I send some from Alexandria?* He humored her when he could and hit back when he thought appropriate. *Rome's greatness, Your Majesty, is that we are willing to listen to rulers of our client states, much like how a kind keeper listens to the grunts of a chimp, and I speak of the barbarians from Syria and beyond, of course.*

Not all she said was an insult. Cicero noticed her agreeableness and sweet praise, and he found himself unable to hide his pleasure at those words. *They say there is no sweeter wine than the Falernian, and no wiser man than Cicero!* or *It appears to me a folly of Roman laws that a learned man like yourself cannot keep the position of Consul for more than two years,* or *My library is the greatest, they say, and yet it softly weeps for it has no works of the great Cicero!*

Cicero's emotions swayed between a dislike for her haughtiness and snark, thrill at her acknowledgment of his greatness, and admiration for her understanding of politics and administration.

Your understanding of politics is good, but I might have something to add about rule and administration on the basis of my profound experience, he once said, to which she responded with, *have you been a ruler of an entire kingdom, Marcus Tullius? I have been, since I was sixteen.*

Finally, after barbs were traded, wine was drunk, Ramesses the cat was petted by all parties, and topics turned mellow (they both stayed away from talking about Caesar who refused to partake in the drinking and continued to do whatever he was doing), Cicero finally ventured to ask. "I have heard much about your fabled library, Your Majesty. Caesar cannot stop speaking about it."

She beamed with pride at the mention. "It is the greatest library in all of the world. Nothing elsewhere comes even closer, Honorable Cicero. Nothing! We have the original scripts of every master you can imagine, and from Egypt, Greece, Babylonia, Syria, and even India. I have spent hours and hours there, lost in the beauty of those words and worlds."

"It is a truly magnificent place, Marcus," Caesar said, helpfully, perhaps knowing it would needle Cicero.

"And you set fire to a part of it!" Cleopatra turned and scolded Caesar. Ramesses hissed to make his displeasure known as well.

"Because your people were trying to kill me!" Caesar retorted and went back to his work.

Cicero felt a pang of jealousy. Would she invite him to Alexandria as a guest? He wondered. He was a voracious reader and being lost in the musky smell of bound papyrus and old linen, sitting among the shadows of the shelves, on rustic wooden benches with just some light streaming in—that was the greatest sensation of them all, except, perhaps, putting his face between the young queen's bountiful breasts, he wondered idly.

"We have Homer, Plato, Aristotle, Euripides, Eratosthenes, Democritus, *Arthabhasha, Vishnugupta*–and thousands more from corners far and wide."

Cicero noticed how she switched to an eastern accent when she spoke eastern names. She was quite the character, a subtle enchantress. No wonder that old fool Caesar was beguiled by her.

"Well, then, if I may say so, I have heard you are to return to Egypt in a few weeks and plan to return again in a few months. Would you be kind to bring me the original works or two from perhaps Plato and Homer?" he asked, feeling vulnerable but unable to control.

Cleopatra suddenly switched topics. "Honorable Marcus Tullius, may I ask you something?"

He was miffed at his question being ignored. But the great Cicero determined that he would not debase himself, asking for it again. He controlled his tongue and let her speak. "Of course, Your Majesty, not that you care for my permission to ask."

She grinned, and then quickly her eyes turned cold and serious. "What is your assessment that Judaea must remain as an independent client-state of Rome? It is ruled by weak men and an unruly Jewish population. Judaea belongs to Egypt. To me. Will you speak to Caesar about that? He refuses to listen."

Cicero was taken aback by the question. He leaned back and stared at her. *Haughty and presumptuous. Why did she think he would take her case?*

Caesar shook his head and kept it down, refusing to engage. *She must have been harassing him to expand her empire.*

"You may know very well that Rome prefers its client-states to be of manageable size. It does no one good if one kingdom, or queendom, in your case, becomes too large and unwieldy, and–"

"And perhaps too ambitious. I know. Rome has nothing to fear from me. After all, my son is a product of Rome. Judaea belongs to Egypt, and Rome will benefit from my investments in the region and improved trade," she said, more forcefully this time.

Caesar pretended not to listen, and instead took a long gulp of water and stared very intently at a map on the table.

You know what is being discussed, you just don't want to be part of it, thought Cicero, amused at the situation. Caesar was behaving like a husband who had had enough of his wife's nagging about a matter he had no interest in resolving.

Cicero would not take the bait. His own relationship with Caesar was on unstable grounds after his support to Pompey, and his loud and forceful denunciations of Caesar's conduct. "That may very well be. It is, however, a conversation you must have with Caesar, Your Majesty. In Rome decisions need the will of the Senate, not by a single man," he said, pointedly staring at Caesar, and then leaned forward to her, "or woman."

"She is certainly not very used to anyone telling her no," Caesar chuckled from the corner and earned an angry look.

Cleopatra leaned back, let out an exasperated sigh, and twirled a loose hair near her ear. Then she rose suddenly, an indication that she was done with this meeting. The cat jumped down and ran. Cicero rose as well, feeling a mix of indignation, admiration, and irritation.

She walked to him and gave him a warm hug. "You are every bit as I imagined. Articulate, wise, and certainly greedy for books!"

He laughed. She smiled that dimpled grin that was certainly attractive, even if she held no candle to the most beautiful Roman women, of course.

Then she whispered into his ears. "And Honorable Marcus Tullius Cicero, I shall return with a few original works for your pleasure next time. But I do expect that you pour into Caesar's ears the benefits of handing Judaea over to me."

As he walked out of Caesar's villa, Cicero was concerned about the power this woman wielded and her influence on an already power-hungry Caesar.

Dear Atticus,

I hope this finds you well. I had the most interesting meeting with the remarkable Egyptian queen. She is quite young, insolent sometimes even, but the Ptolemies know how to educate their women! I would be wary of her, for all her charm and wit, her singing voice and cunning praise, there is a cold and calculated mind that seeks to expand her influence. She has promised me some original works from their famed library, and you know my desire for such artifacts, and I was none too ashamed to make demands, after all, why would the most respected Consul of the Republic not demand the head of a client-state to carry out his desire?

It is cold here. You have to write more, for the days are quite dreadful, and Caesar is full of himself.

With much affection,

M. T. Cic.

CHAPTER 22
ROME
CICERO

Honorable Marcus Tullius Cicero,

Matters of state have kept me busy. I have been unable to procure the books you desired. I seek your presence when the opportunity presents.

Caesar still scoffs at my demands for Judaea; perhaps your power of persuasion has been exaggerated. I only say this in jest. I wait for your acerbic wit and response.

May you live well,

Queen Cleopatra Philopator

Cicero was livid. He cared little for this eastern harlot and all her nonsense. She had sent some emissary to him, with not even the slightest of apologies, stating simply she was unable to procure what he had requested. She was the Queen. She could procure anything she wanted. She could load the entire library on her Navy and shift it to Rome if she wanted. And yet, she had pointedly chosen to embarrass him. Heat rose up his cheeks and shame enveloped him like a hot summer's dusty wind. No foreigner dared treat him like Cleopatra did, like he was some commoner begging on the side of the street. He was a senior Consul of the Republic!

So, Cicero's disdain for Cleopatra, who had left for Egypt and returned again just a few months later, suddenly magnified with this slight. He decided not to visit her, but instead would ensure anyone and everyone who heard of her would get his acerbic opinion on this characterless seductress. He was already fed up with Caesar's increasingly controlling, dictatorial behavior in the last few months. Against sound advice, the *Dictator* was planning a massive invasion of Parthia, that hostile, vast eastern kingdom that would further push Rome towards bankruptcy. No doubt Caesar was partially influenced by the seduction of unbridled power Cleopatra wielded in her land. And he had also not forgotten her greedy request to snap Judaea. And the most worrying thing? She was pregnant again! Another child of Caesar's? And this time possibly conceived on Roman land! That was catastrophic!

It was now March. And there were many murmurs of discontent against Caesar's behavior. Cicero was tired of this man endangering the Republic and looking to become a king every day. *A king!*

And there was no way Cicero was going to let a king and queen rule Rome.

He would have a word with Brutus and Cassius. He penned a complaint to a dear friend.

To Atticus,

Put aside what I have said of the Queen, for she is nothing but a false promiser who thinks too high of herself. I will have nothing to do with her, and she would be a discarded rag were it not for Caesar's arms. I cannot stand her, Atticus. When I have time I shall write more of this sordid affair, but it is a matter of an

attack on my pride, when I have been most
gracious to her unwelcome presence. How is your
health? Have the physicians found an answer to
your confounding cough?

CHAPTER 23
ROME
CLEOPATRA

"He snores as loud as he speaks, it's impossible!" Charmian complained. They were on a leisurely boat ride on the Tiber. It was not terribly hot, and the boat offered a canopy under which she could rest. She was pregnant again, and while Caesar had been busy with administration and the need to be by his wife Calpurnia's side time-to-time, they had still found opportunities to spend time together. She noticed that her fondness for the man had dimmed somewhat—he looked tired, anxious, irritable, increasingly unwilling to listen to her, and completely preoccupied with the planning for the Parthian invasion.

Caesar also struggled in the bed, sometimes quickly giving it up and going back to sleep. But to her, having him by her side was necessary for the self-preservation of her kingdom, and to thwart any other Roman misadventures in the region. She wanted them to leave her alone or make her a joint ruler for the entire Roman domain.

She missed Apollodorus.

In any case, she would be leaving Rome in a few months given that Caesar would be away, at least for two to three years, when he left for Parthia. She could not see herself living in this place, alone, for many months. She wanted the comforts of her palace and people. The more time she spent in this muggy, dirty city, the more she longed for Alexandria.

Alexandria would have to be the capital of the Caesar-Cleopatra empire.

Enough of worrying about politics all the time.

Her mind returned to Charmian's remark. "Well, I can hear both of you when you have sex. In fact all of Alexandria can. I have received numerous petitions from sleepless citizens to make you stop," she said, wagging a finger at Charmian who sat by her, swinging a peacock-feather fan on Cleopatra's face to cool her.

Charmian laughed. "No, you cannot, Your Majesty! All he does is grunt like a pig."

"Oink. Oink. Grunt. Grunt. An ornery pig. Yes, that was what the petitions said," Cleopatra laughed. "As long as he is hung like a donkey and grunts like a pig, you can be happy," she said, continuing their bawdy talk, something she liked to shock the reserved and chaste Roman women with once a while just for amusement.

"But he is rather quick," Charmian whispered.

"Quick?"

"He does not last too long."

"Oh!" Cleopatra exclaimed. "Kadmos, fast with his mouth, faster with his penis!"

"Your Majesty! Please do not tease him. He is sensitive."

"He is sensitive. That is why he is fast!" Cleopatra laughed.

"Please, please, Your Majesty! I should not have told you. Please do not make fun of him," Charmian implored. "Is there something a Royal Physician might do?"

"Oh Charmian, his secret is safe with me. This condition is more common than you think. I can recommend a salve that might help prolong his time."

"Thank you, Your Majesty," Charmian said, relieved.

"Kadmos. Fast with the sword. Faster with the–"

"Your Majesty!"

"You are so dramatic, Charmian. Fine! Do we have a new cook in the kitchen? The roasted boar tastes different. There is too much salt," she said. Cleopatra traveled with her own kitchen staff, including cooks, cleaners, tasters, supply masters, and arrangers, all meant to protect her from assassination attempts.

"No, Your Majesty. It is the same men. Perhaps the salt is different? We have had to buy locally since we lost some of our supplies due to torn bags."

"Just tell him to reduce salt. And I am bored with boar. Tell him to learn something different, something more Roman."

"Should I have him serve Mark Antony?"

Cleopatra slapped Charmian on the wrist. "Behave yourself."

"They say he is Caesar's master of the horse."

"Yes, he is a *Magister Equitum*, Caesar's representative, Caesar holds him–"

She heard someone shout. There were four cavalry riders–two Roman officers and two from her guard, waving frantically at the boat. She ordered the master to stop rowing and head to the bank. *What was going on?*

They waited for her to disembark on the muddy beach and clamber up the low embankment. The men bowed to her.

"What is it?" she asked. The leader, a senior Roman officer, looked agitated.

"You must prepare to leave immediately, Your Majesty. Now."

The hair on her neck rose. What had happened? Was Rome under attack, or was there some disastrous news from Egypt? A new rebellion? Or had Metjen staged a coup?

"Why? What is it?" she asked again.

The men looked at each other. Finally, the Roman spoke. "Dictator Gaius Julius Caesar has been murdered by cowards of the Senate, Your Majesty."

CHAPTER 24

ALEXANDRIA

CLEOPATRA

Cleopatra left Rome soon after the murder of Caesar. The gods, unsparing in laying impediments and sorrow in her path, also took the life of the child growing in her while on her return voyage. A sorrowful queen arrived in Egypt to a still peaceful and quiet kingdom managed by the exceptional Metjen. Hardened by the various travails she had experienced over the years, and having slowly disengaged herself mentally from Caesar in the final months, she worried what his death might do to the stability of her kingdom. She knew from murmurs and whispers that powerful citizens like Cicero had little use for her and thought little of her, and she knew he felt slighted by her treatment. Perhaps she should have dealt with Cicero differently, but it was too late. She was thankful to Serapis, Amun, and Isis, that she was allowed to leave Rome intact, with no harm to her person, and with assurances that there was no desire or urgency for anyone to pay attention to Egypt. Right then, she knew Rome would plunge into a civil war, and she simply cast that wretched Republic away from her mind and decided to focus on her own kingdom.

She first took the time to recover from the arduous voyage before returning to her royal duties. Metjen, she dispatched to the South, to oversee an extensive and complex construction of irrigation canals and river embankments. She spent time with architects to rebuild portions of government buildings along the Canopic way, destroyed by the riots and the unrest. She would bring back the explosion of colors, palm fronds, Pharaonic statues and glorious falcons to the thoroughfares and parks.

Kadmos had fine-tuned her Royal Guard to exceptional quality, even better than Apollodorus had, she silently observed. Simonides did what he could with his forces and reduced the military budget as she balanced spend between civil construction and the military. General Valentinus, while quite despondent at the death of Caesar, remained loyal and stubbornly stuck with the orders Caesar had given him, saying that until he had instructions from Rome with a new master, he would follow the orders of the old. And her husband-brother Ptolemy, the younger brother of the now dead boy-king? He had grown a bit in the last year. Now fifteen years of age, the boy's voice had broken out of his childish tone and he sounded a man. His confidence had grown under Metjen's tutelage and observing the operations of the kingdom. He was no longer that shy around his sister, she noted with some amusement, and not hesitating to argue when needed. He had even once referred to her as his wife and demanded she fulfill her obligations of a wife on the marital bed, only to receive a sound remonstration to never imagine that possibility. Ptolemy was now just a year short of being lawfully appointed Regent, which was the step before assuming authority as king and rightful co-ruler with decision-making authority.

On this day, she and her brother had arrived at the glorious temple of Hathor and Isis at Tentyris near Thebes, almost six-hundred miles south of Alexandria, to bless some ceremonies, inspect Metjen's canal works, meet with the administrators of the southern Nomes, and also conduct a council with officials and commoners. The commoner's council was a new concept she had instituted, allowing farmers and tradesmen to ask questions directly to the Royals without fear of retribution. It allowed her to know what the people were thinking, without their thoughts being conveyed to her by middlemen.

In the orange-yellow colonnaded temple hall it was her, her husband-brother, Metjen, Kadmos, two interpreters, and thirty men and women from the farmlands and local businesses, selected at random directly by Kadmos, to avoid local officials from polluting the pool.

The hearing began after the initial greetings and prostrations, with hesitating and gentle questions from the awed attendants who, in their and perhaps in their ancestors' lives, had never even set their eyes on the royals, let alone be given a chance to *ask them questions!*

"Your Majesty, divine Isis, do the gods speak to you in your dreams?"

"The canals have helped my family and me. We are eternally grateful. Will her Majesty be so kind as to plant a peach tree in her village for them to worship?" (*If time permits my officials make an arrangement*)

"His Majesty radiates brilliance like Ra and has blessed this land!"

And so on, until she prodded them to ask questions on how her administration was performing or what difficulties they faced in their daily obligations and farm production, with no fear. Then the bolder ones stepped into the light.

"Will there be a tax code reform to allow automatic relief on bad harvest instead of forcing us to petition Alexandria every time?" (*Metjen will see what we can do, but we must be vigilant for fraudsters false-reporting produce.*)

"The Jews are undercutting our produce and depressing our prices, will you drive them out of Alexandria?" (*Well,* they may not be citizens, but doing so will create enmity with Judaea, but we will look into this.)

"My local tax administrator demands that he sleep with our wives for tax relief, this is very unacceptable, and my wife is angry!" (*If that is true, I will have him lashed. That is certainly unacceptable.*)

"The roads from my town to the river are in a terrible state and we cannot move our carts to the collection points. Can Her Majesty fund repair?" (*We can. Metjen will look into it personally.*)

"My sheep's wool has a slightly different color than my neighbor's due to his curses, could Her Majesty undo them with the power of Isis?" (*Uh.*)

She enjoyed these candid conversations. Some sad, some amusing, and some downright ridiculous. But as she promised them, she never raised her voice or threatened them. But the meeting also revealed something else—her brother had become more vocal, adding to the answers, and sometimes stepping in even before she opened her mouth.

"Her Majesty carries all the weight of the world to care for her kingdom's children. When will His Majesty reign as king?" a hopeful participant asked.

Ptolemy answered unhesitatingly. "On the first day after my sixteenth year, I shall rule as king, bringing back the glory of my father and his father!"

The many people nodded admiringly and some cheered. Ptolemy straightened his back, and smiled proudly.

Once the ceremonies were completed, they all retired, and Cleopatra called Metjen to converse. The topics finally veered from status updates and mundane administrative matters to the thorny question of succession.

"Do you know that Caesar left nothing for me in his will, and made no acknowledgment of his son?" she said, bitterly, still smarting from the slight. Instead, Caesar had left almost everything to an eighteen-year-old nephew named Octavian. She had never even seen this boy.

"They will rip that boy limb-to-limb soon," she said.

Metjen did not answer.

"What do our laws say, Metjen? Refresh my memories. My brother is now fifteen. What do you foresee?"

Metjen was circumspect in his answer. "He will assume Regency automatically in a few months, Your Majesty, as is custom. He is already a co-ruler, though we all know that you bear the burden. But the people will want the king to begin exercising his rights and issuing decrees soon. They have nothing from him so far."

"And what of my son?"

Metjen rubbed his chin and fixed his dark and intelligent eyes on her. "He must wait his turn as long as king Ptolemy sits beside you on the throne. And in the event you choose to have a child by him, then that child is granted greater legitimacy than your son, who is by a Roman man, who has not acknowledged him."

Cleopatra leaned back and nodded. All her plans for her son Ptolemy Caesar were coming undone. And she too would soon be at risk.

CHAPTER 25
EPHESUS, ASIA–MINOR

He was almost there. He had escaped once again, vanishing into the hostile empty lands and finding his way through Judaea and Syria until he reached Cilicia. His vagrancy had taught him much–how to survive in hostile conditions, how to listen carefully to the chatter of the people to understand how the winds of politics changed direction, and what might benefit him as he sought resurrection to his former glory.

As he came up that hill, near the town of Ephesus, tired and feeling dirty, he finally saw the columns and Doric structure of the beautiful temple of Artemis. There it stood for centuries, historians said, and blessed all those who came to it. The temple stood on higher ground, and it melted into the skies with its white marble facade blending gloriously with the wispy clouds. It was as if the temple reached into the heavens. The rest of the sky was brilliant blue, and it was hot on this day.

He ate the coarse bread and drank some water from his sheepskin before he arrived at the wide, smooth steps of the temple. He would wait here, keeping a watchful eye for the person he was here to meet. He dared not enter inside, should a priest or official recognize him–extremely unlikely, but a chance he would not take. Not just yet.

He sat until evening with no fortune smiling upon him. The person who he had come all this way for had not shown up. So, he found a corner to sleep and wait for dawn.

The flat and wide steps were comfortable to sleep, offering some respite to his back after months of rocky ground. Tired and thankful that there were no guards here to harass him, he fell sound asleep.

With the roosters making a ruckus and the rays of the sun slowly warming up his skin, he woke up and rubbed his eyes. There was a public fountain nearby for him to wash his face, and the reflection in the pooled water showed his gaunt visage, graying hair, and an unruly curly beard. Hopefully, he was recognizable to whom it mattered.

The sounds of morning ceremonies began with bells and chants. Adherents walked in one by one; the old and the infirm, the young, travelers and the tired. Some of the temple staff too began to trickle in–cleaners, priests, cooks. He watched them from afar, sitting on the steps on one side. Finally, his heart quickened its pace when he saw a figure emerge from the corner.

She was graceful in her walk. Lean, beautiful, and her hair tied like a horse's tail. She wore a simple garment of priests–a loose drapery that covered her from shoulder to ankles. She balanced a jug in her hands. Her face was serene and had assumed a certain weariness. Her hips swayed gently, but with the maturity of a woman. Quite different from the raging beauty he last remembered.

He willed himself to stand, and with his heart thudding in his chest, he approached her. She seemed not to notice him, for her eyes were planted on the ground. She stepped aside, perhaps with the intention of letting him pass. But he stood in front of her, smiling. She looked up in surprise, and for a moment her lovely eyes did not register his presence. "Sir, would you–"

And then she stopped. Her eyes opened wide and she hesitated for a moment. Finally, Arsinoe put the jug down and surprised Theodotus with a warm hug.

CHAPTER 26
ALEXANDRIA

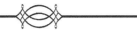

The men walked through the dimly lit corridors of the palace. It was night, well beyond even the hours of workaholics. Guards positioned in intervals along the way to the Royal bedrooms saluted them, for they were known to be part of the Royal Guard and had permission to walk the corridors on Her Majesty's authority.

They moved with purpose towards Ptolemy's bedroom. It was a corridor away from Her Majesty's. Once there, the leader, a large man and Head of the Royal Guard, asked the guards to retire for the day for it was a surprise inspection. Once the guards left, they quietly opened the door and entered.

His Majesty Ptolemy was asleep below fine linen covers on his comfortable bed. The large window was open and let in a gentle white moonlight and a cool breeze that made the lone lamplight flicker and dance. One man quickly strode to the King Ptolemy's bed and got near his legs. Another near the head. The third swiftly removed the glass vial from his pocket. The fourth straddled the boy-king.

The man near the head suddenly lunged forward and put a thick silk scarf around the sleeping king's mouth, and the other two rapidly tied the two legs and hands by wrapping a rope. Ptolemy woke up in terror and began to thrash, his eyes wide open, reflecting the moonlight. But no sound came of him, for his mouth was by then firmly closed, and his legs and hands were made immobile. The fourth man roughly pinched Ptolemy's nose. Unable to move and breathe, the boy-king gasped, which was when the fourth man poured all the liquid content in his vial into Ptolemy's mouth and closed his lips. The third man let go of the nose and Ptolemy gulped all the liquid.

They held him firmly as he thrashed and fought. His body began to spasm and convulse. He began to foam copiously in his mouth. Ptolemy's muscles contracted like a rope being pulled, and eventually, his hands and legs went rigid. One of the men then placed a pillow on his face and held it down until the struggling boy-king finally took his last breath and his body went slack.

The leader confirmed that the boy-king's heart was no longer beating and that his breathing had stopped. Ptolemy's visage was peaceful and serene again, as if he had only been asleep. One man pressed a pillow on the boy's face for several more minutes just be sure.

Once satisfied, they placed the linen sheet back on his body, rearranged his hair, unbound his hands and legs and arranged them in a casual position, and quietly left the room.

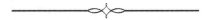

Alexandria plunged into three days of mourning, led by Her Majesty, who let it be known that divine king Ptolemy had become beloved of the gods after accidentally poisoning himself during an experiment gone wrong. She lamented at his unfortunate and untimely death, and arranged for a magnificent funeral. Her last brother was interred in a splendid Alexandrian tomb, where she had him blessed by senior priests.

Ptolemy XIV, Father-Loving, was then buried in a marble and gold-lined sarcophagus.

With the throne of her co-ruler now empty, Cleopatra promptly announced that her son, Ptolemy Philopator Philometor Caesar, son of divine Isis Cleopatra Philopator and divine Venus Gaius Julius Caesar, god himself, was now the co-ruler.

Charmian never asked Cleopatra anything, and Kadmos made no mention of the incident. Metjen knew enough not to investigate, and general Valentinus left it to Egyptian affairs.

Cleopatra was now the absolute monarch. Just that there was that one question of Arsinoe still at large, of course.

And that traitor Theodotus.

CHAPTER 27
EPHESUS
ARSINOE

Arsinoe was thrilled to see him. His presence was like a piece of comfort from home. They chatted happily about "old times," and she wanted to know everything he could tell.

They shared an afternoon meal like they were acquaintances. She had changed significantly–mellowed, almost, still ambitious but without that fiery temper. She had known little of what happened in Egypt, but knew more about the ongoings in Rome through the travelers. He told her of the battle of Nile, disappearance of boy-king Ptolemy XIV, and then created a glorified version of the uprising against Cleopatra in which he had been betrayed and ambushed by the dishonorable Apollodorus. He made no mention of using an impostor. Fabricius became the villain in this story and Apollodorus apparently had unnatural sex with sheep.

Then, Arsinoe told her story, to which Theodotus commiserated appropriately. He was, however, surprised that Caesar had let her go. She was now an attendant for the head eunuch priest of the temple. Him, she saw as a protector, for he had offered her sanctuary when many others rejected her for fear of attracting malcontents.

"Very few know who I am, and I prefer it that way," she said. "Whatever we wish to do, Theodotus, we have to be quiet. If anyone finds out that we have met, you can be assured that my monstrous sister will set her dogs on us."

Theodotus nodded. Arsinoe still resented her sister as she always did, which served him excellently. For all her smiles and smooth talk, Cleopatra was dangerous. The many-tongued enchantress was intelligent as she was ruthless–and he had learned it by underestimating her.

"What do you know of the happenings in Rome?" he asked her. He had heard pieces of information–the best being that Caesar had been assassinated. That was the most joyful news he had heard the last year.

"Rome has descended into civil war. What I have heard is that a coalition of Senators, headed by Senators Marcus Junius Brutus and Gaius Cassius Longinus, assassinated him and soon fled Italy. It seems that the pro-Caesar group is headed by Mark Antony and a certain Octavian, a nephew of Caesar."

"I have never heard of Octavian. What about Cleopatra's son?" Theodotus asked.

Arsinoe smiled. "Caesar's will was read in public. He left nothing for her and did not acknowledge her son."

Theodotus clapped in glee. "I knew it! He just treated her like the harlot she is. She is finished then!"

Arsinoe shook her head. "How many times have you said *she is finished*? She is far from finished. If we must do something, we have to be patient. Our only bet is perhaps finding out if there is a way for us to benefit from reaching out to Brutus or Cassius."

Theodotus pondered and rubbed his chin. "Do you think this is the right time, Your Majesty? Should I make my way to Cassius' camp?"

"Do not call me Your Majesty loudly, Theodotus. You will get both of us killed," Arsinoe said. "They are preoccupied. I have heard they are building armies in

Greece. Perhaps find your way there in a few months. But what do you think our proposal should be?"

Theodotus' chest puffed up with importance. Finally, someone of matter was asking *him* what they should do.

"I think our need and the proposition is clear, Your–. We cannot hope to enter Egypt and foment another uprising. She has a firm grip now. So we either need Parthian help, or Roman help. The Parthians have a cordial relationship with Egypt, and they care more about Judaea. It is unlikely they will do something. Rome is what we should take advantage of. Cleopatra's patron is dead. So we exploit the civil war."

Arsinoe nodded thoughtfully. "Go on."

"We, or rather I, will go to Cassius or Brutus. If they turned on Caesar and are fighting his faction, then they will have no love for Caesar's lover. We put the fear of her in them–that she will use her son to her advantage over time, and that she is actively working to support the Caesar faction against them. And that the only way to stop Cleopatra is for them to dismiss her from the throne and appoint you as Queen instead."

"All that sounds compelling," she said, chewing her lips.

Theodotus leaned towards her and whispered. "You would make a magnificent Queen, Your Majesty."

Her eyes glowed at the mention of being Queen. She rubbed the bridge of her nose and sighed. "I would," she said, softly.

They discussed the details of the plan some more. Theodotus would take a new name and Arsinoe would offer him a job as a tutor at the temple. He would stay here until it was time to travel west to meet the Roman consuls. The heavily traveled route and the stream of visitors to the temple meant they would always have news.

CHAPTER 28
ALEXANDRIA
CLEOPATRA

Cleopatra loved inspecting the shipyards along with Metjen. Her Prime Minister was an expert (among many other things) in operations and craft of building a Navy and a formidable merchant fleet. They walked the yard looking at the skeletons of impressive biremes, triremes, specialized warships, large merchant vessels, little speed boats, and even leisure boats with new sails being installed. All of it provided a welcome change from the rote of meetings, councils, prayers, endless visitor dinners, application dispositions, and anything related to administration. She welcomed the sensation of walking amidst the smell of raw wood and warm cloth, coal-burnt smoke, molten metals, cooked meat, incense, cow and camel urine, and seaweed. To add to those heady smells were the sounds and sensations–ruckus of seagulls, the clanging against anvils, inspectors shouting at the workers, the crackling of fires, the dull *thud* of nails against wood, the sensation of cool sand beneath the feet, the flutter of new masts, the taste of salty air and the occasional bug, the howls of dogs and the clang of bells on the necks of camels sitting and chewing leisurely.

It was magical. If she could, she would be here every week, but such were her pressures that she could afford one trip only once every few months.

She raised her face and let the wind caress her. Then she turned to a group of camels sitting on the side, resting after what may have been a long trudge carrying building materials. "I love camels."

"They are beautiful creatures," Metjen concurred. "My father reared camels and I learned how to milk them."

"Is there anything you haven't done, Metjen?" she asked, looking at her Prime Minister.

"Never hunted a lion, Your Majesty," he said, smiling.

She pointed to a particularly chubby camel sitting nearby, chewing happily and with its eyes half-closed. "Look at the lazy one. Look at his face, uncaring for the world! No worries. No desire for kingdoms. No one trying to murder it. Just sitting and getting fatter!"

Metjen laughed. They both walked to the sitting camel as a handler came running to ensure the animal behaved well. She caressed its hairy neck and scratched its chin, enjoying the serenity of the moment. The camel turned to her and grunted, blowing smelly air on her face. She jumped back, laughing with glee. "By the gods, it stinks!"

They spent some more time by the camel before resuming the walk towards the docks. "How are we doing on the rebuild of the Navy?"

"We have a navy of four hundred ships now, Your Majesty. No doubt Rome will come calling at some point."

"Yes. The dogs are at each other's throats," she said, as she ran her hand on a smooth wooden plank ready for assembly. When she was pleased with a specific construction, she handed small rewards to the excited and grateful workers.

The sun was preparing to set in the West, turning orange and making the Mediterranean turn liquid gold. The light rippled on the waves and she looked out to the sea. As she breathed in and enjoyed the moment, she noticed the crested helmet of her trusted Roman commander. Valentinus' red plumes contrasted with the yellow bands of the sky.

"General Valentinus? What brings you here?"

"I have been seeking you since yesterday, Your Majesty. I have some news."

Here we go.

She nodded. "Well, deliver it, but let me enjoy the scenery and the sounds."

"Of course, Your Majesty," he said, as he drove a wedge between Metjen and her, and stood in the middle. "Consul Cassius Longinus has a message."

It took her a moment to register that Cassius was the consul, who, along with Brutus, had murdered Caesar and then run away to Greece to prepare for a fight with the Caesar faction of Antony and Octavian.

"What does he want?" she asked, angry, knowing that the treasonous scum had ended what could have been a glorious future for her.

Valentinus handed the papyrus. She broke the seal and read the message, an unsightly scribble written possibly directly by the hand of Cassius.

Her Majesty Queen Cleopatra,

Greetings. I ask of the well-being of your child and peace in Egypt. Matters of urgency require your attention. In light of your previous support to Gaius Julius Caesar, I seek to give Her Majesty the opportunity to pledge loyalty to the will of the people of Rome, and require an immediate dispatch of ten-thousand legionnaires, five-hundred ships, and one-hundred tons of grain, to be sent to the port

of Thasos by Philippi, failing which I am
compelled, by the will of the Senate, to march
upon Egypt with my vast legions and institute a
governor of Rome's choice. I wait for Her
Majesty's response.

By order of,

Consul Hon. G. C. Longinus

S.P.Q.R

She scoffed. She then handed the letter to Valentinus and watched the Roman general's face as he read it quietly. He then handed it back to her.

Cleopatra sighed loudly. These fools never understood her. They still thought she was a little dog in their vassal states who would come running to whatever master called her.

"The hubris of men that murdered Caesar and pretend that the people of Rome are by their side," she said, holding the papyrus and waving it. Valentinus did not respond, but Cleopatra knew that the general was despondent by the news of Caesar's death.

"Whose side are you on, Valentinus?" she asked, surprising the general. He had never ventured to declare his loyalties, and she knew that the civil way put him in a precarious position. But she wagered that even the rule-driven Valentinus had certain scruples.

Valentinus smiled wryly. "A day like this would come, Your Majesty. I cannot side with the men that murdered Caesar in cold blood. And I do not support those that threaten you. I am on your side."

Cleopatra nodded to him. "I am grateful, General. Perhaps I do not say it enough, to you. How capable is this man in matters of war and invasions?"

"He is an experienced commander. With Brutus, he will be a formidable force."

"The question is whether Cassius thinks he can march such a distance, all the way from Greece, through Syria and Judaea, into Egypt, when he is also threatened on his western front by Antony and Caesar Octavian."

Metjen ventured. "That would be foolish, no matter how large his forces."

"But why would that be a problem if he moves his entire force, intact, and then occupies Egypt? Antony and Octavian would not have to chase him all over, and they are not ready," she said, knowing the early stages of the civil war.

"I agree with Her Majesty," said Valentinus.

"Would they still make that hazardous march to Egypt, with the hope that you will offer no resistance or bog them down with defensive warfare?" Metjen asked.

"The Prime Minister understands me," Cleopatra said. "For all his bluster, I do not believe Cassius will really force his way through to Egypt. It is too much of a gamble. I have no interest in supplying him anything."

"Yes, Your Majesty," said Metjen. "But surely you are preparing to respond, in some way?"

"Of course. I will give him something, without giving him anything," she said, smiling.

And she also had something else to tell Cassius, just in case.

CHAPTER 29
WESTERN CAPPADOCIA
CASSIUS

Cassius studied the smug man before him. Theodotus had arrived the previous day, loudly seeking audience with the senator and general who was now camped in western Cappadocia, building his army for the long struggle ahead, fighting the factions of Mark Antony and Gaius Julius Caesar Octavian.

"My men say that I must hear your proposal," Cassius said, a small smile rising up his lips. "And of course, you must first tell me about yourself."

Theodotus, puffed up with importance, took his time to describe his illustrious career (*the highest-ranked tutor in all of Egypt, of course*) in the court of the Ptolemies. His tutelage to the royals (*Cleopatra, Arsinoe, the Ptolemy brothers, and even the late Majesty himself learned from me*). His exceptional oratory skills (*I could be of great use to your officers, general*). And his fall due to the machinations, treachery, and betrayal of Queen Cleopatra (*she sees no tutor or patron, no father or brother, and lives her day seeking blood and nights in amoral debauchery*).

"You bring a wealth of knowledge and experience on Egypt, it appears," Cassius said, drumming his fingers on the table.

"I do, general, and my heart thirsts to be of service to your cause. No one in all of Egypt exists with greater knowledge of the inner workings than I," he said, pointing to his chest. Theodotus was a healthy-looking man–

wherever he had sought refuge since his run from Egypt, as he said, had fed him well.

"And what cause is it, Theodotus?"

Theodotus stood, pushing his chair back. He straightened his back, and his voice changed to a stentorian tone, surprising Cassius. It was impressive.

"May I explain my thinking, General?"

"Of course. I am a patient listener," Cassius said, smiling.

Theodotus launched into a speech. "Gaius Julius Caesar inserted himself into the affairs of Egypt, just as he attempted to become Dictator of Rome. His desire to become king was evident in his interactions with Queen Cleopatra. Together, they wished to rule as emperor and empress. What Roman man of principle would not be offended by that?"

"Indeed."

"And you, esteemed general Cassius, took those bold steps to remove Caesar from the realm, while we humbly submit that we failed to remove Cleopatra as well. And now Cleopatra grows more powerful, with her eyes towards Rome itself by using her son for legitimacy. And she will no doubt seek to support your opponents."

"That is true, Theodotus. Egypt's considerable resources, when put in service of my enemies, could threaten the Republic and create an opening to this cunning Queen. I was no great admirer of her, and Cicero had many choice words as well."

Cicero, that blathering idiot who complained like a little boy, because she forgot to bring his toys.

Theodotus beamed. "And with my knowledge and support, you will be able to depose Cleopatra, and in her place, appoint the rightful ruler who will forever be indebted to you."

"You speak of Arsinoe."

"Indeed. Falsely accused and sent away by her own sister. Cleopatra urged Caesar to murder her, but by the grace of god, she was spared. The depravity of Cleopatra is intolerable!" he announced, loudly, his voice rising enough for a guard to peek through the tent.

"So what do you suggest?" Cassius asked, leading back and clasping his hands. And also to get away from the strange smell of the man. Theodotus had applied some rose paste on himself, and the flowery smell mixed with copious amounts of sweat was revolting.

Theodotus returned to his chair. He clasped his fingers and stared into the infinity thoughtfully. He made a great show of shaking his head and sighing, as if there were no choices except what he would propose.

"This is my recommendation, General. With Her Majesty Arsinoe by your side, and me behind you, let us take an army through to Egypt at haste. General Valentinus will take his orders from any Roman Senator and will not fight you. The Egyptian army is weak and hates Cleopatra. Most will defect to you, and the rest will flee. Your victory will be quick and decisive, and with Her Majesty Arsinoe on the throne, you are guaranteed a powerful ally in your endeavors against the pro-Caesar faction."

Cassius leaned back and appraised Theodotus. How confident he was!

"You make powerful arguments, Theodotus. And it seems you are confident Arsinoe will join you."

"She will, Your Excellency," Theodotus said, his bushy eyebrows dancing with glee. "I have already met her!"

Cassius was surprised by the enterprising nature of the man. "That is most impressive. I suppose she agrees with your assessment?"

"She absolutely does, Your Excellency. It is only a matter of your orders."

Cassius sighed. He reached for a papyrus scroll in front of him and opened it slowly. "Do you know what this is?"

Theodotus eyed the document. He looked confused. "How would I know—"

"It is a letter from Cleopatra."

CHAPTER 30
WESTERN CAPPADOCIA
THEODOTUS

Theodotus was alarmed. "Cleopatra?"

Cassius continued. His eyes cold and with no affection towards Theodotus. "A letter from Her Majesty Cleopatra. I received it twenty days ago. She has, as you expected, chosen to side with Mark Antony and Caesar Octavian."

Theodotus felt relieved. "As I said, General! It is then necessary to move to Egypt as soon as we can. Without delay."

"I was already planning to do that. She has been transparent and rather apologetic in her response. Do you want me to read it?"

Theodotus hesitated but his curiosity was piqued. Knowing what was in the letter might even help him make his case stronger. "Yes, General."

Cassius squinted and began to read.

Honorable Senator Gaius Cassius Longinus,

It is no secret that I mourn my husband Gaius Julius Caesar, but my affection for him was not borne of disloyalty to you. My subjects suffer from the ravages of our civil war and meaningful supply to Rome can only be fulfilled if Egypt is healed, and of that I am certain, and for which I am committed and keep myself occupied at this time. My wish is to remain neutral in this conflict, for I have no voice in the affairs of Rome. While I harbor no ill towards your illustrious self, General Valentinus and his legions have pledged loyalty to the Caesar faction, will remain in Egypt, and take no part in action unless Egypt is directly threatened.

Should you prevail at the end of this dark chapter, Egypt will, and has always been, a valuable partner to Rome, and His Excellency Gaius Cassius Longinus will be afforded the warmest welcome and an enduring hand in friendship and trade.

"She says a few more things, but those are of no interest for this conversation. But it seems she will mind her own business, and work with me when this is all over. I am disappointed but I see Her Majesty's argument."

Theodotus was unsure where the conversation was headed. It all seemed amply clear. "You cannot trust her, General."

"And why must I trust you? Why do I need you by my side if I must go to Egypt?"

Theodotus argued his case, about his knowledge, wisdom, and ability to handle volatile Alexandria.

"But if all that were true, why would you be here, like a fugitive?" he asked, smiling.

And if you had all the support of Rome against Caesar, why are you here in Cappadocia building an army, you arrogant bastard, Theodotus wanted to ask, but controlled his tongue.

"As I said, General, Cleopatra—"

"I have no intention of putting Arsinoe on the throne, much less you leading anything. We will place a governor."

Theodotus felt heat rise up his face. This was not how he envisaged this conversation.

"Nothing you have said so far is insightful. I have enough messengers from Egypt telling me all I need to know. But there is something else, Theodotus," Cassius said, his voice now cold and ominous.

Theodotus' response stuck in his throat. His heart began to race.

Cassius continued. "Tell me what happened in Pelusium when Pompey Magnus sought asylum. I have heard that Cleopatra instigated his murder. How true is it? Details are murky because I know King Ptolemy's forces were in Pelusium as well."

Theodotus broke into a sweat. He had suddenly found himself in treacherous territory. How close was Cassius to Pompey? How much did this matter to him? Was Cassius testing him with a lie like how Cleopatra had lied about Ptolemy's mole?

"They may have lied to you, Your Excellency," he said trying to sound sincere. "The decisions to deal with the Great General Pompey was made in King Ptolemy's camp."

Cassius cocked his head slightly. "Go on. What happened there?"

Theodotus sighed deeply. He shook his head with sadness. "To even think of it makes me profoundly sad, General. There was much debate on how to handle the general's request. Pothinus, the Regent, finally decided that Pompey should die. I resisted heavily, Your Excellency. I told them why killing a venerable Roman Consul on Egyptian soil was a terrible idea. Queen Cleopatra may have influenced Pothinus, but I was not privy to that decision."

"Then why did you gleefully present Pompey's head to Caesar?"

Theodotus' fingers went cold. He stammered. "Coerced. Your Excellency! Surely you recognize that one sometimes does what one loathes to, when under constant pressure and the eyes of tyrants!"

Cassius leaned back and stared at Theodotus who blabbered some more about how Cassius should take his assistance, in any way, in any manner, and if His Excellency were not interested, then Theodotus would be on his way.

Cassius did not respond. Instead, he nodded at someone behind him. Before he could react, Theodotus felt two strong arms seize and yank him off the chair. Theodotus protested loudly but they dragged him outside the tent, with Cassius following.

"General! What are you doing? Let me go. I am here to help!"

But Cassius did not respond.

Theodotus kicked around frantically, unsure what was happening. *What is going on?!*

They dragged him to a small mound and what he saw on it chilled him to the core.

A cross.

Crucifixion cross. Lying flat on the mound.

Theodotus began to scream and fight his guards. "No, General! Why? I shall live quietly, please, no!"

How could he have gotten this so wrong? Why did he listen to Arsinoe?

They dragged him as he thrashed and kicked, shouting for mercy, and soiling himself in intense fear. Someone punched him in the stomach causing him to collapse. They dragged him onto the cross, stretched his hands to the sides and tied the wrists with rope. Likewise, they tied his feet. Then, even as Theodotus begged and implored, they hoisted the cross on its pit and implanted it firmly to the ground.

Cassius stood before a gasping and heaving Theodotus. "I would also have you scourged. But here you are, with some intention of helping me, and I shall spare you for whips. You said dead men don't bite, did you not Theodotus?"

Theodotus struggled against his restraints and fought to breathe. "It was–"

Cassius shouted at him. "Quiet! It was your plan to end the life of a man I so highly regarded. You had a Roman consul murdered with not a whiff of concern and supreme arrogance, knowing that such violence would invite Crucifixion. You had his head hacked off and presented as if it were a trophy. Do you think of me as a useful idiot to whom you can lie and take advantage of?"

"No, no General, my intentions were pure, I–"

"I loved Pompey. I was distraught at his death. Cleopatra mentioned your role in the letter, perhaps guessing you might come to me. And what she says is the same as what I heard from other credible sources," Cassius said, looking up to a terrified Theodotus.

"It was the heat of the moment and fog of politics, General!" Theodotus sobbed, having lost all his energy, shaking in terror and fear of what was to come.

"And greater men see through such fogs," Cassius said, coldly. "Men!"

An impaler walked forward with a hammer and several sturdy and rusted long nails. Theodotus began to bellow with fear.

They drove the nails through his wrists and ankles, crunching his bones and rupturing the ligaments. Theodotus screamed and screamed until he turned delirious. Cassius left him there, gasping and moaning until sunset. Theodotus begged for all the gods for his life to end, and for him to return in the next as a tutor, and one who would stay out of intrigue. Finally, as the sun began to set, well before how he may have died otherwise, Cassius ordered a man to end Theodotus' life.

Theodotus welcomed the tip of the spear as it rammed through his ribs into his heart, and he left this realm of the living, his mission unfulfilled.

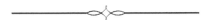

Cassius thought long and hard about Cleopatra's letter. She had further politely insinuated that should Cassius march south to Egypt, she would declare allegiance to Antony, and establish robust defenses that would bog down Cassius' army and deplete him. *No one knows Egypt better than me, honorable Senator,* she had said.

He decided to hold his march south and instead focus on building his army for a standoff. Meanwhile, he responded to Cleopatra anyway, informing her that he would call upon her after matters were settled with Antony and Octavian. He also noted the end of Theodotus and the fact that he had met with Arsinoe.

With this sorry affair ended, Cassius turned to the larger matters of his world.

CHAPTER 31
ALEXANDRIA
CLEOPATRA

"That leaves us with Arsinoe," she said, as she handed back to Metjen the missive from Cassius. The Roman general had responded to her message. He had curtly thanked her for the frankness, and that he valued her continued relation should they prevail. Cassius had called off his potential march to Egypt due to other developments.

This brought great relief to Cleopatra, for she knew that without Mark Antony or Octavian's help, she would be destroyed if Cassius and Brutus came her way. That was two months ago—she did not know the situation at the moment. Cassius also told her that Theodotus had arrived before him and had been executed. However, most alarming was the fact that Theodotus had met Arsinoe who apparently still nursed the idea of returning to Egypt.

But now was not the time to worry about Arsinoe—she had nothing and no one to come after Cleopatra.

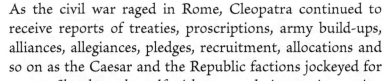

As the civil war raged in Rome, Cleopatra continued to receive reports of treaties, proscriptions, army build-ups, alliances, allegiances, pledges, recruitment, allocations and so on as the Caesar and the Republic factions jockeyed for power. She threw herself with renewed vigor to improving Egypt's financial standing—the currency had become stronger, trade stabilized, and Alexandria was now back to its glory, hustling and bustling with people, parties, and spectacular constructions.

But many months since Cassius' letter, there was a missive from Rome, seeking her support. For men and materials. For warships and coin. For copper and tin. She knew it wouldn't stop. The pressure would build.

She summoned Metjen and Simonides to consult. She had Valentinus join as well.

"I have no intention of sending overt support to Cassius or Brutus. To that I reckon you will all agree. But what do you think I should do to Mark Antony and Octavian's demands of supply?" she asked, looking at her most trusted senior men. For this occasion she had shunned her throne room, instead preferring to sit below a gorgeous open marble dome set by sea. The wind was cool and comfortable. A difficult conversation could be made more palatable amongst the cries of seagulls and the sound of crashing waves.

Metjen crossed his legs and leaned forward. "We have no clarity on who will win this, Your Majesty. I would suggest we wait and not respond."

Valentinus shook his head vigorously. The grizzled general was now a veteran of Alexandrian affairs and never afraid to speak his mind. "That would be a mistake. Mark Antony is an exceptional commander, and I have heard that Gaius Julius Caesar Octavian is astute. If they request help, Egypt should forthwith lend a helping hand. It also ensures, Your Majesty, that you are still by Caesar's side."

Simonides joined. "But we are receiving reports from Greece and Cappadocia, that Brutus and Cassius are amassing a formidable army. It also appears those senior Senators have considerable backing. Why are you so sure, general, that Caesar's faction will win?"

"Because Mark Antony has spent years fighting for Caesar. No one else has that richness of experience."

Cleopatra stepped in. "But Valentinus, I have heard Mark Antony to be profligate and having little control over his emotions and actions. He may have been effective under Caesar, but what makes you think he will do well on his own? I have deep love for Caesar, but he is no more, and I have a kingdom to rule while dealing with constant interference by Rome."

"Because General Antony has adroitly managed to survive and build his faction after the murder, Your Majesty. That shows a man capable of rousing admiration and support. His men will follow him. They love him, just as they loved Caesar," Valentinus said, his pride in his former commander still strong and unwavering.

Metjen rubbed his skull and squinted in the sun. "It is easier to feign inability and seek forgiveness for not being overtly in support of either faction, than make explicit gestures and fall afoul of the winning one."

"And that may be a slight the winner may not forget," Valentinus said. "And some are not so forgiving, Prime Minister, for not all are Caesar."

Cleopatra stood and the others did as well. She smiled. "The meeting is not dismissed. Walk with me."

They trailed her as she touched each baluster on the edge of the high ground. "I am condemned if I do, condemned if I don't," she said. "We have just managed to turn around our shipbuilding capacity, we have repaired our harbors and dredged our derelict canals. And just when I have brought peace and stability, I must again send precious resources to some warlord or the other. I may have been more amenable if Caesar or Cicero handed me Judaea."

The men kept quiet, knowing her resentment about being left out of Caesar's will and inability to finagle the rich provinces of Judaea.

She continued. "I know what Antony purports to do–he will aim to finish what Caesar didn't. Subjugate Parthia."

Parthia. That vast and powerful eastern kingdom that had not bowed its head to Rome. Caesar had hoped to pave his way to India after adding Parthia to the Roman empire. He wanted to do what Alexander couldn't. She knew that. But Parthia would be a terrible drain, and she knew that Rome would come knocking on her door for resources. *It was one after the other!*

"Metjen, do you still strongly believe we must wait?"

Metjen nodded without hesitation.

"Valentinus and Simonides, have your positions changed?"

Valentinus said no. Simonides said it was prudent they wait, but then offer assistance once the direction of the winds of victory became a little more evident. Valentinus and Simonides traded friendly barbs of one being stubborn and the other a vacillating weakling.

She held the railings and looked out to the vast and deep blue sea. "I have decided," she said, turning back to them.

"We will do nothing until we receive several more requests, and then offer meager assistance until the fighting men of Rome settle their affairs amongst themselves."

They bowed to her in acceptance.

She would know sooner or later whether her strategy was the most prudent. For now, she would focus her energy on Egypt. She had recently created an academy of arts, summoning the greatest philosophers, mathematicians, cartographers, physicians and sculptors, and provided them food, quarters, and royal audience, all to further their capabilities. She enjoyed their company, and spent hours debating or inquiring various subjects.

She had recently taken an interest in two subjects—one was mathematics, and the other was poisons.

CHAPTER 32
ALEXANDRIA
CLEOPATRA

"Enough. Execute him," she said, turning away from the man writing on the floor, his mouth foaming and eyes turned up so that only the whites were visible. But an hour later, she was pleased with a result where a different prisoner went to sleep quickly and died quietly.

Cleopatra had developed an interest in poisons–and the purpose was manifold. The primary benefit was to recognize symptoms of poisoning so as to protect herself from assassination attempts. And then the study of antidotes to save oneself in the event of poisoning. But the study extended to other useful purposes–use of poison to paralyze areas around wounds to reduce pain, as medicine for specific conditions, and to hasten death in cases where there was no hope for a diseased or wounded person. Arrows dipped in poison could also act as powerful enhancers of damage to the enemy. Her physicians had scoured the magnificent library to bring to her treatises on use of poisons from nearby, including her kingdom's rich past, from Pharaoh Menes to minister Imhotep, the studies during Philadelphos' time, Mithridates of Anatolia, and even from faraway lands like India, where a saint named Sushruta described poisons and antidotes in great detail. She mused how the world was endowed with so many ways to produce poison–belladonna, strychnine, copper, arsenic, antimony, and opium amongst the choices.

She also considered the speed of the poisons in ending life, and if there were ways for one to die without much suffering and their bodies intact as if they were asleep. Cleopatra had been disturbed by the details of her brother's poisoning effects. And therefore, she subjected some condemned prisoners to various dosages and cocktails of herb poisons and snake venom, to observe time and the condition of the body. Where suffering was obvious, she ordered a quick death. Contrary to the romanticization of poison in the tomes, most failed to act quickly, and some produced terrible symptoms. But after many trials, a specific herb cocktail was found to induce a sense of disorientation, sleepiness, and then a quiet death. She decided she would use it sparingly to lessen the suffering of wounded officers in battles, should such days arrive, and one day, perhaps on herself.

CHAPTER 33
EPHESUS

ARSINOE

Arsinoe waited for months hoping Theodotus would return, but there was no news from the Rhetorician, not even a message, let alone a physical presence. Her vague inquiries yielded nothing–it was as if he had vanished after having discussed bold and brave ideas. Had he been murdered on the way to Cassius? Or captured by Cleopatra's agents? Did he abandon the cause after further thought? Whatever it was, the winds whispered nothing.

Meanwhile, the travelers to the temple brought steady news of the drums of war beating louder, with the armies of Cassius and Brutus building to fight those of Antony and Octavian Caesar. While all this was happening, Arsinoe's thirst to return to Egypt had dimmed slowly, having met a wonderful man, and learning of Cleopatra's absolute power in Egypt. She had once dreamed of marrying great kings, and yet the man she yearned for was a modest trader and farmer. And it was by his cajoling that she had asked the head priest to relieve her of priestly duties and relegate her to temple administration, thereby allowing her to break requirements of celibacy. Many nights, Arsinoe lamented how her life had changed from the opulent palaces with arches of gold and cushions of red silk, to dwellings with simple reed mattresses and hay roofs. But in a way, she was happy. This was simple. No one died and no one murdered someone else on a daily basis. There was no intrigue, no violence, no constant stress of who might conspire to kill her. She woke up, cooked food, drew water from a well, went to the temple, cleaned the altar, welcomed visitors, closed the gates at dusk, met her man for a few hours, went home to eat, and then she slept.

As those weeks passed by, Arsinoe finally resolved to leave her past behind.

This little village, this beautiful temple, and that simple man were now home.

CHAPTER 34
ALEXANDRIA
CLEOPATRA

Cleopatra received a steady stream of news over the next several months. That Mark Antony and Octavian had amassed their armies to go up against Brutus and Cassius. Over the months, she received many summons and urgent requests for help, whether money, grain, people, ships, timber, copper, medicinal salves, clothes, footwear, horses, camels, and more money. Most she ignored. Sometimes she sent modest grain shipments and some clothes.

The news continued, and she learned more as time went by.

And that the men were likely to fight somewhere in Greece.

And then that a battle was impending at a location known as Philippi.

And then that the pro-Caesar faction had prevailed, and Cassius and Brutus were dead. She received this with some relief, and sent messengers with congratulatory notes to the victors.

Antony had assumed role as lord of the East, from Italy, and Octavian the West. And that meant domains of interest to Cleopatra were now Antony's. As a client-state of Rome, Cleopatra was now answerable to Mark Antony, a Consul of Rome, and former commander of Julius Caesar.

Cleopatra then received two successive missives from Antony.

To,

Her Majesty Queen Cleopatra,

Honorable M. Antonius, Consul of Rome, hereby demands her Majesty's presence in Tarsus to explain Her Majesty's performance and conduct during the war between Honorable M. Antony and Honorable G. Caesar Octavian., and murderers of G. Julius Caes., G. Cass. Longinus and M. Brutus. You are summoned to answer the charges of lack of support to the men who have fought for G. J. Caes., expression of support to the opposite faction, and reluctance to respond to previous summons.

Consul, General, Protector of the East,

Hon. M. Antonius

She ignored them.

"General Antony sends his greetings, Your Majesty, and demands your presence in Tarsus," the man kneeling before her said. The slim and tall Quintus Dellius, a close friend and advisor to Mark Antony himself, had arrived in Alexandria the previous day with a new summons from Antony. He was a pretentious man, his nasally voice drawing out every Greek word in the most torturous manner until she put an end to his misery and switched to Latin. He had cropped his curly brown hair short, and wore an elaborate toga with maroon borders.

After pleasantries they turned to the urgent matter at hand.

"I have received summons from him before, Dellius, what now?" she asked, without harshness, as Metjen watched. "I am not in the habit of responding to orders."

Dellius smiled. "He has sent me, Your Majesty, and Lord Antony does not send me except for the most pressing matters, or to the most important people."

"And what does he want, specifically?" she asked. "More coin? Ships? Grain?"

Dellius stood straight. "He makes no demand for men and material this time, Your Majesty."

She hid her surprise. *What now?* "Then?"

"He seeks your presence, without further delay, to answer three charges—that you supported Cassius, you failed to rise in favor of Antony and Caesar Octavian, and that you have willfully ignored prior summons—all that cause much concern."

Same thing again.

Cleopatra's heart palpitated. She could not feign ignorance or pretend that the developments in Rome were of no import. She conferred briefly with Metjen before turning her attention to Dellius.

"I have nothing to answer. His charges are frivolous, and my conduct is as it should be," she said.

"As the case may be, Your Majesty. But I have no authority to judge those far above my station. I am only a messenger from the General," he said, bowing. He wiped his head and arranged his hair, reminding her of Caesar's habit.

"And what if I refuse to go? I am no servant of his to run on his summons. I am the Queen of Egypt."

And if you keep up with this insolence I will have you drowned with a rock tied to your ankles. Idiot.

Dellius bowed in acknowledgment. "Queen you may be, Your Majesty, but Queen by his support. You are still, after all, a client-state of Rome, and Antony is the new master."

He irritated her enough for her to want to slap him for his insolence, but his words had truth. Unless she magically expunged Rome from her life, she would always have to balance Rome's demands with her aspirations.

Cleopatra told him that she would answer him tomorrow. She hosted a magnificent ten-course dinner with fowl, boar, pig, wine, beer, bread, peach, grape, a heady concoction made of date, figs, honey candy, Persian and Indian spiced goat, fish, oysters, and sweetened milk. The dinner ended with a dance and flute performance that Dellius very much enjoyed. He frankly admitted that he had never experienced anything like it before. Dellius also sang praises about her intelligence (*I see why Cicero was jealous of you!*) when she lectured him about Rome's history.

Two more meals and perhaps you will tell Antony to come to me, instead. Idiot.

He also assuaged her fears that Antony sought to punish her. "Lord Antony is a very forgiving man, Your Majesty, much like Caesar before him. He will accept rational explanations, and I assure you that he will have seen no one like you. No woman that matches the wit and wisdom, and none with such power and grace. You have nothing to fear! Go to him with humility and seek forgiveness!"

How convenient of him to forget beauty, she thought. But Dellius' forceful declarations that if she were to go to Tarsus as a chastened supplicant and gave her reasons for her behavior during the civil war, Antony might be highly inclined not only to believe her, but also bestow upon her, the things she desired. Dellius seemed to be on her side, at least for now.

What kind of a man was Mark Antony, she wondered. She had barely spoken to him even while in Rome, and all she had heard was his loose and amoral ways, temperamental attitude, lack of control with money, and excessive reliance on unreliable men. But how ruthless was he?

That night she was restless. The soft silk cushions and feathered mattress offered no comfort, and neither did the cool breeze that came through the expansive windows that looked out to the sea. Should she go? What if the quick-tempered Antony turned on her? Romans were often brutal in the treatment of their supplicants, and would he see her as one? What if he announced that she would no longer rule Egypt, or worse, arrest her for defiance?

She tossed and turned. And in the early hours of the morning, she finally summoned Metjen. She needed his counsel. Metjen arrived, bleary-eyed, worried that something had happened. She assuaged his fear and explained the tortured thoughts and her predicament.

"What do you think, Prime Minister, speak your mind," she said, lying on her bed sideways and facing him.

Metjen contemplated and she let him be. When her Prime Minister was in deep thought, he usually came out of it with brilliant insights.

"Have you forgotten what you evoked in Caesar, Your Majesty," he finally said, smiling.

"What do you mean?"

"Remember you told me about the story of the Indian King Porus who faced Alexander after his defeat?"

She squinted her eyes. "And?"

"Porus was brought before Alexander as a prisoner. When Alexander asked Porus how he wished to be treated, the Indian said *As a king*."

Cleopatra smiled. "This is why I woke you up at this hour, Metjen."

Metjen bowed. She was glad that he was by her side.

The next day she decided not to see Dellius. *Let the man stew and wait.* Instead, she asked Charmian to join her in the botanical garden in the central part of the complex. The garden was a place of healing for her, a place to go to calm her mind and make momentous decisions.

And of all the people, Charmian was the dearest. With her lady-in-waiting, she could speak freely of matters other than politics and rule, which could be exhausting. Charmian was now not only managing all the affairs of the palace, but she had also been entrusted with bookkeeping for one subdivision of the Nome, setting her up to be a senior administrator one day.

"The rose is the prettiest," Cleopatra said. "Look at the petals! So beautiful."

"I like lotus more."

"Rose is prettier."

"Lotus."

"I command you!"

"Fine. Rose. But it is not fair Your Majesty that you order me to like what you like."

"Who are you going to petition?"

Charmian grinned. "Mark Antony?"

Cleopatra snapped a small branch and whipped Charmian playfully. "If it was anyone other than you, Charmian, I would have them buried in the sand."

"If I was anyone other than Charmian, I would not have said that," she said, laughing.

"Where is Iras?"

"Arguing with some maid about her dress, no doubt," Charmian said, smiling, as she grazed the chrysanthemums with her palms. All around them was an explosion of colors, flowers of all kind, lovingly managed by the horticulturists.

Iras, now fourteen, was a faithful minor attendant. Her job was to inspect Cleopatra's bedroom after the maids did their job. She was in charge of conveying orders to the kitchen, folding Cleopatra's evening clothes, applying perfume after the bath, and occasionally, under Charmian's supervision, issuing palace administration orders. But she talked so much that Cleopatra or Charmian would often scold her to be quiet and listen.

"So, this Dellius thinks I must go to Antony or there will be serious repercussions," Cleopatra said.

"Will you be safe?" Charmian asked.

"He promises that I will be."

"I remember seeing him when we were in Rome, but did you ever speak to him, Your Majesty?"

"No. He was mostly outside Rome and I greeted him in some gatherings. I never spoke to him or this new boy, Octavian."

"What did Prime Minister Metjen say?"

Cleopatra relayed Metjen's advise and her plan. Charmian approved of the idea with some hesitation. As she thought, she snapped a rose from its stem and held it for Cleopatra to sniff. Then she inserted it into the Queen's hair.

"Go as a Queen you must, Your Majesty. But they have seen Queens."

"What do you mean?"

"If you must truly make a mark, then you cannot go as any Queen. Just as you invoked a surprise in Caesar, you must make an unforgettable impression of Antony that he does not even think about punishing you."

Cleopatra looked at her astute lady-in-waiting. Cleopatra had no family left, except her sister who no doubt only wished death on her. She leaned to admire some light pink water lotus.

"You say intelligent things maybe once a year, Charmian."

"I seek to impress Her Majesty with two intelligent things next year. It would still be better than all your other advisors."

Cleopatra laughed. "How is Kadmos?"

Charmian giggled. "He is such a character. But he cares for me, is kind to Iras, and even though I see him eyeing other girls in the palace, he seems to be faithful."

"He is getting fatter. Feed him less. I want the Head of my Royal Guard to be able to run to my protection, not roll."

"He eats four or five meals and won't stop!" she rolled her eyes. "He burps but goes for the next helping. With Her Majesty's grace we have a bathhouse but he won't go unless I force him to."

"I told you not to marry a pig!"

"He is not a pig, Your Majesty, just a little stubborn," Charmian said. Cleopatra enjoyed hearing Charmian's marital complaints. She wondered if she would ever be in that situation. Would kings and queens behave that way at all?

She sat on a bench and inhaled the pleasant aromatic air. "Have Dellius appear before me, tomorrow."

The next day she gave Dellius her response. She would travel to Tarsus and meet Lord Mark Antony to make her case.

"Be bedecked but be humble, Your Majesty. Be a respectful and remorseful supplicant," Dellius advised.

She stared at him. "To go like a supplicant is to be treated as one. I wish to be treated as a Queen."

PART II

Her Majesty Queen Cleopatra Philopater, having graced the people for **twenty-eight years** since her arrival from the heavens, has ruled her subjects for **eleven years** after ascending the throne as Regent.

CHAPTER 35
TARSUS, CILICIA
MARK ANTONY

Antony was smitten by her. First, it was that spectacular entry into Tarsus, on the gold, silver, silk, and rose bedecked barge with music piping from its sides, while dressed as Isis. The people had gone berserk at the display and she received an adoration he could only hope for. Then, it was his time on her barge, summoned there instead of her coming to him, and entertained in a way that defied description. For two nights he had been intoxicated out of his mind and his officers had to revive him in the morning. And finally, it was her intelligence and wit (*you may be a Lord but the East is quite a stretch*), her bawdy words without reserve (*even if a beautiful girl had her mouth on Valentinus' flag pole, he would look to Caesar for what to do next*), and that little dimple on her face, that had won him over. Cicero, that old, thorny bastard, now long dead, was right about his fear of her. She was bewitching and could drag any man to ruin. No wonder even Caesar, a great man and a lover of many women himself, had been enamored by Cleopatra.

But after all that pomp and gay revelations were over, his advisors reminded him that she was here to answer his charges, and not for him to behave around her like an infatuated teen.

So, finally, he issued a stern order to her, still on the boat, that she must formally appear before him to answer for her conduct. And there she was, sitting in front, somber in a dignified Greek attire, a sky-blue diadem, and a single, spectacular pearl necklace, staring at him with those cool gray eyes.

The only person with her was her lady-in-waiting, the woman named Charmian, lovely and pregnant.

"As the Queen of Rome's client-state, and as one placed on her throne by Caesar himself, you must account for your conduct," he said, trying to sound harsh. He deliberately lowered the tone of his voice with the hopes of sounding ominous. Like a lion threatening the deer before it.

"I am here to answer your questions, Lord Antony. But you must recognize that it was I who gave Caesar valuable advise that helped him extricate himself from the mess he created in Alexandria," she said, unflinching, fixing those glass-gray eyes on him. Her auburn hair shined in the morning light. Antony felt his pulse quicken at her sight.

"As that may be. What of the reports that you supported Cassius?"

She flicked her wrist and rolled her eyes. "Lies and unfounded rumors. I did no such thing. I assisted Dolabella, who was a man of your faction, and he lost to Cassius. General Cassius threatened me, and yet I did not relent."

"So you say."

"Because so it is," she responded haughtily.

"And why did you not rise up to support me?"

"The seas were unfavorable to send a fleet, and it would have been wasteful to send legions via land. The question, Lord Antony, is not whether I was for or against you, but whether I am with you from hereon. I was always for you, but unable to help for reasons beyond my control. But I am here now. And you have Egypt's cooperation, and my divine support, for your plans for Parthia."

Antony was taken aback at the mention of Parthia. How did she guess his intention? He had not discussed Parthia with her. He argued some more with Cleopatra, but she refused to admit her failings and stuck to her position: she did nothing to help the enemy, and she was constrained in her ability to help him directly via sea. But with Antony controlling the east, she would find it easier to support him financially and logistically. He really needed her, she assured him, for without Egypt's vast reserves, Parthia would only be a dream.

"You seem to know of my plans. Parthia is still a while away. We have to speak of your grain and onion shipments to my legions."

"What of them?" she asked, putting on an innocent tone.

"You are deliberately raising prices when we need it the most. They have gone up almost an eighth in the last year. This is price gouging."

"It is supply and demand," she said, cocking her neck and flicking a wrist. "Surely you know, Lord Antony. If I were price gouging, I would have raised prices by a fifth or a third."

"It still impacts my finances."

"Then why are you charging us a tenth higher for wood supplies from Anatolia? What you pay higher for my grain, you seek in your wood."

This woman!

Antony eyed Cleopatra. He had never talked to a monarch who could rattle trade terms and fractions, and this one was a woman. He turned to his attendant who struggled to control his smile.

"You seem to be unwilling to relent on any position," Antony said, a little irritated.

Cleopatra looked at him coolly. She finally responded. "The volume of grain we send is far higher than the quantity of wood we import, so I recognize the impact of higher prices. We will honor prices to the level just after Philippi, if you agree to reduce prices of Anatolian export and also Italian wines."

Antony turned to his accountant and whispered. "Is she making idiots out of us?"

The man responded. "She is right, sir. Though Octavian controls the exports out of Italy."

Antony turned to her. "I do not control prices on Italian wines. You must write to Octavian. But yes, I can control Anatolian exports."

He was satisfied that he got something out of the exchange. It was remarkable that she haggled like a crusty shopkeeper, only that her scale covered countries.

Then Antony turned to Egypt's supply of linen and people. While she would agree to increase production and supply, she would not commit to sending people. "We have spent years dealing with our internal strife, so do not ask me to create further unrest, Lord Antony. If you take people from me, you should accept disruption to your grain and linen supplies."

It took until evening, but Antony, not one given to recriminations and by then thoroughly impressed by the haughty and clever Queen (even if sometimes condescending and puffed with self-importance of her own divinity), gave up on his accusations. Instead the conversation turned to when Antony would grace Alexandria and partake in a welcome ceremony to recognize his victory. They ended the day with a desire for each to seek the other's company, and Cleopatra left with her retinue, giving him a crooked smile as she swung her hips and walked out.

Dellius teased him that night that even the great Antony had not been able to get Cleopatra to his bed. *You impressed her enough, but not enough for her to disrobe,* he teased. But Antony smiled–the visit to Alexandria would give him plenty of chances to visit the forbidden land between her thighs. She brought a strange excitement to him, but she was also strategically critical for his invasion plans. It was true what Caesar said; she was nothing like the Roman women. Perhaps her allure was her intelligence and immodesty combined with the fact that she was a true Queen, and the richest woman in the world.

The next day they spent time in leisure, discussing Antony's life and his background, her rule in Egypt, and why the coming together of two divinities (he was, after all, Dionysus and she was Aphrodite) was good for the world.

But she had something more in her mind. In the evening, Cleopatra sat by his side, wearing an almost transparent gown, alluring and forbidden at the same time. She ran her fingers through his curly, thick hair. It felt wonderful.

"Lord Antony, you care for our relation, my well-being, and safety, do you not?"

He was puzzled. "I care for the well-being of all my subjects, client-states, and soldiers. Anyone who has been under my command can attest to that."

"But me. Do you care enough for *me*?" she said, pouting. Cleopatra was almost fifteen years younger than him, and some of her ways felt immature and yet endearing. Antony's wife, Fulvia, on the other hand, was all fire and heat.

"I do. Very much. You are of great importance to me, strategically," he said, paused, and completed. "And personally."

"Then you must demonstrate it with a small act. Easy to do and entirely within your domain."

Antony furrowed his brows and switched to his side. He placed a palm beneath his cheek and rested his head on it. "I am not giving you one more piece of land, you have enough," he said, grinning.

She did not smile. Her cool eyes bored into his. "Ephesus is now under your control, is it not, Lord Antony?"

CHAPTER 36
EPHESUS

ARSINOE

Arsinoe finished her work for the day, which ended with washing several of the marble statues, closing the side gates, clearing the floor from debris, picking up flower petals and other offerings from the ground, and dousing the night lamps. It gave her a sense of calm and peace, and she had begun to settle into this routine. Egypt–home–felt like it was only a figment of her imagination, as if that life of hers, as a Princess and future Queen, never happened.

She had recently learned that Brutus and Cassius were dead, not that it mattered anymore for she had settled down to a simple, idyllic life. She had cut her hair short and changed her look.

Arsinoe mopped a section of the floor once again because it looked dirty. She then knelt before an idol of a local goddess, a derivation of Artemis, and prayed. Once completed, she rose to leave. The head priest, a eunuch named Megabyzos, one who had welcomed her on arrival and cared for her, had just left for the day.

It was beginning to get dark. Chilly air wafted through the open door and she walked towards it, raising the hair on her hands. Arsinoe felt as if someone was watching her. Theodotus had warned her that she should always carry a dagger, and Megabyzos had given her permission, knowing that she was never completely safe being a potential successor to the throne in Egypt, no matter how she carried herself.

She stepped out of the temple and dragged the two doors close. From the corner of her eye she noticed that three men, with scarfs around their nose and mouth, were waiting near the footsteps. She stopped to stare at them.

Who were they?

And then they sprinted towards her, jumping multiple steps at a time. Arsinoe recognized danger immediately. She screamed loudly for help, while at the same time reaching down to pull her dagger.

But they were quick. She managed to slash one on his hand, but the others overpowered her. One man pulled her hands back and held them, and then kicked behind her knee causing her to buckle and fall to the ground. She screamed again, but no help was forthcoming. With her lying on the wide marble step, he sat on her back, yanked her hair roughly, and exposed her throat.

No, no, no, no, no.

Arsinoe saw the glint of a blade below her chin, and then a sharp, incredible pain as it sliced her neck. Her blood gushed and stained the pristine white slab. And thus ended the life of Arsinoe, only twenty-six years of age and once in line to be a Queen of Egypt.

CHAPTER 37
CLEOPATRA
ALEXANDRIA

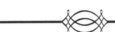

Antony arrived in Alexandria and was welcomed with much pomp and celebration. He stood on a ten-horse chariot flying insignias of the Roman eagle and Ptolemaic Ram, while standing beside a beaming Cleopatra dressed as Isis. The slow ride through the grand Canopic way adorned with flags, cheered by a packed crowd that showered them with rose and lotus, was nothing like Antony had ever experienced, Cleopatra was sure. Valentinus' impressive all-red cavalry paraded in the front, while Simonides' infantry, bedecked in blue, green, and golds, marched behind to the beat of drums and melody of trumpets and harps.

He was an exceptionally handsome man with his broad face, powerful body, curly hair, and affable nature. She watched him as he basked in the adulation as bystanders showered rose petals on him. With Caesar gone, Antony had suddenly become important to the preservation of her own power, ambition, and safeguarding her kingdom from excessive Roman interference. He had already done what she asked—Arsinoe had been assassinated on his orders. Antony also had the temple eunuch Megabyzos arrested and brought before him for giving Arsinoe sanctuary and acknowledging her as a queen. But Cleopatra had received a petition from the temple to pardon the Eunuch, and she had magnanimously done so, with the condition that Megabyzos now serve in Alexandria. The grateful priest was now assigned to a temple of Serapis in the eastern quarters.

"This is a different Alexandria than what you saw when I was young," she said, as she acknowledged the kneeling subjects as she passed them.

"And how!" he exclaimed, as he dodged a bunch of sunflowers headed his way. "You know how to welcome a guest!"

"A god," she said, deferentially. "Dionysus himself."

He smiled and raised her hands with his for another loud cheer from the onlookers. The palace loomed ahead, and Lord Antony would soon learn what Ptolemaic splendor was all about.

Antony settled comfortably in Alexandria, partaking in the festivities and luxury. She could see his nature clearly now, up close, and he was very different from Caesar. Antony was exuberant, loud, quick to temper, flirtatious (*much to her irritation*), and had astonishingly poor habits. He often ate and drank to senselessness, slept late, woke well after the city was up, lazed around and received his messengers late into the evening. He was also exceptional and tiring in bed, but her fondness for him grew each day, even if she had reservations with his conduct.

But Antony was no fool. Beneath that veneer of a man given to largesse was an astute politician–this he made amply evident when they sat to discuss affairs of states.

"Octavian is no doubt painting you as a whore and me a reckless fool," he said, as they lounged outside, playing dice, surrounded by their servants. Iras, her trusted junior attendant, waited by her, as Charmian had taken over larger roles of running the palace.

"How is he? I have never met him. He is so young. Why did Caesar choose him?" she asked.

Antony sighed and drummed his fingers on his chest. "I suppose you are upset, as am I, that he left us out of his will. Octavian is his nephew. He is a calculated, cunning man, using the name of Gaius Julius Caesar. He lacks in his respect for my abilities."

"You are far more capable and popular, Lord Antony, why do you not claim supremacy over the Roman realm and depose him?" she asked, throwing her dice and watching it clatter on the board.

Antony snapped his fingers to order a snack–he had an irritating habit of having the kitchen at his beck and call at all hours. He was putting on weight and she had already teased him about it. *Lord Antony, fattest commander of the Republic! If he cannot stab you, he will sit on you!*

"Even with all your education, Your Majesty, you think Rome is like Egypt. I cannot depose a man who is not king. He has his factions and armies, the backing of a good portion of the Senate, and legitimacy for his name by Caesar."

She rubbed her chin and did not respond. If not now, she would wait years if needed, to find ways to help Antony become the undisputed ruler of the entire Roman sphere of influence, and with him, her as the empress.

Antony continued. "And the Senate does not yet recognize the legitimacy of your son by Caesar."

She nodded. Caesar, for all his kindness towards her, had ultimately betrayed her and left her with no standing in Rome. She would have to rebuild it all again with Antony.

"What do you want to do today? Hunt? Fish? Go to the town dressed like a commoner and get into drunken brawls?" she asked him. A few times, they had ventured into the city dressed like peasants to see how life was, and Antony had gotten himself into drunken fights until his identity was revealed and he had to be taken out of dangerous situations by his bodyguards. But his public, carefree behavior made him even more endearing to the people of the city, who were now reporting his sightings far more than when he actually ventured out. *Every big Roman acting like a fool is now Antony,* she had grumbled.

Antony had also taken to dressing himself as Dionysus and lording over the court proceedings, much to her irritation. He sometimes thought yelling gibberish at applicants (pretending for it to be Egyptian) was amusing, and the other times he wore garish makeup and long Persian gowns and pretended to be Darius. Sometimes she tolerated his silliness, and other times she shifted the location of the court and never told him. They fought over his behavior, and then he was adept at cajoling her into giving in for more of his shenanigans. She agreed privately with Charmian that with Lord Antony there was never a dull day–the day may not be happy, but it was never without adventure.

Antony leaned forward and held both her hands. "You have imprisoned me here in Alexandria with your charm, Your Majesty," he said, fixing his dark eyes on her and grinning mischievously. "Should I relinquish my rights to all possessions and stay with you?"

"If Lord Antony has none of his Lordship, then Queen Cleopatra will have to banish him as a legionary in her forces, for what use is he to her?" she said, with mock anger.

"Is Her Majesty implying that Antony has use for her beyond his adventures in her bed?"

She slapped him teasingly. "Speak no matters of ill omen, Lord Antony. You are the master of the East, and may you never look down upon what you have conquered."

He grinned affably, as always, and held her palm to his cheek. "My levity hides my iron will, Your Majesty," he said. "You forget that not only was I a supreme commander of the great Gaius Julius Caesar's forces, but I am also a Consul of Rome."

She appraised him. He was a lovable rogue, and her sentiments on him swayed like a turbulent trireme on troubled waters. Even as others watched, he pulled her to his embrace as they lay together to watch the birds and the blue seas as her maids fed salted boar pieces to them.

"I deserve Judaea," she said, forcefully this time, for they were in another of their lover's quarrels. Her nostrils flared with anger, rare for someone who kept her composure even in the most testing times. "It was Egypt's from the time of our greatest Pharaohs!"

"Well, your greatest Pharaohs are dead!" Antony retorted. "It is Hyrcanus' and I prefer it that way. You want to swallow everything in the east."

"Did I say everything, Lord Antony? I have only asked for Judaea. Caesar would not oblige. And you are stubborn. Why is it in better hands with a stupid princeling than with the Queen of Egypt?"

"You should control your greed before it engulfs you, Cleopatra!" he said, wagging his finger. "It is not that I do not wish to bequeath Judaea on you, but how it will be perceived in Rome!"

She pouted and sat in a corner, not speaking. She stayed away from him for the night, and refused to engage with him the next day. She knew that he hated her silence and distance, so Antony, the ever loud and unstoppable character, came to her to reconcile.

He held both her hands and took her to a couch as she looked away, not speaking still.

"Cleopatra?"

Silence.

"Your Majesty, my life, beautiful Cleopatra, bountiful between the shoulders!" he said, while comically eyeing her breasts.

She guffawed, unable to resist the silliness. Antony knew then that he had broken through her anger. He placed her palms on his cheeks–something he did when he wanted to speak serious things to her.

"Listen to me. You think I am a loud fool, but there are reasons why I cannot just hand over Judaea to you."

"Explain," she said, gently, caressing his rough stubble.

"Remember that each step I take on your benefit is an arrow in Octavian' quivers. I know that. He pours poison into the Senate's ears while I am here. We must be careful. If we must have a great future, one with a significantly expanded realm, then you must be patient."

She sighed. "Perhaps you are right."

"I am always right."

"No, you are not. You thought you could scold and threaten me in Tarsus and extract concessions," she said, smiling, tapping his cheeks.

"I did extract a place in your life," he said, his eyes twinkling.

In the preceding months she had somehow managed to get him back to his military discipline. He practiced his arms every day as she watched him get leaner and stronger.

He conducted military drills and annoyed Valentinus endlessly, much to her amusement. He lectured Simonides about the lack of his troops' discipline and personally conducted training sessions for them. And Simonides, thrilled by the prospect of being taught by none other than the great Mark Antony himself, made the best of their time. Antony admonished Kadmos for his uniform, his walking style, and his manner of speaking. He managed to make the loud and uncouth Kadmos coy around him. He flirted with Charmian much to her embarrassment until Cleopatra put an end to it by shouting at him in front of everyone. He engaged Metjen in matters of politics and understanding of the Egyptian and Ptolemaic system of administration–and after one of Metjen's lectures, told him, *I understood nothing, but it is clear you know everything.*

"And I in yours," she said. She knew of his wife, Fulvia, a powerful woman in her own right, causing much headache to the Senators in Rome. But Fulvia was, after all, a noblewoman at best. Not a Queen. Not the richest woman in the world. Not descended from the gods.

Not Cleopatra.

And when she kissed him, it felt like her life had finally put behind the tumult and retributions. Antony was a different man–and each day her strategic equations were dulled, chipped away little by little, by her genuine affection for him. And perhaps his behavior, willingness to spend time here, in Alexandria, was an indication that he valued her companionship. As she looked at him, she mused on her past relationships. Apollodorus would always be her dearest–her affection for him came from no expectation of status or ambition, it truly was simple, and she had never quite experienced it before or after. With Caesar, it was cautious, respectful love, one created from awe of his stature, the need for his protection, and the desire for her self-preservation. But Antony was like a combination of Apollodorus and Caesar. He brought to her the simplicity of passion, and yet the complexity of the dance between kingdoms and heads-of-state.

"How long will you stay in Alexandria?" she asked, knowing that he had matters to take care of in Rome and elsewhere. As much as she wanted him here, his lack of focus sometimes meant he underestimated dangers. For both of their sake, she wanted him to leave and stabilize his control.

Antony watched her face quietly, and smiled knowingly. "In a fortnight. News from Rome and Greece create pause. I have to go away for a year or two."

"I ache for your return," she said, sincerely.

"To hear that from the great Queen of Egypt, Pharaoh and Isis, is music to my ears," he said, laughing.

"You make fun of me."

"No, I mean it," Antony said, as he pulled her into his characteristic fiery embrace. "After all, you will soon be the mother of my child."

CHAPTER 38
CLEOPATRA

ALEXANDRIA

The maids dressed the two whimpering babies by wrapping each in a fine white linen gown. Then they placed thin golden bracelets around the babies' wrists and dabbed small drops of Lotus perfume on their cheeks. Charmian carried the boy, and Iras held the girl with the utmost care, as they brought the babies before their mother. The head priest of all of Lower Egypt was in attendance, and so were the senior officers of the court. Cleopatra, dressed as Isis for the occasion, held her hands out so they could place each infant in the crook of her arm. She looked at them affectionately even as they cried, bunching their little fists, with their eyes still half-closed.

With her twins in her hand, Cleopatra nodded to the head priest who came before her and prepared to bless the children as she read their names to the record keepers.

She first looked at the boy, and then raised her head to announce loudly and clearly. "My son by the divine Dionysus Lord Antony, Alexander Helios Philometor Philopator!" *Alexander, the Sun, Mother-Loving and Father-Loving.*

A great cheer arose in the hall heralding the birth of a son who was a product of two great houses.

She then turned the girl, her cheeks pink and wet from the tears. She gently placed her forefinger on the baby's lips, which caused the infant to try to suck on the finger. Cleopatra smiled. And then she announced her daughter's name. "My daughter by the divine Dionysus Lord Antony, Cleopatra Selene Philometor Philopator!" *Cleopatra, the Moon, Mother-Loving and Father-Loving.*

For the next hour priests performed various rituals in celebration. Senior officials of the court and visitors walked in procession to kneel before the new additions to the Royal family and to receive her benedictions as manifestation of Isis. It was a tiring affair, but a momentous one, and it would no doubt create news in Rome.

Messengers would soon leave Alexandria carrying the news of her children's birth to relay it to Antony and to the Senate in Rome. The last they had heard from Antony was he was in Athens, and it was unclear when he would return to Egypt or plan his invasion of Parthia. The birth of her twins was without difficulties due to the blessings of the gods and the exceptional midwives and physicians at her service.

Ptolemy Caesar was now nearing four, and with Antony's children, she had a strong case for her legitimacy to Roman aspirations. It was now up to her and Antony to cement their relation and convince Rome, which she knew was a difficult task. Many members of the Senate hated her, and she was aware of the vicious propaganda already circulating in the western sections–that she was a conniving harlot who had seduced two great Romans, and that her sorcery and evil eastern ways had waylaid their great warriors and so on. She cared little for those stories, for those were the ways employed since her great-grandmother's time.

Her only failing, she thought, was that even with all the relationship-building, she had *still* been unable to extract from her Roman lovers the piece of land she knew belonged to her. Judaea. While the province itself held no great affection for her and she cared little for the Jews, the bitumen rich lake and the balsam producing farms were of great trade value that would help her coffers. It could strengthen her position, create an easier trading post with the Parthians (until Antony destroyed Parthia and added that to her), and further enhance her influence. For now she had to wait.

And in that state, opportunistically, came calling Herod of Judaea, the Idumean Arab who had become Jew, and a supporter of the current Hasmonean ruler of Judaea who was under pressure from Parthian mischief in his backyard.

Herod was a strange man. He was excitable and hummed with nervous energy–he tapped his feet, drummed his fingers, bit his nails, shook his head, scratched his ears incessantly, darted his eyes at all and sundry as if they were out to kill him, and often shot air from his mouth, making a grunting sound like a bull.

"Alexandria is magnificent, Your Majesty, *bufff*," Herod said, as his sandals made a clapping sound on the floor.

"And I have heard you wish to make Jerusalem a glorious city as well, Prince Herod," Cleopatra said. She had avoided passing through Jerusalem when she had gone to build her army years ago, knowing that Herod's father was no great admirer of her and cared not to intervene in Egypt's troubles.

"I wish to! I wish to!" he said, and tugged on his earlobe. His eyes shot between Metjen, Kadmos and Cleopatra.

"And what brings you here?" she asked, leaning back and appraising him.

Herod was a tall man. He sported a mop of dark, shiny curly hair. He rubbed his thick beard. He entertained no mustache, much like many from his region. Herod, she had learned, was thirty-five years of age, older than her, and if it were not for Roman patronage, would be her subject.

Herod cracked his knuckles. "The Parthians! They are at our border and have helped put an illegitimate man on the throne. This is just a prelude to them taking over Judaea, taking over, taking over, *buffff!*"

Cleopatra was aware of Parthia's incursions in the eastern fringes of Judaea and Samaria, none she was too concerned about, knowing Antony's plans.

"I see that it distresses you much. Are you seeking asylum?" she asked, as she directed a servant to go and fan the profusely sweating Idumean. Herod had been a general under the previous ruler Hyrcanus and had proved his worth as an exceptional commander; brave, loyal, and ruthless.

Herod shook his head vigorously. He placed his palms on his chest and leaned forward. "I seek assistance, Your Majesty. Parthia at your borders is no good, just as it is no good for us. No good. Help me get rid of Antigonus and we shall have a long-lasting collaboration! Long-lasting."

Cleopatra shot a look at Metjen. She needed to confer with her Prime Minister, because this situation opened possibilities as well as dangers. She assured Herod that she would consider his request, but as such matters needed much thought, he could enjoy the hospitality of Alexandria for a few days before she responded. Herod huffed and grunted, but accepted the invitation and went away to his quarters.

What a strange, high-strung man!

The next day, she summoned Metjen and Simonides. "I have no intention of sending him an army. Antony will deal with Parthia when the time is right. I have cordial trade relations with the Parthians and no reason to worry that they will march through Pelusium. If they take over Jerusalem meanwhile, let them. I do not trust Herod."

Metjen and Simonides both concurred.

"Besides, Egypt is too important to Rome for them to watch idly if Parthia attempts to invade Egypt," Metjen said.

"And if we must act urgently, then Valentinus and I can march at the shortest notice and hold them, though it is exceedingly unlikely that will come to pass," Simonides said.

"But I have another idea," she said, and Simonides and Metjen listened to her intently.

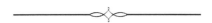

Herod, red-eyed from the adventures of the previous night, appeared before her again. Perhaps it was his permanent state of being, for he was still agitated and could barely sit on his chair without bouncing off it.

She offered him some wine which he accepted. He gulped some greedily and wiped his mouth with the back of his hand.

"You are a formidable general, Herod. Many accounts attest to your skill."

Herod grinned. "I am glad my fame has spread and reached the ears of the Queen of Egypt! Queen. Queen. *bufff.*"

"As good deeds and the story of strong men do," she said. "So I have a proposal for you. It is perhaps not one you desire, but one that may be of interest."

Herod was curious. "I wait for Her Majesty to describe," he said, and began biting his nails.

"I have interests in Ethiopia, and yet we do not have full domain over them."

"Uh huh. Uh huh."

"Many rulers have tried to control and subdue that lawless land. The great Pharaohs. Even my own forefathers. Yet complete control evades us. Even the Persian King Cambyses tried and ran back because success proved elusive."

"Uh huh. *Bufff*," Herod said, narrowing his eyes and rubbing his beard as his feet danced.

"I need a highly competent commander of an army to lead them to Ethiopia. A job only for the astute, clever, and skilled."

"Uh huh. Uh huh," Herod said, shaking his leg and cracking his neck.

"And yet I am stretched thin when it comes to highly experienced generals."

"I see. I see," he said, distracted by one of her maids walking nearby.

"Would you like to be a commander in my army, Herod? You will live a life of prestige and power."

All of Herod's body movements stopped. "Your army? *bufff!*"

"Yes. You will command some of my legions and bring me Ethiopia. I will appoint you governor of the conquered lands and more."

Herod stared at her unblinking. His dark eyes sparkled with manic energy. Then he shook his head vigorously many times and tugged on his ear lobes.

What do those gestures even mean! She wondered.

Finally, Herod kept his eyes to the ground and spoke. "No, Your Majesty. My home is Judaea. They are my people. My people. People. I have no desire. None in fact. To be your general. I say this respectfully."

"Your people will go nowhere, and you are not their king. Why do you hesitate to serve me?" she asked, without raising her voice. She knew Herod could be a difficult man. She flicked a fly that intruded, and a servant went chasing to kill it.

Herod shook his head like a bull about to charge. He cracked a few knuckles (and it reminded her of Pothinus) and twisted his torso to crack his back. "I wish to be their king, Your Majesty, and then have wonderful relationships with Egypt, but I have no desire to be in Egypt, *bufff*."

"Would you like to think about your position and answer me in a few days?" she asked, still willing to give him the opportunity, as she picked up a cat lounging by her feet and caressed its head.

But Herod would not consider. "I cannot accept that generous offer, Your Majesty. Generous. What use is a commander if he cannot put his heart to the mission at hand? Mission at hand? *bufff*."

He rubbed his palms together and itched his ear. "But I must respectfully ask if you can spare some legions to help me push the Parthian puppet out of Jerusalem."

Cleopatra gently put the cat back on the floor and it looked at her with disdain. She stretched on her couch and paused to drink some water. She stared at him without responding. Herod became more anxious and began to tap his leg on the floor while breathing loud and hard. *What an odd man.*

"And I must respectfully decline, Prince Herod. Egypt has enough to worry about than send legions against Parthian incursion. Why would I signal hostility towards Parthians when they have never shown such inclination towards me?"

Herod looked miffed. "What kind of neighborly relation is it that you abandon us at the hour of need!" he yelled excitedly. Drops of his spittle flew across the gap.

She was taken aback by the outburst. "Watch what you say, Herod, this is not your home in Jerusalem!"

Herod bit his lip and began pacing. "The Parthians will destroy all of us and you are not supporting us, Your Majesty. Not supporting. I need your legions."

Cleopatra stood and raised her voice. "You are not getting my legions. It is up to Rome what they want to do with Parthia so do not drag me into your quarrels, Prince Herod. I give you two days to think and decide what it is you wish to do. If you wish to leave to Rome to make your case with the Senate, then as a good neighbor I am willing to sponsor your expedition and give asylum to you and your family, but no more," she said, and walked out of the room, with Herod still complaining loudly about her lack of support.

Eventually, he came around, thanking her for sponsoring his travel to Rome. She gave Herod two ships, two hundred guards, some money and grain, and ordered the establishment of a safety post for his family should they desire to defect to Egypt. He was welcome to return to Egypt from Rome, should he desire, and a position in her army would always be waiting. Herod left Alexandria in a hurry, sailing to Rome to make a case for support to drive out the Parthian puppet.

Months later, she learned that the Roman Senate had inexplicably thrown its support behind him and nominated him "King of Jews." Not only that, Antony, who was then in the east, had begun operations to put Herod on the Judaean throne.

She knew it would not be the end of dealing with this strange Idumean.

CHAPTER 39
ANATOLIA
MARK ANTONY

Dear Lord Antony,

I desire to be by your side, as you have
expressed the desire to be mine. The weather
and the water have delayed me. But I am on the
way to Anatolia. A. Helios and C. Selene wish
to see their father.

May this letter find you in anticipation,

Queen Cleopatra

Antony waited impatiently for Cleopatra's carriage to
arrive. A messenger had conveyed that the Queen had
landed and was on the way. He could not understand the
minor palpitations in his chest and the hollow in his
stomach. *Did she still have affection for him? Did she still
favor his strategies?* It had now been nearly three years since
he had seen her. He also wished to see his children by her,
for he had not set his eyes upon them since their birth. And
now, at the cusp of launching the greatest invasion of his
career, against the powerful eastern Parthian empire, he
needed her more than ever.

For the health of his mind, through her companionship.

For the strength of his army, through her vast resources
and wealth.

The other eastern client-states were either too small or too poor to assist him beyond supplying men, and war needed money, lots of it.

He had implored her more than once to come to meet him in Anatolia, but now, months after his requests, she had finally sent word that she was on the way. Her delay irritated him, but he knew she never responded well to threats, so all he could do was wait and fume. But he had confidence in his relationship with Cleopatra; no doubt she would give him the support, and she would want something in return. He smiled at the thought of arguing with her, it was always an interesting sport.

He watched the windy road that snaked up the hillock on which he lived in a villa relinquished by a nobleman. His legions were set up in a vast circle in the plains around the hillock, as far as the eye could see, preparing for their toughest mission yet. Only Alexander the Great had made victorious inroads into Parthian lands, when it was the Persian empire, all the way to India. Caesar sought it but never had the chance to embark on the invasion. Marcus Crassus, an influential Consul and "the richest man in Rome," had died fighting the Parthians.

Antony would do what none of them had done. He had heard that his plans sent such fear to vast distances that even the Indian kings were preparing for his arrival, though, of course, Antony knew enough not to trust everything he heard.

There!

Finally, a procession came around the bend, with one-hundred horses leading in the front. Trumpets and bugles heralded her arrival. Then came one-hundred archers mock shooting arrows in the air, followed by swordsmen swinging their swords and dancing to the drums. There she stood, on a chariot, similar to the one she greeted Antony in Alexandria, surrounded by exquisitely dressed women beating drums. Behind the chariot was another cavalry with flags and signs. Antony walked out with his generals to greet her. Soldiers lined the road watching the spectacle as the Queen of Egypt arrived in full splendor.

The procession came to a halt before him, and Cleopatra descended from the Chariot, wearing a tight gold-lined Egyptian gown wrapped just above her breasts, and sporting the red crown of Upper and Lower Egypt. She held a crook-and-flail across her chest. His men and soldiers watched mesmerized as she walked gingerly towards him.

Behind Cleopatra walked Charmian and Iras, each holding the hand of Antony's twins.

She stood before Antony and smiled. He bowed to her and she did likewise, and then, to the cheers of his troops, she walked with him into his well-appointed headquarters.

"I have so longed to see you, Your Majesty," Antony said, holding her by the arm.

"And so have I, Lord Antony. But first, you must meet your children," she said.

Her ladies-in-waiting brought forward the shy and fearful Alexander Helios and Cleopatra Selene, now nearing three years of age. He knelt before them and opened his arms wide. But they resolutely stuck to Charmian and Iras until Cleopatra cajoled them. Antony held them gently. They had his looks! The curly hair, chubby cheeks, the eyes, the nose, all of it. And maybe a little of the mother, he mused. Then Cleopatra Selene began to struggle and make noises of unhappiness until Iras gently led her away.

"How was your journey?" he asked Cleopatra.

"Uneventful, though I hate coming by ship. But I am here with what you desired, apart from myself, of course," she said, grinning. Antony dismissed her ladies-in-waiting, and over Cleopatra's coy objections, dragged her to his room.

CHAPTER 40
JERUSALEM
HEROD

"You will drive me utterly mad, mad, mad! *bufff*!" Herod railed on his mother-in-law, Alexandra. The old hag was incessant about getting her nephew appointed as high priest, an influential position in Judaea, so that she could claw back some of her influence lost after Herod had been appointed king of Judaea. But he loved her daughter, his wife, Mariamne, the light of his life, gorgeous, sweet, and not kind to him due to her mother's incessant meddling.

"You are greedy and amoral, Herod! Aristobulus may be a boy but he deserves the position for the good of all our dynasties."

"Your dynasty! Not mine. Why should he be chief priest? He is too young. I will find someone myself!" Herod yelled, rapidly tapping the pillar by his side. He hated his mother-in-law, *hated* her, but she was too influential for him to get rid of her. He loved his wife so much, but she reflected the mood of her mother. When it was not Alexandra haranguing him about appointing her son to the post, it was his wife, Alexandra's daughter, refusing to even touch him until her brother was appointed.

Arrogant bitch of a mother-in-law, what had he done to deserve her?

Alexandra came from the Hasmonean dynasty that ruled Judaea for a hundred years before Herod. He knew that she resented her rise, and the entire drama around installing Aristobulus was nothing but hoarding power.

That was it. The role of the Chief Priest came with several benefits: a faithful and rabid following, control over the temple treasury, influence over the priests in Judaea and Samaria, and even a willing ear of influential generals in the military who venerated the position.

Alexandra, tall, elegant, beautiful and regal, leaned back on her chair. She made him nervous. "You will have no choice. You just watch, Herod."

"Why? What will you do, you hag? Gather an army of bandits and launch a war?"

She laughed. "You are as uneducated as I always thought," she said, purposefully poking him where it hurt. She enjoyed causing him distress. "Why do I need to gather an army when I can influence one to march on you?"

Herod chewed his nails. *Was she bluffing?* "Which fucking ruler will send an army on me? Who? Keep your mouth shut and make no more seditious comments! *buffffff!*"

"You tell me, son-in-law, who put you on the throne?"

Herod bristled at the direction of the conversation. Of course she knew that it was Mark Antony who helped him get rid of the Parthian puppet and got him Judaea. "And why does that matter to you?"

"Because if you do not grant my request, I will go to Antony!"

Herod laughed. He rubbed his slick, sweaty beard and grunted a few times. Then he stomped his foot a few times. "Why will Antony listen to a pompous arrogant old hag like you?"

She smiled and smoothed her luxurious silk gown. "He does not have to listen to me. And I do not have to *physically* go to him."

Herod stared at his mother-in-law. *What was this high-born whore planning?*

"Then? Do you have a flying magician who will convince Lord Antony to waste his time on your nonsense?"

Alexandra stood and adjusted her many gold necklaces. He eyed her voluptuous body and she perhaps even knew of his unholy desires. Whatever the case, she stared at him until he lowered his eyes.

"Queen Cleopatra is about to embark on a journey to Anatolia and she has agreed to put in a word for me," Alexandra said, coolly, as she walked away.

CHAPTER 41
ANATOLIA
CLEOPATRA

Cleopatra spent the second day idling in the villa and recovering from both the trip and from Antony's bedroom energy. Did he really miss her that much, she wondered, or was it all a show to keep her by his side and get her to accede to his endless demands of ships, coin, labor, grain, oil, soldiers, horses, camels, and more. Nevertheless, she was happy and invigorated by the cool air. This time away from her life in Egypt also gave her some personal time with her children, and Antony, surprisingly, took the time to sit with her in the garden and watch the twins. The son by Caesar, Ptolemy Caesar, now almost eight, remained in Egypt under Metjen's care.

"My son will grow up to be like me, handsome, clever, strong!" he said, leaning on the bench and adjusting his red cloak. He had dressed up to go to his troops but decided to stay back. She had so far refused to meet his generals, saying she needed some time to recover before jumping into politics and war again.

"Maybe I should be the one saying that, Lord Antony. I hope he is not lazy and impulsive like his father," she said, grinning.

"Or stubborn and manipulative like his mother!" he retorted, without malice. "Selene is very pretty, *not* like her mother."

She crinkled her nose and slapped him gently. "What kind of a man insults his Queen?"

"They are both beautiful, just like their parents," he said, holding her by the waist. "I wish for them to have a long and successful life ruling our great empire."

She looked at him with affection.

"No, don't, Selene! Not there! It has thorns!" he yelled at his daughter who was curious about a lovely rose bush.

Cleopatra giggled. "She knows about roses, don't shout. She spends many hours in the palace gardens. Selene, come here!"

The naked little girl ambled to her mother. Cleopatra placed her on her lap. "Can you tell us what those flowers are?"

Cleopatra Selene, in a sweet little voice and perfect Latin, pointed to each flower and described them, including in which seasons they bloomed.

Antony was delighted. "Very clever. I must apologize for my failure to note your skills, Little Majesty!"

"They are learning Greek and Latin at the same time," she said, proudly. "They will not have the accent I have."

"What about Alexander, what special skills does he have?" Antony said, ruffling Selene's hair. The little girl squirmed out of her mother's lap and went back to the garden.

"He can recognize all the kingdoms and client-states on a map. Alexander, come here!"

Charmian, who was attending nearby, dragged the protesting boy to them. Antony held Alexander's reluctant little hands and waited for him to calm down. "Quiet! Or I will spank you!" he said, in his scary-father voice.

Alexander stopped wailing and looked at his mother with his big about-to-cry eyes.

"Tell him all the states you know! You are clever, tell your father!"

Alexander Helios suddenly became excited. He stood in front of them like a pupil before their teacher, put his hands behind his back, lifted his chin, and began. "Britannia, Hispania, Gaul, Germania, Italy, Greece, Egypt, Libya, Cyprus, Cappadocia, Cilicia, Judaea, Samaria, Nabataea, Ethiopia, Nubia, Armenia!"

Antony threw his head back and laughed. "Wonderful!"

Cleopatra Selene, who stood near her twin brother, shouted as well. "I know them all too! I know them! He did not say Parthia and India!"

A delighted Antony grabbed his daughter and planted a rough, stubbled kiss on her cheeks. She squealed. "Of course you know. Now, both of you, do you know which ones belongs to your mother?"

He let go of his daughter who jumped up and threw her hands. "Everything! Mother is Queen of the World!"

Alexander, not to be outdone by his sister, "Yes! Even sun, moon, stars!"

Antony laughed loudly. "Really? Well, it appears you are teaching your ambitions to them," he said, turning to her.

"I have told them many times to say that all those lands belong to father and mother, but what can I do?" she said, grinning.

Iras, who was hovering nearby, said politely. "Lord Antony, they can recite some of Homer's poems too."

"Can they? Well, maybe after lunch. Come, come on, let's eat," he said, standing up and ushering them to the dining hall. "This is nothing like your palace or your famed kitchens, but you should be comfortable. I have recruited cooks for you."

Cleopatra shook her head. "No. Charmian has to vet them all. I have my own cooks and food-tasters. As long as I am here, Lord Antony, Charmian runs this villa."

Antony made a face but agreed. "You worry too much."

"You forget my life history, Lord Antony," she said, poking at his chest.

Antony called the head of the kitchen and ordered that Charmian was now the mistress of the house and would take over all arrangements in the villa. On Cleopatra's request, Antony had already reconstituted security by mixing his Roman legionnaires with Kadmos' Royal Guard and went so far as to put his men under Kadmos' command, to some irritation.

"Well, looks like you are already invading my camp," he said.

"Lord Antony, my invasion is to help yours," she said, walking with him, with her ladies-in-waiting in tow with the children. They had to wait for the kitchen to be ready and for Charmian to inspect arrangements, and chatted idly about the local attractions (*beautiful seaside villas*), food, and weather.

For a man about to embark on a monumental invasion, Antony seemed surprisingly upbeat and casual. She had many things she wanted to talk to him about, but looking at the happy faces around her, the giggles of her children, and Antony's handsome and joyful face, she decided to wait.

That night they visited a local Greek amphitheater to watch a play organized by the citizens of the region and enjoyed the hospitality of the nobles who were dazzled by her. Antony noted with some jealousy that her presence ruined the adulation for him, and if she could please wear a fish bag next time. *Not that it mattered to Caesar* she retorted. "You keep thinking that it is my gown or my necklace that enchants them, Lord Antony, have you still not figured out why?"

And when she embraced him that night, she let her mind float in clouds of bliss rather than in the fires of conflict.

CHAPTER 42
ANATOLIA
MARK ANTONY

Antony called his senior council for a meeting, with an intention to introduce them to Cleopatra and discuss the strategy to invade Parthia. In the last few days, he had realized that she was a significant source of his happiness. She was also one of his most significant financiers. Cleopatra had insisted that she have a place in the council and be part of the conversation. *You cannot take my money, Lord Antony, and pretend I am just an ornament,* she said.

They came in one-by-one, King Artavasdes of Armenia, commanders Oppius Statianus and Flavius Gallus, and several other senior military and logistics officers. He was in a good mood, ready to begin finalizing elements of his invasion and also make a few announcements.

His commanders knelt to Cleopatra (they had grumbled), and the aged and dignified Artavasdes bowed to her as a co-ruler. She was graceful and surprised him with her Armenian. Artavasdes laughed and said, "everything I hear about Her Majesty is true then!"

With them seated comfortably in his central hall, Antony outlined his expedition. Nearly 55,000 legionnaires, and over 30,000 cavalry and other support forces. They would march through Armenia and enter Atropatene, a Parthian province, before going deeper into the empire. He would split the baggage train, taking only most essential items with the main force and the rest separately. The men seemed to be aligned on most decisions, and Antony was surprised that Cleopatra had remained quiet for most of the conversation.

But when they began to discuss dates to begin the march, she finally spoke. "Is separating the baggage train a wise decision?"

Artavasdes, with his long flowing beard and a tall Median cap, spoke softly. "It will go through my kingdom, Your Majesty, and it is safe."

"I worry about Parthian cavalry harassing them," she said, not convinced.

"Perhaps Her Majesty can give us instructions on how to move our legions," Oppius said.

"Perhaps Lord Antony should tell his Legate that his legions are financed by me," she said, icily. Antony reprimanded Oppius to remain respectful. But the men were adamant that the plan was the best that could be, and Cleopatra, while unconvinced, had no standing to make them decide otherwise.

The invasion would begin in a few months as the vast army completed its preparations. No doubt that Phraates (*Farahad*), king of kings of the Parthians, would be doing his own preparations.

As the meeting came to a closure, Antony rose and announced. "I have a major announcement to make. Gather your senior Centurions and invite the senior noblemen of the legion tomorrow."

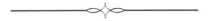

Antony, dressed as Dionysus, and Cleopatra, dressed as Aphrodite, holding her children's hands, stood on a grand podium. Below stood senior commanders of Antony's force, luminaries from Anatolia and Armenia, high priests and other administrative officials of Antony's client-states.

A strong-voiced announcer stood on a stool to make an announcement.

"Before the assembly of his beloved people, Lord Antony, Dionysus and Ruler of all East, declares his everlasting love to Cleopatra, Queen of Egypt, Goddess Isis, Father-Loving and Fatherland-Loving."

Charmian and Iras gently brought forward Alexander Helios and Cleopatra Selene, dressed in bright white ceremonial gowns and little diadems, and had them stand between Antony and Cleopatra.

The announcer pointed to them and continued. "Lord Antony, Dionysus, Consul of Rome, Ruler of the East, hereby declares to the world, to all his people, that he wishes to declare and claim Alexander Helios, Father-Loving and Mother-Loving, as his son by Queen Cleopatra, and Cleopatra Selene, Father-Loving and Mother-Loving, as his daughter by Queen Cleopatra!"

The murmurs and surprised looks gave way to loud cheers. Antony knew that his men adored him and no personal announcement from him was ever greeted with anything but approval. How would this be received by Rome? By Octavian? He would know in time.

Then, Antony and Cleopatra moved closer to each other and held their hands. The announcer continued.

"Let this also be known to the world and his beloved people, that Lord Antony, Dionysus, Consul of Rome, Ruler of the East, beloved of his people, declares his eternal love to Her Majesty Queen Cleopatra of Egypt, Father-Loving and Fatherland-Loving, and declares her his wife!"

Horns blared, drums beat, cymbals clanged, lyres played, and whistles rented the air as the stunned lookers absorbed this momentous announcement before a massive celebratory roar filled the air. Antony knew that many would take offense to this, for he had not yet divorced his fourth wife, Octavia, sister of Caesar Octavian. But then every man in Rome knew that his marriage to Octavia was for reasons of diplomacy and not love, as he had for Cleopatra. There would be questions in the minds of the Romans, for Rome did not recognize such a marriage between a citizen and a foreigner, especially a Monarch.

Antony and Cleopatra had mulled these decisions for days, putting matters of the heart aside and discussing the strategy and impact of such an announcement. But eventually, they had come to an agreement that to declare marriage would force the hand of many, and cement an alliance like nothing else in the world. They both had reservations, but her cool and calculated logic melded with his temperamental and passionate emotions to arrive at a decision both were willing to stand behind.

Antony looked at her, beaming. Cleopatra smiled, what he perceived as genuine, with that beautiful dimple, and squeezed his hand. They raised their hands in blessing, and the senior council by the podium knelt in obeisance.

Antony was not done. As the audience waited, he asked the announcer to step down and he stepped up to the announcement stool. "Let this be known to all that in securing her hand in marriage, for the stability of my eastern rule and as a loving gift to the great Queen and my wife, I hereby bequeath to her the entirety of Cyprus, confirming her authority over the island. I also bequeath to my wife, Queen Cleopatra, regions in the following domains: Cyrene, Coele-Syria, Crete, and most cities on the Phoenicia. The nobles, kings, chieftains of regions mentioned shall now abdicate or kneel to the rule of Queen Cleopatra!"

This announcement came with a smattering of cheers but mostly bewilderment at his generosity. Cleopatra had become, without doubt, the richest monarch in the entire Roman domain.

As he looked at his beaming wife, Antony could not help thinking that together they would be an unstoppable force.

CHAPTER 43
ANATOLIA
MARK ANTONY

Antony was at his wit's end. They had had a wonderful four months, enjoying each other's companionship and experiencing a marital bliss he had not had for a long time. Having Cleopatra and the children with him as he shored up his support and finalized his invasion plans gave him unusual calm. He had surprised many around him, including himself, that he could be a dutiful father and a husband, having been known as a womanizer with lack of self-discipline. Even Dellius, who often played the role of procuring beautiful women for Antony's pleasures, was surprised by his control and refusal to indulge in his carnal desires so long as Cleopatra was around.

But this came at a cost. Cleopatra, who was difficult enough to handle as a mistress and a Queen of Egypt, could be excruciating as a wife! She was haughty and demanding, argumentative, and devilishly stubborn at times. As she was now, when he was *this close* to beginning the expedition. The topic? The same darned subject she was unwilling to let go like a dog after a particularly delicious bone.

Judaea.

What was it with her and that province? Why did it matter? He had already given her so many provinces all along the Mediterranean coast and Libyan coasts! How much more did she want?

After a particularly tender moment of harmony, he had generously given her several portions of the eastern Mediterranean coast, adding to her list of provinces that made her the largest single landowner and the richest ruler of all his known world. And that had not been enough.

And there she was, for the last two days, pouting, not speaking to him, refusing to see him, even refusing to eat, and putting on a sad and forlorn look. He hated it. He really *hated* the silent treatment. He could not stand it, and how strange it all was, he thought, that he would feel this way for her. What was it? Besides, he desperately needed her continued support and could not risk alienating her over this issue. Worse, having already declared her his wife and showering her those regions in front of his legions, he could not take anything back! How clever she was!

"Cleopatra, my love, you are the empress of Egypt and the Mediterranean coast. You are the wife of Mark Antony. You will soon own all of Parthia along with me! Why are you so adamant about Judaea? Talk to me!" he implored her, sitting by her side on the comfortable bed. She had her head down, her hair disheveled. Was it an act? Was it sadness? What was it?

This was his fifth attempt at speaking to her. He was close to giving up. She finally looked up at him, her lovely eyes wet with tears. He had rarely seen her this way. "My dear husband, Lord Antony, do you still not see my request for what it is?"

"What is it? My love. What is it that I do not see?"

In the past, she had only argued and fought with him that Judaea belonged to the Ptolemies and to the great Pharaohs of the past, and that it was immoral for Rome to keep it away from her. It was about *dignity, legality, morality,* and whatnot. But he had not been swayed by it.

The Senate had confirmed Herod King of Judaea. Antony had blessed the confirmation and helped Herod drive out the Parthians. And besides, it was Herod's father who marched to save Caesar! Did she not see it?

"You think my ownership is only borne of a desire for more land. But I will have all the land I want when you conquer the east," she said, softly, sadly, holding his hand.

"Then?"

"I am a ruler, Lord Antony. You are a conqueror. You are the snatcher of provinces, cities, and domains. It is you who marches to the far and unknown, bringing them to kneel before you. You are a warrior."

He was glad to hear such a ringing endorsement. But what was she implying?

"A conqueror conquers. A ruler rules. What makes a conqueror happy, Lord Antony?"

"To find new enemies to fight, to show his ability, his mastery," Antony replied. It began to dawn on him what she was implying.

"And likewise a Ruler must have lands to govern, to secure trade, to ensure the safety of her citizens, to finance defense, and," she paused, staring into his eyes, "supply all that a conqueror needs."

Antony listened quietly.

"I need rich and continuous lands, Lord Antony. Judaea has many things that benefit my trade, and I am a far better administrator and trader than Herod. The Parthian invasion will be expensive and take time. Do you not want me to bring stability to the lands you leave behind, and supply you without interruption?"

"Why not support Herod?"

"He does not like me, Lord Antony. I have not forgotten his slight when he came to Alexandria. Will you allow an uneducated loutish little king to slight your wife? You have seen the man—he is nervous, skittish, and does not have the temper to rule with a steady hand."

Antony sighed. He knew and accepted that Cleopatra was simply a better ruler with vastly more experience and highly effective administrators and tax system. In comparison, Judaea was a mess. Herod was skilled as a fighter, but he had yet shown no temperament to bring order to Judaea. Antony needed money. Lots of it. And perhaps it was time to cede a little.

He slid next to her. "My love. You know that I cannot depose Herod. He has significant support in the Senate. I simply cannot. But what if I have him accede the areas you like? He can deal with the Jews, the politics of Jerusalem and surroundings, while you enjoy control of the trade-worthy regions, will you agree to that?"

She wiggled and made a show of unhappiness, but he could easily see she was softening. He grabbed her and planted a few kisses, the way she liked. And then, nuzzling against her perfumed neck, he made a concession. Herod would not be happy, but such was the nature of life.

"The army moves in a few weeks, my love. We will cross the Euphrates, and as I march towards Atropatene, you can turn south to return to Egypt via Judaea."

CHAPTER 44
ARMENIA
CHARMIAN

"You can hold it, you can slide on it, you can sit on it, you can kiss it, you can–"

"Husband, you are so disgusting! Be quiet! Anyone may hear outside," Charmian scolded Kadmos, who sat on a chair, his legs spread, his penis out, as he sang an idiotic bawdy song which he thought was clever and witty. *What would people think!*

"Oh, is it, my dear, CHARMIAN SAYS SHE CAN HOLD IT, CHARMIAN SAYS SHE WANTS TO SIT ON IT," he began to yell. She was sure there were guards outside. She almost ran to him and punched him on the chest, and Kadmos, too big and strong for her, pulled her onto his lap and she squirmed.

"Quiet, shh, be quiet, I will do whatever you want," she said, laughing. Kadmos' eyes danced. He made a few obscene gestures as he dragged her to the bed.

The deed completed, she lay exhausted and placed her head on his hairy, smelly chest. How many times had she told him to shower at least once in three days? The gorgeous Euphrates was just half-a-mile from the camp! The river narrowed here and flowed through a canyon. She had accompanied Her Majesty several times with the children to frolic in the cool waters. Charmian's son, now just three, remained in Egypt under care. She missed the boy. By the time they returned, her son would be seven months older at least. Kadmos was the most unlikely husband–as rough and loud he was, he was kind, caring, made her laugh, fiercely protective, and very rarely beat her–even then lightly. Perhaps it was because of her stature and closeness to Her Majesty. The gods smiled upon her.

"When do we return?"

He ran a finger on the bridge of her nose. "In fifteen days. Lord Antony's forces will cross the river and head to Media. We return through Judaea by land."

Charmian was surprised. She was not aware of the return-by-land plan. Her Majesty had been preoccupied with Antony and had not shared much with Charmian in recent weeks. She thought they would return to the Syrian coast and take a ship back home. "I know Her Majesty prefers not to take a ship but–oh!"

"What is it?" Kadmos asked, taking her wrist, and forcing her to scratch his beastly beard. She often wondered if rats hid in it.

"You should tell no one," she said, narrowing her eyes to him.

"I have told no one that you have big big–"

She closed his mouth with her palm. "Enough! This is serious. Listen to me."

Kadmos grinned and acquiesced.

"Her Majesty is pregnant again," Charmian whispered. "She lost a child during the last return trip from Rome through the seas. That is why she must have decided to go by land."

Kadmos nodded. "I was certain she was pregnant, I am not that much of a fool!" he said. "But I do not think that is the reason."

"What is it then?" she was curious.

"We will be spending time with King Herod in Judaea. Her Majesty's empire is about to expand even more. She will be conducting negotiations with him."

Charmian chewed her lip. She had heard Her Majesty speak of Judaea many times, sometimes venting about how the Romans wouldn't accede it to her. It seemed Her Majesty's tenacity was paying off.

Kadmos held her hand in his giant palms. "Does she really like Lord Antony? Or is this all because he is important for her to keep the throne and expand her domain?"

She was surprised by his frank assessment. Hopefully there were no spies listening in on them!

"I think she is very fond of Lord Antony. He is a likable man, not like you, Kadmos."

Kadmos promptly pointed to his penis. "Is his this big? Huh?"

Charmian laughed. "Bigger. It stretches from Rome to Greece."

Kadmos shook his head. "What do you really think, after all these months?"

Charmian stretched her back on the bed and sighed. "With Her Majesty, it is always both. I think she really likes Lord Antony, but questions whether he would ever come be by her side and live with her. And she wants to expand as much as she can, and ensure she has his support."

"It is exhausting, the constant balancing," he said, looking at the patterned tarp over their head.

"You are more exhausting," she teased. "Do you think our son misses us?"

He shrugged. "I hope. He is being taken good care of. He gets to eat as much fruit as he wants, which he would get little here."

"I hope they clean him well when he soils himself. I have to keep telling them because he gets rashes."

"A few beatings will help," Kadmos suggested.

"All problems deserve beatings according to the Idiot Head of Royal Guard," Charmian pinched him.

"No problem not solved without a sound beating."

"We are lucky, Kadmos, to have Her Majesty's grace," Charmian said.

"I never imagined she would recruit me."

"You were so clumsy in how you were flirting with her in those early days!"

He laughed loudly. "One must try!"

"Should I try with Lord Antony?"

Kadmos wrapped her in a bear hug and over many protests proceeded to prove why his medicinal salve was working.

CHAPTER 45
CLEOPATRA
SYRIA

Cleopatra prepared to leave Antony with a heavy heart. The last few months had brought them closer, and he was thrilled to find out that she was pregnant again. But they could not spend more time, for it was time for Antony to move his forces. And finally, as the season became warmer and days longer, Antony ordered the invasion to begin. His magnificent force would cross the narrow channel and cross into Parthian territory, and she would take a slow but purposeful trip back to Egypt.

Antony had already sent messengers to Jerusalem for Herod to prepare for her visit, and to Egypt for the return of the Queen.

When the day arrived, they bathed together, received blessings from the priests, and he sent her off with significant protection. She had arrived with half of Valentinus' legion and half of Simonides', but Antony added two legions to her force and a five-hundred horse Cappadocian cavalry to ensure her safety through the gorges, ravines, and sparse lands of Syria and Judaea, and from any shenanigans by Herod.

She stood on a makeshift podium as Antony's glorious legions marched by to the sound of horns and whistles. Cavalry, infantry, baggage train, siege equipment, all beautifully disciplined and marching to orchestrated sounds. Antony sat on a magnificent horse and he waved and bowed to her as he passed. Tears welled up as she watched his maroon cloak and red plumes recede in the distance. For all his failings and largesse, Antony she loved, and she hoped he would succeed in this mission and return. Cleopatra had reservations on the timing and tactics of the invasion, but what did she know about large wars? She wondered if he ever thought that her desire for territory and expansion of her domain was greater than her affection for him. If so, he had never talked about it.

She wanted both–the territory and his affection–and could not understand why anyone would see those at odds. These regions belonged to her. It was hers by right. By her divine need.

The trip South through Syria brought her memories of the long past, when she had built a mercenary army and marched on her brother. But this time, she returned as an empress, with the combined power of Egypt and Rome behind her.

"Reminds you of our shaky carriage a decade ago, does it not?" she asked Charmian.

"It does, Your Majesty. But we never saw Jerusalem!"

"All it has is Jews and Herod, neither excite me very much," she said. Jews in Alexandria had given her enough headache, she never liked them, and they didn't like her. Metjen often advised her that it was her bias that created resentment, but she was adamant that it was their behavior towards her that caused it in the first place. But she tolerated them. And they tolerated her.

"I wonder if there are nice things to see," Charmian said.

"I doubt it," she scoffed. "But there are regions I am very interested in. We'll see."

"Do you feel well, Your Majesty?" Charmian asked.

"Don't keep asking me that! I am fine!" she chastised Charmian who fell silent. She wondered if her sharpness was due to her general dislike of Herod and the impending meeting with him.

"I am fine, Charmian," she said, gently, this time. Charmian relaxed. And they both sat and watched the Syrian sunset in the vast, unforgiving desolation.

She patted her growing belly.

They would arrive in Jerusalem in two weeks, and she would finally get what she wanted.

CHAPTER 46
JERUSALEM
HEROD

Herod greeted Cleopatra near the walls of Jerusalem. He gave her a Queen's welcome with an honor guard, musical procession, and gave her and her entourage a large section of his palace. *She called it an interesting fortress-palace, not quite a palace, not really a fortress. Bitch.*

Since he had seen her nearly a year-and-half ago, she had put on weight, and she walked around as if she owned Jerusalem. Just because she was fucking Antony didn't mean she had control over *his* land! Sure, she was his wife now, but then Lord Antony had many wives and so what.

For three days Cleopatra rested, and she gave audience to many in his family, including his horrible mother-in-law, Alexandra, who was ecstatic to meet Cleopatra. Also his wife, Mariamne, who had many nice things to say much to his irritation. But then Mariamne had a tendency, just like her mother, to say hurtful things to him. Many of Jerusalem's elders met her too, including the Jewish high priests who he made sure to make them complain to her of her treatment of Jews. No doubt that ruined some of the arrogant cow's happiness.

Finally, Cleopatra summoned Herod for an important council meeting to discuss matters of state between Egypt and Judaea. That's right. The Egyptian harlot, living in his palace, summoned him to her presence! A bristling Herod humbly accepted; what else could he do, given the message directly from Lord Antony himself to demonstrate necessary respect and indulge in a meaningful negotiation to the satisfaction of Cleopatra. The gods had his balls in a vice and Herod was frustrated.

And there was nothing he could do!

Herod walked the stony corridors of his palace which had none of the grandeur of Cleopatra's in Alexandria, past the stone pillars and small rooms with little square openings. Someday, he thought, he would surpass Egypt's buildings with magnificent creations of his own. Herod fantasized about the many grand residences and fortresses he would build. He dreamt of them. He sometimes fantasized about his glorious structures. But now, he had no time, and Antony's mistress was here to squeeze his balls and get something from him.

He arrived at a large, cavernous chamber that he usually used for campaign discussions. Cleopatra was already there with some of her entourage, and so were a few of Herod's officials. He bowed to her, and she did likewise. He was relieved to see she was not wearing her traditional suffocatingly Egyptian Pharaoh's garb, a sure sign for headache-inducing pomp. Instead, she wore an elegant silvery gown, a grand pearl necklace, a bright white diadem with pearl studs, and a few silver-and-gold bracelets on her wrists.

Herod, himself wearing a long Arab gown and a tall cap with a bird feather, took a seat positioned opposite her. His officials sat on his either side.

"Her Majesty appears rested," he said, forcing a smile. *Appears dead would have sounded nicer.*

"Your hospitality is appreciated, Lord Herod," she said, switching to Aramaic, causing many of his officials to go gape-mouthed. Idiots.

Herod eyed those around Cleopatra. That little Egyptian, the Prime Minister, he forgot his name, was not here. The lady-in-waiting sat beside Cleopatra. When did maids sit beside the Queens? A distinguished-looking man sat on the other side.

"How may I be of service to Her Majesty? It would be my honor to show you the beautiful vistas and attractions of Judaea before escorting you to the borders of Egypt."

Hopefully in a coffin, arrogant diadem-head!

Cleopatra smiled knowingly. "You are generous, Lord Herod. I am sure there will be time for leisurely visits. But as you know, Lord Antony, *my husband*, is on his way to Parthia, and we have more pressing matters to address."

Herod tapped his fingers, shook his leg and grunted a few times. This woman stressed him. "Of course. Lord Antony's requests are my commands. My commands. *buffff.*"

"Well, as you may have seen from the missive, Lord Antony, *my husband*, and I, as Queen of Egypt, wish to open negotiations for you to relinquish specific areas in eastern Judaea including the Great Asphalt Lake, and all portions from fifty-miles south of Jerusalem," she said, holding his eyes steadily.

Herod, who was taking a sip of wine, almost spat it out in shock. What in the god's world was this Brother-Fucking, Sister-Murdering whore talking about? Give up the only few regions that were of any worth to him? Antony's message before Cleopatra's arrival said nothing of the sorts, only telling him to please her! This was not supposed to be the "pleasing" agreement; it was like stripping him of his entire kingdom. It was cutting the tongue of a singer and telling him to sing!

Might as well slice off my balls and give it to her for dinner, why not demand that as well! Bitch!

Herod, breathing hard and almost choking, controlled himself from lunging across the chair and stabbing her. His men looked mortified at what they heard, but Cleopatra sat there, with the slightest smile on her face, looking at him coolly as if she had asked for a few trees and a well.

Once he composed himself, Herod countered. "If Her Majesty will consider, that is like asking a man to part with all his limbs. I am sure Lord Antony intended a negotiation. And Her Majesty remembers that my father garnered much help to help the great Caesar, and by the act, even Her Majesty."

Cleopatra bowed slightly. "Indeed, Lord Herod, and I was indebted to your father. And that I have paid by giving you refuge in Alexandria and financing your travel to Rome, by virtue of which you gained the title of king of the Jews. Our debts are paid in full."

By all the gods he knew he hated this arrogant, pretentious, "I-am-a-goddess" posturing bitch who got *her* throne because *his* father saved Caesar! And she had no respect for any of that. How he wished he could slap that smile off her face. She was a few years younger than him, and yet the insolence!

"And if that were so, Your Majesty, you negotiate from a position of unfair demands!" Herod said, feeling outrage hug him like an otherworldly demon.

He grunted and cracked a few knuckles, waiting for her to respond. He tugged an earlobe and stretched his neck. She barely moved.

Finally, Cleopatra spoke. "Very well, Lord Herod. I am willing to reduce my demands, but before we engage in difficult conversations, I must relay my happiness at meeting your wonderful family!"

Groan. Not my family.

Herod nodded rapidly and bit a nail and spit it at the feet of one of his men. "Uh huh. Uh huh."

"Your wife is so beautiful, Lord Herod. She is like a goddess on earth. And your mother-in-law, Alexandra, has many wonderful things to say about you."

"Uh huh. Uh huh."

Of course she is much more beautiful than you, big nose thin lips.

"Lord Herod, if you prefer, we can dismiss others in this room and speak of family and their desires," she said, flicking her wrist and pointing her fingers towards a far corner.

Herod began to worry, but he had no interest in his senior men listen to whatever this woman would spew. Only Herod and Cleopatra remained with his bodyguard and her Head of Royal Guard. He looked big and dangerous, so Herod's impulse to maybe stab Cleopatra might not be a viable option.

Cleopatra leaned forward. "Your beautiful wife desires happy relations with you, Lord Herod. And I think that would make you a happier ruler, and a better partner in this region."

That was true. He longed for Mariamne's affection so much, but received so little. If he was happier, perhaps he would be a better king?

"She spoke of the fond days when you met as teenagers."

"She did? Uh huh."

"And as Lord Antony's wife and Queen of Egypt, it is also my interest that you are not distracted by family feuds,

Lord Herod, for who better in the world to know the life of complex families?" she said, self-deprecatingly.

"Indeed, Your Majesty, and yet you have prevailed. I do fine with my family."

You prevailed by murdering all your siblings, you bloodthirsty market whore.

Herod had, of course, murdered much of Mariamne's family as he worked to secure his power, and she was not too happy about it. And now this Roman-seducing sorceress was getting involved in his affairs.

"Not how I see it, Lord Herod. You say you wish to negotiate, and yet you hesitate to listen. I am willing to concede on my demands for your land, and in return I expect that you hear my proposals."

Herod, uncomfortable and already frustrated, nodded and chewed more nails. "Uh, huh."

"I desire stability in the great House of Herod. Nominate Aristobulus as the Chief Priest–"

Herod almost jumped up. His mother-in-law, damned gossipmonger and daughter of a street dog, no doubt she was behind this! "That is my decision to make!"

"And I ask that you make that decision soon, or I will return to my demands of your land," Cleopatra said coldly.

Like that's any surprise, donkey-face coarse-hair.

"What if I do not accept? Lord Antony has great affection for me, and I will send word to him!"

Cleopatra stood, signaling her intention to leave. "Lord Herod. He may have affection for you, but you do not have children by him, nor are you his wife. Think about that. Besides, he is away with the far greater issues that demand his attention and has no time for two-bit little kings like you. Neither do I. Think carefully."

Herod, now livid, and his temple pounding, stuttered. "I am, I am, am, a competent general! If Antony is away and busy, I can take on you! I can!"

Cleopatra laughed. "As you wish. I have three heavily armed Roman legions with me, a gift from *my husband*. I can summon all of Valentinus' experienced legions–"

Herod started something when she insolently flicked her wrist to silence him.

She continued. "And, I have my entire Egyptian army trained by Simonides and Valentinus. Is that who you will fight? I leave you today, Lord Herod, think. I shall call on you tomorrow to decide the details, should you desire. I will now go and spend some time with your wife, for she is delightful company, unlike you, Lord Herod. And better educated."

With that, the haughty bitch glided out of the room, leaving Herod with a painful constriction of his chest, a pounding head, and a deflated penis. The whole world was against him, the whole world! His wife, his mother-in-law, and this witch from Egypt. And she had to bring up his education. How that burned!

Herod cursed liberally and left, it was time to call his council.

CHAPTER 47
JERUSALEM
HEROD

"She wants my land! She wants my brother-in-law, who is too young, to be nominated head priest!" Herod railed to his council. The elders, including senior regional administrators of Judaea, Hasmonean and Jewish priests, senior commanders of his forces, all had assembled to deal with this crisis.

"That is preposterous, Your Majesty," said one of his men.

"What is strange," said Herod, looking every man in the eye, and straightening himself, "is that this harlot thought she could seduce me!"

The men looked at him quizzically but said nothing.

Herod continued. "She comes here, believing herself a Queen, but she is nothing but a common whore who was simply gifted everything without doing anything except to promise to spread her legs! She did that with Caesar. She did that with Antony. And she tried it with me! How shameless, *buffff*, that she would so boldly tell me that she would pleasure me in various ways if I grant her request! Her offer was which man could boast of sleeping with a Queen of Egypt, how disgraceful!"

One of the priests coughed, and the others nodded sagely. Surely they believed him! They better!

Herod knocked on the table with his knuckles and shook his leg. He then wiped the surface and chewed a nail. "I am not the one to succumb to such cheapness, not I! Have you seen my wife, have you? Those who have seen Mariamne would never even consider this Egyptian woman of no virtue! *bufffff.*"

A senior advisor finally spoke. "It is the gods' blessings that we have His Majesty to fight such temptations and debauchery. Now that you have shown her her place, Your Majesty, what do you propose we do next? She is no doubt a spurned woman, and a Queen of such character is no doubt now burning with revenge having failed to secure His Majesty's affection."

A few others nodded vigorously.

Herod was pleased. "It is true we cannot fight her with our armies, no matter how brave and bold we are. She outnumbers us greatly. How about fomenting a civil war using the Jews in Alexandria?"

Another man spoke. "Alexandria is a very large city, Your Majesty, and it is extremely unlikely we can create a meaningful unrest with the relatively small Jewish population, and besides, they are not too popular in the city and will receive little support."

Herod grunted and scratched his curly sweaty hair. "Uh huh. Well, then we must do what is possible, and do it quickly."

The men looked at him puzzled. These men, the council, indeed, had no creativity in them. Bunch of hapless, feckless fools he would have the deal with later.

Herod looked at them and grinned. "She is here, in Jerusalem, in our palace. We will assassinate her!"

CHAPTER 48
JERUSALEM
CLEOPATRA

Cleopatra enjoyed speaking to Mariamne. While Mariamne's mother, Alexandra, could be a little overbearing and annoying, the daughter was delightful company. She was a radiant beauty, with a high forehead, shining black eyes, hair that cascaded down to her waist, a pert nose, and full lips. No wonder Herod was obsessed with her. But Mariamne, while not educated formally like Cleopatra, had borne the wounds of familial conflict, and many of her family had been murdered by Herod. While she bore no great resentment to these facts, Mariamne cared for her brother Aristobulus who, she believed, should become Chief Priest. And to Cleopatra, having these Hasmoneans by her side could be helpful strategically.

Mariamne knew much about Jerusalem and she enjoyed speaking of the city. Her voice was soft, and Cleopatra had to often ask her to speak up or repeat herself, but standing on a fortress turret and looking down at the city and hearing her speak was enjoyable.

"Is that the great temple of Solomon?" Cleopatra asked, pointing to a swath to her right. There stood the ruins of a large complex, with broken walls, a large rectangular central structure, and a few relatively newer buildings with cut stone paths leading up to them.

"It is," Mariamne said. "They say the Persian King Nebuchadnezzar, the son of Nebuchadnezzar, destroyed it. Herod says he wishes to rebuild it to its past glory."

She was surprised. Herod the builder? "Is he interested in building?"

"He is. He often speaks of grand projects, like palaces, granaries, fortresses, temples. He was very influenced by your city, Your Majesty," Mariamne said, smiling.

"Your husband is rather temperamental," she said, leaning over from the wall and looking down on the stony ground below. A gentle warm wind caressed her face and neck.

Mariamne laughed. Even her laugh was soft and seductive, Cleopatra mused. "He is sometimes a child, only a dangerous one. He gets angry and rages, and a day later pretends as if nothing happened. If one offends him, he threatens all manner of pain and then invites them to dinner the next day. With those he likes, he is forgiving, Your Majesty, but he is a difficult man."

Cleopatra nodded. "He is like Antony with a bad temper!"

The two women laughed and commiserated over their husbands' oddities. And then complained about their heating habits and flirtatious behavior. *No shame, none at all.*

"How did you meet him? Was this an alliance of houses?" Cleopatra asked.

"It was, Your Majesty. I was twelve when my mother chose to marry me to him, but we married only four years ago, when I was fifteen."

"You have no children."

"I lost one. Affection has been difficult with the tension over Aristobulus. With Your Majesty's help I hope to gain my family some influence, and also have a child!" Mariamne said. She picked a stone and threw it over.

Cleopatra looked over at this girl, who was now the same age when she had built her army in Syria and was heading back through these very lands to fight her brother. She felt a strange kinship to Mariamne. "He was exceedingly angry at my demands. But I wish for you to know this, Mariamne, that I seek no harm to Herod. I desire for him to engage in a meaningful exchange."

"Of course, Your Majesty."

"Should you ever decide that you no longer desire to live with this man, then you shall be granted residence in Alexandria, along with your mother and brother, to live comfortably."

Mariamne knelt before Cleopatra. "I am most honored, Your Majesty. I shall be by my husband's side but remember your generosity."

Mariamne stood. She then paused and pushed a curl behind her ears. "But you should be careful, Your Majesty."

Cleopatra furrowed her brows. "How so?"

"He... He is not averse to assassinations. If, as you say, he thinks he has no other way, then he might consider the easiest means to end someone without the need for battle."

A chill descended on her and enveloped her like a freezing blanket. *How did she not consider that?*

"Can you find out? Is there a way you can infer his move?" she asked.

How right I was in striking a kinship with this girl, for she is key to Herod's dark heart.

Mariamne nodded.

CHAPTER 49
JERUSALEM

The leader of his assassination squad walked silently along the barely lit corridor of the fortress. Almost seven-hundred feet long, the corridor connected the main living complex of Herod and his family to the guest quarters for dignitaries. He knew that the Egyptian Queen stayed in a vacated portion of Herod's main complex (much to Herod's displeasure) for a few days, but two days ago had shifted to this far corner to experience how it would be to live in a true fortress setting.

Earlier in the night, the guard messengers had dispatched a series of confusing instructions that misled Queen Cleopatra's Royal Guard and sent them to an entirely separate section during a shift change. The assassination squad would have no resistance elsewhere in this confusing maze that he knew intimately. How *stupid* of this Queen to distance herself from the safety of central palace!

It was quiet everywhere, except the sound of howling dogs. There were so many dogs in this city, in every street and corner, roaming in menacing gangs. And at night, when one looked at the moon and let out a long howl, legions joined it, creating a symphony of howls. The leader called it the Jerusalem Orchestra. And the Jerusalem Orchestra provided sufficient cover to their quiet footsteps as they covered the distance with purpose.

When they neared the room, isolated at one end of the corridor, they saw the guards–Queen Mariamne's protection providing cover this evening–and signaled them. The two men, already bribed, left quietly, signaling to the leader that it was all clear and that the Queen's personal guard had not yet arrived. They vanished in the darkness.

He and a companion gently pushed the door open. It was not locked from inside, as expected, as protocol to allow swift entry-and-exit should an emergency arise. All of which worked to his advantage of course. The heavy cedarwood door made a creaking noise and the hinges groaned under the weight. He sensed no movements inside, and if intelligence was right, there would be no one. No one would hear clashes here, in this isolated section, but he hoped to execute the order with as little noise as possible. He knew the layout of the space by heart. It was a large rectangular room interrupted by several square stone pillars, and the flat granite bed was in one corner. The ceiling was under construction and several wooden planks hung from the roof to allow for workers to patch and paint. There were only two flickering little lamps on the corners that barely illuminated the area.

He signed for four of his men to move in, leaving three outside to watch the long corridor.

They entered and closed the door. They stood quietly waiting for any movements or sounds, and to let their eyes adjust to the darkness. If there were any guards waiting inside to ambush them, they would have rushed him by now. But it was all quiet, except the Jerusalem Orchestra.

They tiptoed quietly, their soft leather sandals tied securely by threads to their ankles making no sound. They began to inch towards the bed, where the Egyptian Queen slept fitfully. He was surprised to hear a low snore from this distance. Even the great Queen of Egypt snored, how delightful!

The plan was to converge on the bed from two sides, lunge on top and close the mouth, and suffocate her. King Herod did not want her blood spilled in Jerusalem. Once she was dead, they would leave her as-is, place a poison vial nearby as if she had killed herself, and leave. In the worst-case scenario, her Royal Guard would be here in the next few minutes before he was done, in which case there would be a battle in the corridor and then it was up to His Majesty to resolve the mess.

As they neared the bed, his heart beat harder. He was proud to have been called for this duty. No one would know it, but the king would forever hold him in high regard, and he would change the fate of kingdoms! He dreamt of a fine little house in Jericho, amongst lush farms, surrounded by admiring relatives and leading a comfortable life with the patronage of the king.

But something began to worry him.

The smell.

The chamber was musky, the smell of wood and dust permeated the air. He expected the presence of a *Queen*. What about a fragrance? The smell of rose, or lilac, or even the heady aroma of balsam? What of Myrrh? What of the sweat of a woman? What about food? The aroma of warm bread, or cut fruits, or the rich waft of spiced goat? There was none of that. Were they in the right room?

But he persevered. It would be over soon. As they neared the bed, he heard a slight creaking of a wooden board somewhere above him.

What–

———————◇———————

Kadmos watched the five men walk into the dim room below him. He and his four men lay flat on wooden planks suspended by ropes from the stony roof. So, it was true, Herod was stupid enough to try an utterly immature assassination attempt. Kadmos almost laughed at how easy it was for them to learn the details of the potential murder and prepare accordingly. And now, the idiots were just below them, looking around the room, walking quietly.

When they neared the bed, with about ten feet to go, Kadmos moved a little, causing the wooden board to creak. The men nearby looked up, but it didn't matter. With a loud yell Kadmos leaped from the plank and jumped down, and the others did the same. From the corner of his eye, the figure under the blanket rose as well, his sword glinting in the yellow flicker.

The men were taken by complete surprise and shock. Two died even before they tried anything, having been stabbed right through the heart from the figures that dropped from the sky. Kadmos felt their blood spring like a fountain and drench his cloak.

Kadmos took on a large man, possibly the leader, and hit his side with the broadside of the sword. The man was a trained professional. He charged Kadmos.

Kadmos realized his disadvantage for fast and close combat, so he dropped his sword and watched the enemy as he crouched again. The two danced around like wild cats until he lost patience and rushed the man. The enemy swung his knife which sliced Kadmos just below his chest, only a glance, but painful enough. Kadmos took advantage of the assailant's forward momentum and punched the man's throat with tremendous force. He fell gasping, clutching his throat.

Kadmos kicked the man's chest and then straddled him. He then twisted the assailant's neck until he heard the spine crack and the man stopped struggling. The man's whites of the eye were visible even in this darkness. Meanwhile, his men had butchered the other two, having cut off one's head and impaled the other on a short spike, and he still writhed in his death throes, stinking the air with his urine and loose bowels. Irritated, Kadmos reached out to his neck and snapped it like a twig.

The dumbest assassination attempt in the history of dumb assassinations was over even before it really began. The five men lay dead. Kadmos' orders were clear—spare no one to tell the tale.

They quickly wrapped up the bodies and dragged them out. And soon, moppers arrived to clean the floors as best as they could, and helped carry the dead out of the corridor. When it all was done, it was as if the assassination squad never existed.

CHAPTER 50
JERUSALEM
HEROD

Herod sat before Cleopatra, and this time the scenery had changed. They met in an open area, as demanded by her, and behind her stood a heavily armed Roman contingent, along with her full Royal Guard. Herod brought his senior council, and Cleopatra said she wished to have this negotiation as an affair between two great states and that the pomp and show was to give it an aura of importance.

Of course, Herod did not believe an ounce of it. Something had gone wrong last night. His council had strenuously objected to sending an assassination squad, telling him that the ramifications could be deadly to the entire province, but Herod had quietly decided to gamble. But what had happened? He had no idea. The assassination squad never returned, and Cleopatra had made no mention of the attempt. No one knew, and he had no idea why. There was dried blood on the floor in the room, but no bodies.

The man who planned the assassination, one of his lieutenants, now stood beside Herod, his face ashen. He had no answers to the failure.

And now, she looked serious, and just to annoy him she was dressed in her "look-at-me I am a Pharaonic Whore" garb, with the golden vulture gown, Uraeus crown and even the pretentious crook-and-flail. Herod hated it all. He had won his throne from the Hasmoneans through hard work, ruthlessness, and his unswerving loyalty to Rome, and now this woman was trying to take away what belonged to him.

"May we begin, Lord Herod?"

Do I have a choice, fat thighs?

Herod bowed and nodded. He shook his feet and tugged at his ears. It was as if a python constricted his chest; he could hardly breathe, he was that angry and anxious.

"But first, a ceremony of wine, one that we Egyptians do before great dialog," she said, with a crooked smile.

What now?

He had never heard of whatever this ceremony was, but who knew with these ritual-obsessed Egyptians?

"You may not be familiar with this ritual, Lord Herod. The God Amun leads my hand to a member of your delegation, and offers him a cup of fine wine from your own orchards, as an offering of cooperation and blessing."

Fine. Fine. I see Amun sitting on your shoulders.

"A very fine gesture, Your Majesty. My delegation is glad to receive such an honor."

Cleopatra nodded and turned to her side. The lady beside her, whatever her name was, handed a golden cup filled to the brim. The Queen then held its stem in both hands and closed her eyes. She swayed gently. The delegations were so silent that all one could hear was the smattering sounds of the people clearing their throat or taking deep breaths.

She then opened her eyes and looked around at the audience. Her extended hands pointed towards Herod, but she spoke no words.

Herod was confused. *Was she pointing to him?* He clumsily got out of his chair and began to walk, and watched him coolly. But when he neared her, she retracted her hand, causing Herod to stand awkwardly before her.

"Not you, Lord Herod. I did not speak your name. The god seeks someone else," she said.

Herod's face flushed with embarrassment. He trudged back to his chair. Cleopatra extended her hand again, but this time with firm purpose, and she pointed it to the man by Herod. His assassination planner.

What the-

"You," she said. "You gain the blessings."

The man, looking concerned, took his steps forward. He looked back at Herod, perhaps waiting for his King to intervene in some way. Herod said nothing.

Go drink the stupid wine.

The irony of this pretentious hen offering wine to the man who planned her assassination was not lost on Herod. He found it amusing.

The man knelt before the Queen and accepted the cup. He quickly gulped the content and the Queen's attendant took the cup away. She nodded at him, and he rose to his feet and returned to Herod's side.

It was now time for the negotiations. Herod's stomach felt tight, as if a giant ape squeezed him from the sides.

Cleopatra finally spoke. "My demands remain unchanged, Lord Herod. The Great Asphalt Lake in the east, and all land south of fifty-miles."

"You have already said that, Your Majesty, and it is an unfair ask. You wish for me to relinquish my kingdom."

She leaned back and looked at him coolly. It was unnerving. He remembered his one encounter with Caesar years ago, when Herod was much younger, and Caesar did the same. He stared at those before him until they simply ceded. It seemed like Caesar's expensive mistress had learned a tactic or two from the great man.

Suddenly, there was a loud choking sound next to him. His man, the planner of the assassination and the one who drank the wine, suddenly fell to his knees. He clutched his neck and began to gasp. White foam exploded from his mouth and he collapsed. As Herod's attendants rushed to him, Herod himself was frozen. Cleopatra looked on without emotion and no one from her delegation moved.

It was as if they knew this would happen.

The man continued to roll about some more, discharging more of his stomach, and then with one arched back and a gasp, expired in front of horrified onlookers.

Cleaners made quick work of dragging away the body and wiping the dirtied floor. Herod sat where he was, unsure what to do, but an understanding germinated in his mind.

He could not breathe.

He could not scream.

This bitch knew! She knew all along they were planning to kill her! It is true that this mad woman experimented with poisons!

Finally, a frightened silence descended in the space.

Cleopatra addressed him. "The great Ra moved my hands away this time, Lord Herod. But who knows how long his patience lasts?" she said, icily.

Herod felt like a large hairy man was squeezing his throat. He finally managed to eke out a weak acknowledgment. With no more words spoken, everyone quietly contemplated the situation, drank some water, and waited.

Finally, the Queen spoke again. "Are you aware of this land's history, Lord Herod?" Cleopatra asked, sitting straight, regal, with a smirk on her face.

"Yes, I know!"

"I do not believe so, for there is no shame in admitting, Lord Herod, that your education is inadequate, and that you do not come from a long lineage of noble kings."

May god rain fire on this arrogant Brother-Fucker!

Herod almost burst a blood vessel in his eye and his temple pulsed. He breathed slowly and clenched-unclenched his fist. These bloodsucking bitches looking down on his education again. It must have been his mother-in-law whispering into Cleopatra's ears.

"My education is adequate, Your Majesty. More than adequate. *bufff*."

"This land belonged to our Pharaohs long before you existed. The Great Pharaoh Ramesses won it long ago. It belonged to the Ptolemies, my ancestors. This is Egypt, and yet I am allowing you to keep a portion."

As she said that, Ramesses walked by her feet and rubbed himself on the chair. She petted him. "His name is Ramesses."

May I strangle the cat and throw it into a firepit, Your Arrogant Majesty?

Herod raised his voice, hissing, crackling. "It has not been Egypt's for two-hundred years!"

"That may be. I want the people here to know something," she said, as she rose to her feet and raised her voice theatrically. Just like how Theodotus had taught her long ago, and how other rhetoricians had since honed her craft.

She came closer to Herod's line of men. "My husband stands beside me. His legions stand behind me. My army is ready for my command. My people worship me. But I am reasonable. So reasonable that should even Lord Herod were attempting to assassinate me, I would still forgive that and make a reasonable negotiation. What does Lord Herod wish to do?" she said, now staring at him. *I know what you did, but I shall let it go one last time,* that was what this witch was telling him.

Herod's heart slammed itself to his ribs and his ears burned. He had little choice. "I am willing to make concessions, Your Majesty," he finally said, slowly, rasping and struggling for words.

Thus began the haggling. She was a difficult negotiator, unwilling to concede much and countering everything he said with something he didn't like. Don't want to give the Asphalt Lake? Then handover half of Jerusalem. Don't want to give South of Jerusalem, then relinquish rights to everything in Jericho. Not ready for that? Give up the throne and take a position in the Egyptian military. She was relentless, knowing his disadvantage having tried to kill her. If that news got to Antony, it would all be over for Herod. However, for some inexplicable reason, she had not brought up the assassination. He had no idea why, but it was clear that she was extracting her measure of flesh, which had now doubled.

And finally, after hours of exhausting arguments and her unrelenting energy, Herod finally accepted the final settlement. The Great Asphalt Lake with its rich and hugely profitable bitumen deposits would go to Cleopatra and she would lease it back to Herod for a big fee. *Fucking whore bitch!* She also got the lush balsam and frankincense farms and oil presses in Jericho with no lease clause. Herod felt castrated; some of his richest revenue-producing areas were gone, and all he had left was the canyons, sand, and rock. He would never forget this misery she heaped on him.

But she wasn't done.

"And then there is the final question of a just resolution for your beautiful family, Lord Herod," Cleopatra said, smiling. That knowing harlot smile. Herod wheezed to relieve the pressure in his chest and tugged on his beard until it hurt. He had lost appetite to argue more. He just wanted to be done with this and send her away. Away!

"I approve the nomination of Aristobulus to the position of Chief Priest. I have always intended to, but his youth prevented me. But I shall accept this desire of all the parties," he said, trying to gather some authority, as if he was granting it rather than being forced to do so.

Cleopatra smiled. "You are considerate and a skilled negotiator, Lord Herod!"

He nodded and grimaced. How could he smile? He would smile if he drove a shank up her throat and watched those eyes lose their brightness. But for now, the ordeal was over.

That night Herod drank himself to unconsciousness, cursing Cleopatra and his miserable situation. Two days later, he arranged a tour of the Asphalt Lake and the Balsam farms so that the new owner could see the beauty of and richness of these lands. *Fucking bitch.*

CHAPTER 51
JUDAEA
CLEOPATRA

Cleopatra, accompanied by an overjoyed Mariamne, took an entourage to first visit the vast and spectacular Great Asphalt Lake. The lake stretched as far as the eye could see, and while Cleopatra had heard much about it, she had never actually seen it. Surrounded by hills and desolate vistas, the Lake, many said, had remarkable properties.

She walked beneath a large umbrella with Mariamne on her side, and Charmian following nearby. "It is beautiful, Mariamne!"

Mariamne acknowledged. "I enjoy this place so much, Your Majesty. Herod wishes to build a palace a nearby, on top of a hill. We call it Masada."

Cleopatra squinted at a gray-orange hill far behind her. The imposing structure rose tall from the yellow desert and had a flat top. It would make a formidable fortress, she thought.

"They say the water is so salty that one can float here," Cleopatra said, running her toes through the ribbed sand.

"It is, and some say it heals afflictions of the skin."

The ground had floral and snake-crawl like patterns everywhere due to the weather and erosion patterns. Thick salt deposits bordered many spots where the clear water lapped the shore. The fascinating landscape had deep orange pits in blue-white salt and sand swathes, lone trees with deep green leaves sprouting from hostile ground, little mounds of sparkling salt with sharp edges.

She put her hands on her hips and looked out. The orange-yellows of the surroundings contrasted with the brilliant green and blue of the lake. Pebbles shimmered under the sparkling water. The bitumen clumps, perfect for building water-proof boat floors, were further south and she wanted to see them as well. They spent an hour walking on the shore, chatting.

At one point Charmian waded into the water and brought back a fist full of crystal salt. "There is so much of it!" she said.

"You have been of service to me, Mariamne. I shall not forget how you divulged the details of the ambush," Cleopatra said, looking at the young Queen.

Mariamne smiled. "Of course, Your Majesty. I could not support his impulses. Herod was livid that the plan leaked."

"The entire attempt was amateurish," she said, laughing. Charmian had joined her by then.

Cleopatra continued. "Did you know that he told his council that I tried to seduce him?"

The ladies began to giggle.

"Would he be aroused by your pregnant belly?" asked Charmian and they all laughed. And when Mariamne briefly walked away to dip her feet in the water, Charmian said comically, "Oh, My Queen, your nice big round belly, oh! oh!" causing Cleopatra to swat her and laugh some more. They both shut up when Mariamne returned. After all, humor on someone else's husband was only tolerated so far, and Cleopatra did not yet know how Mariamne thought of her husband. She wanted Mariamne by her side.

For now, it appeared that Mariamne held no great regard to Herod, but that might change if there was peace, and if Mariamne's brother was finally formally appointed.

The retinue proceeded further south to see the bitumen clumps. She was amazed at the tar floating on the water. Egypt paid a handsome sum to procure this wonder, and now, with her owning it and leasing it back, she would make a handsome profit for her coffers.

Some of her senior advisors, and Charmian too, had asked why she had not held Herod accountable for his attempt on his life, and simply annex Judaea. She had explained the political sensitivity of doing so, for it would go against Rome's senate, and Antony had no desire to create more enemies behind his back when he was away leading the biggest expedition of his life. So, knowing Herod knew what happened, she knew she could get the best negotiating outcome, and she got what she wanted, dangling the threat of exposure. It all had worked wonderfully.

After a night's rest in the magnificent desolation, under black skies and a million twinkling stars where they enjoyed some singing and swapping stories, they proceeded to the Balsam farms further north. These expansive agricultural units produced the fragrant oil used in ceremonies, embalming, fashion, and social occasions. The oil was also highly treasured by physicians who used it to treat various afflictions of the skin, bladder, reproductive organs, and problems with the stomach. The people, spellbound by her presence, arrived in droves to watch her procession and gain her benedictions as she was seen as goddess herself. Cleopatra cherished the time, walking amongst the lush green bushes, inhaling the smells of the produce, and listening to the cheers of the crowd lined up.

After two days in the region, enjoying the hospitality and the beauty of this harsh land, Cleopatra reconnected with her legions and began her final trip south to the borders of Egypt. Herod came to send her off, and she knew all his affection was fake and forced, but they parted ways cordially, with assurances that they would treat each other with kind consideration.

As the hills and mountains of Samaria vanished, and the plains of Sinai receded, Cleopatra remembered the blazing sun years ago when she had arrived here, with her mercenary army, unsure whether she would live or die, let alone become the Queen who rivaled the greatest Ptolemies–with ownership and power over Egypt, Libya, Cyprus, Crete, Judaea, portions of Syria and Eastern Mediterranean coast.

Queen Cleopatra Philopator had come far from being the one hounded out of her palace and hunted.

CHAPTER 52
EGYPT
CLEOPATRA

While Antony was away waging war on the Parthians, Cleopatra settled back at home with her four children, having given birth to Ptolemy Philadelphos soon after her return from Judaea. Taking charge of affairs and the benefit of relative peace, she proceeded to make a few announcements.

Simonides had fallen ill on account of his age and the stresses of managing and maintaining an army, so Cleopatra replaced Simonides with a new man named Attalus, picked from general Valentinus' officers. Kadmos was declared the commander of all Egyptian forces.

Then, she elevated Charmian to be a senior advisor to herself, therefore keeping Charmian close as she always did, but putting value to Charmian's words and advice. Iras she elevated to lady-in-waiting, replacing Charmian.

General Valentinus, now having served nearly eight years in Egypt, had accepted this land as his new home. He married an Egypt woman of high birth, half his age, causing many to joke that the Roman general had done what his master Caesar had with Cleopatra. The union had her blessing and Valentinus received a reward of a villa in Western Alexandria, a large plot in the fertile delta, and exemption from tax for ten years. The grizzled general, still a stickler to his rules and his odd ways, retained his position as head of the Roman army in Egypt.

Her children were growing well. Ptolemy Caesar, now eight, had a measure of dignity around him, and his life was busy with studies. She wished to bestow upon him all the knowledge she had gained herself and knew the benefits of such wisdom. To him she assigned Rhodon, a competent mathematician and teacher of philosophy. To little Alexander Helios and Cleopatra Selene she assigned appropriate tutors of elementary education. The children experienced splendor that even she had seen in her tumultuous childhood, for their mother was now richer than their grandfather or his father. Some said she was the richest of all Ptolemies, including even the great founder Ptolemy Soter, and his illustrious son Philadelphos.

But even as she was settling, she received an urgent request from Alexandra, Herod's mother-in-law, that Herod was making it impossible for them to live happily, and that he was risking her and her son Aristobulus' life. She begged for asylum. Cleopatra knew that letting Alexandra run away and stay with her would enrage Herod, but not letting Alexandra come would turn her allies and eyes-and-ears in Herod's inner life away from her. As much as she detested the man, he had eventually stuck to his end of the bargain, and she knew Antony held Herod in high regard. There were only so many times she could nudge Antony about the Idumean.

But after careful consideration, she summoned Metjen and asked him to execute a plan—a most delicate one.

CHAPTER 53
JUDAEA
HEROD

Herod watched quietly, hiding beneath an arch of the decrepit south-western gate, standing over one of the abandoned routes out of Jerusalem heading to the coast. His men stood behind, ready to protect the king from an ambush or unforeseen resistance.

The Jerusalem Orchestra, that beautiful symphony of howling dogs, gave them cover from any sounds. The old oil lamps flickered, illuminating the barest of patches on the dusty, rocky ground below.

Where were they?

As he stood there, quietly, waiting, his mind raged. What had he done to deserve the disrespect from his wife and mother-in-law? Sure, he randomly had them locked in their quarters, shouted at them, threatened death or banishment, but they were just words! Just words to scare them, to shut Alexandra's mouth, to force Mariamne to give him the affection he deserved. But no, these cold women, and Alexandra's pretty son, Aristobulus, had such disdain for a wonderful man like Herod.

Amidst the howls, he thought her heard the soft tinkle of bells. The type tied around donkeys. He held his breath as he saw a little lantern swinging in the darkness. His men waited for signal. There would be no premature movements, just in case this was a scout or a diversion. The bell grew louder and the *clop, clop* of the hoof came closer, and so did the rumbling sounds of wooden wheels on stone. He receded into the darkness to watch.

The little procession came beneath the arch and continued, blissfully unaware of the watchers in the dark. There were two carts, each holding a crude coffin. A few armed men walked along, with a lone figure holding the lantern in the front.

Herod let the group proceed and walk further, entering into a lone stretch that would descend gently until it reached a well-trodden path to the coast. He tapped the shoulder of the man beside him, and he another, and Herod's men trotted silently towards the group, aided by the gentle yet sufficient moonlight. It took them little time before they split and surrounded the caravan, which was still clueless. There were five armed men with the caravan, and Herod had thirty with him.

The men seemed to have noticed, as some of them whipped their heads, peering into the darkness, and they pulled their swords out.

Herod shouted. "King Herod orders you to stop!"

The men, on hearing his familiar voice, gave up immediately. They dropped their swords and fell to their knees. Herod and his men closed on the group.

"Control the beasts!" he screamed at the terrified handlers who fought to stop the frightened donkeys. It took some time to bring order.

Herod walked to the coffin. He gestured to one of the kneeling men. "Stand up!"

The man, trembling, got to his feet but kept his head low. "Open the coffin."

Without a sound, the man flipped a small latch, and with some effort pulled the lid out.

And there, inside, with her eyes wide open with a fearful look, was his mother-in-law Alexandra.

"Hello, my dear mother-in-law," Herod said.

CHAPTER 54
ALEXANDRIA
CLEOPATRA

Cleopatra heard a few weeks later that Herod had intercepted Alexandra's escape and stopped her and Aristobulus being smuggled out to the sea. Who had leaked the news of their escape, or the means of their attempt, was never revealed. Cleopatra was secretly glad Herod kept his side of the bargain—in return for the reveal, he would not punish Alexandra or Mariamne, and he would not delay announcing Aristobulus to the priesthood. First, she heard that they had all reconciled and Herod had forgiven them for the transgressions. And months later, that Aristobulus had drowned in a palace pool. She suspected that Herod had engineered the murder, but Cleopatra had by then tired of dealing with Herod's family affairs.

She knew from her spies that Herod hated her with all his being, and a tense truce prevailed between them, with Antony still away.

Cleopatra kept her mind away from Herod's machinations in Judaea and turned her attention to something she desperately wanted to do for a while. The work on central Alexandria had fallen behind, after an initial surge soon after her throning by Caesar.

The magnificent Canopic Way, running East-to-West, nearly 100,000 feet in length, from gates fittingly called Helios and Selene, the Sun and Moon gates, would be turned into nothing that existed. The smooth cobblestone pathway, nearly twelve-chariots wide, had been abraded in many places, opening giant potholes that endangered chariots and nightwalkers alike. Many of the government buildings along the way had been damaged in riots and the siege years ago, and never been restored due to lack of funds. The harbor was in poor shape, and the plaster on the great lighthouse had chipped, giving it ugly white-and-gray splotches. These she determined to restore to glory, through a range of road and building works. The Canopic way received a central divider lined with night lamps and falcon statues. The sides received rows of sycamore and palm trees. The buildings received paints with an explosion of colors—rich ochre, purple, and blue, and the roofs that needed mending were replaced with bright red brick. As the year progressed, the entire section along the palace and the Canopic way screamed the glory and beauty of Alexandria, and people from near and far came just to walk on this magnificent way, shopping, strolling, and simply gawking at wonder, as they stepped away from their squalid worlds with running sewers, pig and cow stench, and tightly packed mud brick homes.

She also raised three twenty-foot granite statues, one depicting herself as a Pharaoh, one with her as Isis holding her son, and another as a mother with her children. One they placed near the palace, and the other two on each end gate of the Canopic way. She made several donations to Taposiris Magna in West Alexandria and the temple of Osiris in the South, adding new sections, chambers, tunnels, repairing walls and roofs, and permitting new tombs beneath the temples. She also had her and her son Ptolemy Caesar's images carved onto the southern section of the great temple of Hathor in Dendara as part of her prayers and patronage.

Cleopatra also instituted judicial reforms, relegating more power to the local Egyptian courts, establishing a more codified means of appeals so that disputes not resolved at local courts could be taken up to the regional Ptolemaic administrators, before they were escalated to the Royal Court. She also enhanced penalties to errant tax collectors and local judges to reduce corruption. All Ptolemaic courts were also ordered to submit the written final orders in both Demotic and Greek, for all cases resolved in their courts. She replaced several poorly functioning officials and expanded civil works. While the primary purpose of the administration had always been maximizing tax revenue for the throne, she realized, just like her illustrious forefather Philadelphos, that a happier, well cared population produced more than one that was not.

As she busied herself in restoration and reform during this quiet period, the news from Antony's campaign was anything but positive. The first message received in months was that the invasion of Parthia had not gone according to plans. Antony had failed make any meaningful progress or captures, and that his legions were being harassed by the Parthian cavalry. As it is in the fog of war, it was hard to know truth from lie, and whether those accused of treachery were victims of war or truly in the wrong. And thus she waited patiently to hear more, even as her anxiety rose, knowing that if Antony survived and returned, there would be renewed demands for money and troops.

And finally, months later, a message from Antony arrived.

To, my beloved wife, goddess, Queen Cleopatra,

I have returned with glory to Sidon, and it is my pleasure to have my dearest wife near me, of whose assistance I seek, for fifty-thousand rolls of linen, fifty-thousand footwear pairs, medicines for wounds and dysentery, bandages, a thousand talents for rewards and prizes, two thousand gallons of wine, ten supply ships, five-hundred flat supply carts, and two tons of copper. These I ask for while Parthia is beaten like a mule, there is still more work on my return.

But reasons of war aside, my loving, beautiful queen, I most desire to enjoy your company, gaze into your eyes, listen to your words, and hold you, for I have so missed you in this year of war, and I long for you to be by my side. I beg you to acknowledge and prepare your journey.

Mark Antony

She smiled wryly. He longed to be with her of course, as long as tied to her waist were all the supplies he wanted. Still, she felt a sense of longing to see him, and her cheeks felt a soft heat in them.

Oh, Antony, you clumsy lover and warlord.

CHAPTER 55
SIDON
CLEOPATRA

Her heart sank when she saw him. Antony was not the man he was when he left her a year ago; his eyes were sunken, the cheeks flat, his hair showed many streaks of gray, and his spirit so broken she worried if an impostor had replaced her dear husband and the great warrior Mark Antony.

His army was in tatters. They had lost thousands to the brutal marches in the winter and constant Parthian harassment. He had won many little battles, but the Parthians held fast, and Antony was forced to retreat. Never had she seen him so dispirited, his mood only elevated somewhat by her presence, and by her bearing gifts of clothes, shoes, medicines, and gold coins to be handed as reward to the bravest.

The night after her arrival by ship, by herself without her children, Cleopatra sought to cheer Antony. "What ails you so, husband?" she asked. "It is but the nature of conflict that some may be lost but the will must go on to win the war!"

Antony was distraught. She knew how he loved his men. He first complained like a petulant child that she had delayed her arrival, to which she responded that collecting the necessary supplies took time and that it was winter, and sea was unkind to travel, what did he expect? Would it help him if she drowned?

For all his experience, Antony never really paid much attention to the complexity of logistics and what it took to amass supplies for large scale conflict. Cleopatra understood it better than any man on Antony's team, and his complaints frustrated her. *You never appreciate my role in bringing you what you want, Lord Antony. You forget that without my money your army would grind to a halt in two days!* She had scolded him once.

Cleopatra learned the truth of Antony's campaign. It was a failure, even though the steady drumbeat of battle successes he sent to Rome painted a different picture.

"The gods did not smile upon me," he said, sighing loudly. "So many dead. Brave, gallant men. And yet they still look upon me to subdue those bastards."

She smiled. So long as he had the support of his officers, Antony could regain his footing, recover from the ordeal, and renew his efforts for mastery of the east.

"What will you do next?" she asked him, as they lay embracing, his musky sweat enveloping her, and her lavender fragrance no doubt elevating his spirit.

Antony was quiet for a while. "Recover, my love, and then beat Parthia decisively. With your help, and my wife Octavia's, I shall have enough—"

"Is Octavia coming here?" she asked, abruptly. Antony had married Caesar Octavian's sister for matters of policy and to maintain truce between the two most powerful men in the Roman Republic. Cleopatra knew that Antony barely spent time with Octavia, though she had heard much about the woman—pious, kind, generous, beautiful, younger than her, and much was said in Cleopatra's ears that might invoke jealousy.

Antony, perhaps realizing the precarious condition he found himself in, attempted to backtrack. "Oh, Cleopatra, have no fear of competition to my affections!" he said, laughing. "She is my lawful wife, and crucial to maintain my relationship with Octavian. She is aiming to send supplies to me to help wage the second expedition to Parthia."

The news was like a little candle lit in her belly, burning it from inside and filling the hollows of the body with unpleasant smoke. Was Antony lying? Was Octavia simply supplying Antony or was she personally coming here?

"Why does she need to come here, Antony? Do you not realize how her mind might change if she sees us together?"

But Antony cajoled and assured her that there was nothing to worry, and the obedient Octavia would do as she was told. He also told Cleopatra that he would arrange his schedules in a way that they would never cross paths. She relented somewhat, and then decided to return to the task of healing Antony.

After she comforted Antony and spent two days bringing his spirits back by her wit, the games of dice, a walk by the local fortress, tales of her children, and constant praise for his capabilities, Cleopatra decided to speak to Quintus Dellius, Antony's friend, and a well-known procurer of women for Antony's pleasures–a behavior that angered Cleopatra though she cared less for it. She had accepted the reality that her men may do what they wish, and she would do what she wanted.

She simply could not put aside the business with Octavia.

Quintus Dellius was the ever unctuous, suspicious character, squinting at her as she made polite conversation with him. Antony was away on camp inspection and she had invited Dellius to join her. The topics meandered from her life, to his campaign, to Quintus' hardships, to the subject of supplies to Antony and his plan to return to Parthia.

"If an army has such hardship inflicted upon it, Quintus, though I may know nothing of leading large military campaigns, it seems to be that an extended rest is warranted. Why is he insistent on returning already?"

Quintus relaxed and leaned back on his flat seat. His toga was dirty, and he made no excuses for it. He swirled the wine goblet. "General Antony believes the Parthian king of kings is in conflict with many of his noblemen, and that he can take advantage of the situation."

"Families that quarrel amongst themselves will fight outsiders together," she said, and before Quintus responded, Cleopatra smiled. "My family is perhaps an exception."

Quintus threw his head back and laughed. "You read minds, Your Majesty. Yes, you may be right about them putting behind their quarrels and fighting the General with a united front."

"And if reports are true, then treachery by Armenians is not something that will heal quickly. And you need more time to build siege trains because hardwood is difficult to get and transport so quickly."

Quintus smacked his lips and inhaled the ripe aroma of the red wine. "You know much about the tactics of battles, Your Majesty. And this wine you have brought has been made by the gods themselves."

Cleopatra took a sip herself and let the warmth bloom in her throat. "A ruler must often opine on the budget, scale, and scope of requests made of her, Quintus, and while I may not be at battle, I know much about what it takes to wage them. Oh, and the wine, well, the best wine for the best men!"

Quintus bowed. "How are her Majesty's children?"

"They are doing well. They wait for their father."

"What of the son by Caesar?"

"He does well too. The quality of his thought shows him to be the son of his father," she said, proudly.

"And his brilliant mother," Quintus said, raising his goblet. He did that irritating smack again, his lips tinged with red. He had by now downed several goblets.

"So, tell me, great Quintus, were my supplies adequate?" she asked, smoothing her hair and twirling the ends.

Quintus, relaxed now, and slightly inebriated, slurred slightly as he answered. "A large army needs more than whatever supply it receives, Your Majesty, but then you know that."

"Indeed. Well, I am glad that Antony has the support from those he holds dear, whether me, or those in Rome," she said, not looking at him and sipping slowly. "He should have all he needs for the campaign once his wife Octavia arrives with her supplies."

Quintus, feeling very comfortable, adjusted his toga and took another swig. He burped and picked a few dates from a bowl and chewed on them thoughtfully. "Caesar Octavian has permitted her to travel with support. We expect her to be in Athens in a few weeks. And then she makes her next leg of the trip by sea."

"I have never seen Octavia. I would have enjoyed meeting the sister of Caesar and the other wife of my husband. Why is she stopping in Athens instead of coming here with haste?"

I have no desire to see her. None at all.

Quintus raised his cup again. "You may have a chance to meet her, if Her Majesty is still here in a month's time. Our messengers leave in a day or two to Athens to convey Antony's message to proceed. Athens provides a chance to replenish the supply and rest."

"Well, I wish I could send a few words of welcome to her. If she will be here, it almost feels inappropriate that the Queen of Egypt does not acknowledge the wife of Lord Antony," she said.

"It might be too late," he slurred, his eyes rolling gently. "I think Antony prefers to keep his wives separate to avoid any mischief!"

Quintus laughed at his own astute observation and hiccupped several times. He swooned and then adjusted himself. She let him come back to his senses.

"Of course. The talk of war can be tiring. Tell me about your family, Quintus," she said.

Quintus Dellius, already puffed up with importance from her attention, and half-drunk, told her about his family back in Rome, his exploits, Antony's worries, more details of the messengers going to meet Octavia, and Antony's genuine affection for both Cleopatra and Octavia. She listened quietly and let him speak, while encouraging him with sweet words and smiles.

They sat late into the night, until guards had to carry him away. Cleopatra retired to her room, her mind full of thoughts and worries.

to Metjen

I seek to return to Alexandria in a month with Lord Antony, may the palace be prepared for his quarters, may the Lighthouse receive a coat of paint for it has lost its luster. The appeals of Kaistos and Emutawe on their trade disputes

I could not dispose before my departure, and I
authorize you to resolve them at your
discretion, but may the ruling favor both
parties for they are critical, so report to me
at my arrival. For the moon procession, I order
you to announce pardons for one-hundred
prisoners, so long as they have not committed
the sin of murder or rape, and may they all be
from the Southern Nomes.

These I command, and so shall it be,

Queen Cleopatra

CHAPTER 56
GREECE

The horses carrying the messengers from Antony galloped leisurely through the well-worn path that descended from Macedonia to Greece, on the way to Athens. With a missive from the Lord of the East, and carrying a flag that gave them free and unfettered passage throughout the Roman domains, they planned to deliver the message to Octavia, wife of Mark Antony, sister of Caesar Octavian.

They loved this route with its lush mountains to the right and the deep blue Aegean to the left. The cool wind on their faces and the steady rhythm of the horses' hoofs beneath them was magical. A thick leather bag hung from the leader's shoulder, bouncing as they made steady progress.

As they turned a bend, the leader, who called himself Quintillus, thought he caught something from the corner of his eye. *Riders?*

He signaled his companion to slow down and they both looked back. And for sure it was, there were three riders coming fast, waving a white flag. They too held Roman messenger standards. He was a little confused–bandits masquerading as messengers? That would be a dangerous and bold move, for such men, if apprehended, could be crucified, a risk most were unwilling to take.

He patted the luxurious mane of his horse, signaling it to stop. His companion stopped as well, waiting for the riders to come closer. They both pulled their swords out, just in case.

The riders came near and halted at a speaking distance. The two men, looking more like Greek stock than native Roman, saluted them. Their leader, a tall, hefty, clean-shaven man with a crested helmet addressed Quintillus.

"Am I speaking to Quintillus?" he said.

Quintillus, puzzled, raised his hand. "You are."

The man raised his hand in peace. "We bring a new message from General Antony, to be conveyed to Her Excellency Octavia."

Quintillus was surprised. What had changed since they left? "What message? Why do you think we are meeting Her Excellency?" he said, still unsure of who these new actors were.

The man shook his head and scoffed. He threw his hands up. "I understand you seek to verify our credentials, Quintillus, but you know fully well where you are headed with a message from the General. How would we know that?"

Quintillus would not relent. "How do I know you are who you say you are? Perhaps you learned of General Antony's message plan from somewhere and wish to subvert that."

The man laughed. "I will convey to the General that he chose well. You are right to suspect us, Quintillus, so let me prove our credentials."

He dismounted from the horse and extended his hand to show a wax-sealed document. And on Quintillus' instructions he gently placed it on the ground and stepped back. With sufficient distance between them, Quintillus dismounted to pick the rolled parchment. He inspected the red wax-seal. It seemed to be intact, and he was surprised to see the signet imprint of Antony's ring, for Quintillus was familiar with it.

He broke the seal as he kept a watch on these visitors, but they made no move. Quintillus read the short message. "Accept the new order," that was all it said.

That is it? He flipped the parchment to see if he was missing something.

He squinted and examined the parchment–it looked genuine. He called his companion to take a look, and he too nodded that it looked genuine, though so short and puzzling.

"This looks odd–" Quintillus began.

The visitor clapped his hand loudly, startling him. "I do not dictate messages to General Antony, and I have no idea what is in it. You are wasting both our times."

Finally, Quintillus relented. "Fine. Give me the new order."

The man grinned. "Well, now I have to confirm that you are who you are!"

Quintillus nodded. *These protocols!*

The men verified a few details from him–that he was going to Octavia (check the location), that they had one item from Antony's personal collection that Octavia would recognize (a scarf), their names, and where their family was from. They made some more small talk, learning about each other. Quintillus told them how he had been a messenger for the Republic for two decades now, serving many masters, with Antony being the latest. He had not yet met Octavia or her brother, Caesar Octavian, but he hoped to, through this expedition.

"Are you not returning after conveying the message?" the man asked, surprised.

"No. I plan to rest for a few months, and then perhaps go see Caesar for a new assignment," Quintillus said, looking forward to the orchards and wine.

But somehow, he felt uneasy about all this, for the men's attire was not exactly like those of Antony's Roman legions. The gold pins and the way they wore their sands were more like the men he had seen around Queen Cleopatra. Who were they?

"Are you sending a message from Queen Cleopatra?" he asked.

His counterpart's eyes flashed, but after the briefest pause he shook his head and answered. "We sometimes guard Her Majesty," he said, evasively. But Quintillus could see that man getting agitated.

What was going on?

He finally dismissed his thoughts and shook his doubts. Both parties satisfied, they all dismounted and gathered together. It made Quintillus nervous that he was outnumbered two-to-three, but so far this transaction was like a hundred others he had done as part of his service.

The visitor reached out to his bag to pull out another larger parchment. "The orders are for you to take this additional message, and deliver both. We do not seek to replace yours."

Quintillus relaxed somewhat. If there was no intention to replace his order, then that was a sign that all was well. He held out his hand, at which point the man, with lightning speed, pulled out a gladius and tried to grab Quintillus' arm.

Shocked, Quintillus retracted and attempted to turn and run, at which the man grabbed his cloak and pulled it hard, breaking Quintillus' flight and causing him to fall. Quintillus' companion, having seen this, tried to mount the horse but from the corner of his eye, Quintillus saw that the two other men were already upon him.

These men were trained soldiers!

Still on his back, Quintillus tried to pull his gladius out. But the enemy swung his weapon and severed Quintillus' arm with tremendous force. Quintillus screamed with shock as blood spurted from the stump like a little fountain. His severed arm teased him from near his ear.

Quintillus could barely understand what was happening as he drowned in a red haze of pain. Another sharp blow to his neck ended his confusion.

CHAPTER 57

SIDON

CLEOPATRA

The ancient fort at Sidon made for spectacular viewing of the Mediterranean from its tall rampart. Cleopatra and Antony walked the broad rock and mortar pathway, dressed comfortably in loose gowns. The cool southeasterly wind caused welcome goosebumps, and Antony held her by the shoulders to warm her.

"Have you bathed in the last two days?" she asked, "or are you trying to become Kadmos?"

Antony grinned. "What is bathing?"

Cleopatra pinched him. "Disgusting men. Speaking of which, I see most of your men dressed sharply in clothes made of my linen."

"They are very thankful for your gifts, Your Majesty," Antony said, bowing comically.

She leaned on the parapet to look at the waves lapping on the boulders below. "My ships are the best on this sea. The best."

"Everything about you is the best," Antony laughed. His mirth had returned, and the last month had done much to improve his mood. His men were rejuvenated, and continuous news that the Parthians were squabbling had renewed hopes that they could be beaten in the next invasion. But his determination, with Cleopatra's concurrence, was to wait until things got worse in Parthia before he returned again.

Antony had grown wiser. And their relation had grown stronger, more informal, and more infused with a sense of playfulness and mutual affection.

"Of course it is," she said, grinning. "Have you decided to come with me to Alexandria, *husband*?"

Antony did not respond. This was a topic of contention, and they perhaps touched upon it twice a day. "Oh, dear wife, you know that I must at least meet Octavia when she is here and arrange for usage of her supplies. Why must you be so impatient?"

"Because it takes time to go to Alexandria, rest, and return to restart your invasion. How long must I wait here?" she said, turning away from him. "And why must I meet Octavia?"

"I will not ask you to meet her, Cleopatra. You can leave before she arrives, and I will follow you soon."

What a stubborn oaf.

Cleopatra had heard much about Octavia, Antony's fourth wife and Caesar Octavian's sister. She worried that if Octavia arrived with rich supplies and more favorable news from her influential brother, then Antony might abandon her and return to Octavia to nurture his ambitions.

Did Antony truly love Octavia, or was he in the relation for the benefits she brought?

"So you wish to stay and make me go. Perhaps your affection to me–"

"No," Antony said, forcefully, grabbing her shoulders and roughly turning her to face him. "It is you I desire, Queen Cleopatra. I have affection for Octavia for she has been loyal and kind, but I am her husband in deference to the desires of the Senate, and not mine. You have nothing to worry about."

"You keep saying that. And yet I am your fifth wife!"

He laughed. "You are jealous. You are truly jealous," he teased, hopping like a monkey. "Queen Cleopatra, goddess of Egypt, Pharaoh of the Upper and Lower Kingdoms, Empress of the East, is jealous!"

She slapped him on the shoulder. "Your guards will see you, idiot! I am comfortable in my standing, Lord Antony!"

"She. Is. Jealous. She is jealous," he kept on, now grabbing her by the waist and leaning to kiss. How scandalized would Rome be if they saw his behavior! As if they have not been spreading enough lies about her already. Schemer. Sorceress. Demon. Harlot. Whore. Brother-Fucker. Murderer. Husband-Stealer. Ensnarer. Eastern barbarian.

She finally laughed. "On the wings of Horus, maybe a little. For the whole world wants Lord Antony. How can Cleopatra live if Antony leaves her?"

"The whole world is not Cleopatra," he said, earnestly, looking into her eyes. The loud squawk of a gang of unruly seagulls interrupted their romantic interlude.

Cleopatra decided to end the discussion about this topic before it turned into an argument. Instead, they talked about how the children were doing and the new theater she had built in Alexandria for the masters of the craft to display a spellbinding rendition of Homer's tales.

But where was Euaristos?

CHAPTER 58
ATHENS

QUINTILLUS

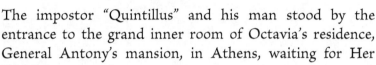

The impostor "Quintillus" and his man stood by the entrance to the grand inner room of Octavia's residence, General Antony's mansion, in Athens, waiting for Her Excellency to arrive.

The older sister of Caesar Octavian, Octavia was the fourth wife of General Antony. He had heard much about her–a religious, gentle, chaste woman known for her virtues and loyalty. She had stood by General Antony, and was here in Athens with supplies of clothes, arms, medicines, and money, to help Antony return to Parthia.

But then the impostor Quintillus' allegiance was not to General Antony but to his Queen, Her Majesty, goddess Isis, Pharaoh Cleopatra. He had helped her during her travel to meet Caesar, and she had in return repaid his help with generosity–pulling him from a life of mediocrity and poverty to that of luxury and comfort, with some expectations of course.

He heard a ruffle behind the curtains and stood straight. Octavia stepped out and looked at him. She was Patrician in her demeanor, dressed in an elegant white Chiton with curved blue borders. She wore long earrings and bunched her hair tied by ribbons. Octavia, he thought, had a lovely face, not bewitching, but not wanting for men's glances. She had a long nose and gray eyes that radiated gentle authority. The gentle waft of her pomegranate perfume filled the space. The impostor Quintillus surmised that Her

Excellency was of a similar age to Her Majesty Cleopatra, who, he knew, was about thirty-three years.

Octavia stepped forward, and he saluted her with his fist on his chest.

"Quintillus, Your Excellency, with messages from Consul and General Mark Antony, now near Sidon."

Octavia nodded. "I am pleased to receive you, Quintillus. I have waited for my husband's words."

Quintillus turned to his assistant and reached out his hand. He placed two wax-sealed parchments in Quintillus' hand.

"This is from General Mark Antony, Your Excellency," the impostor Quintillus said, handing her one. As confirmation he also pulled the silk scarf from his bag and handed it to her. She examined the scarf quietly, with a smile, and placed it on a stool nearby.

Octavia opened the parchment carefully, and while "Quintillus" could not read the message, he watched her face. Her expression changed from one of hope and joy, to that of sadness. She frowned twice and sighed as she finished the message.

She turned her face away from them and looked elsewhere. "My husband leaves it to me to proceed or stay, but to send the supplies," she said, disappointed.

Quintillus maintained a stoic demeanor, for it was not for him to comment on the decisions of his masters. It was for him to deliver.

"And there is one more, Your Excellency, from the, the," he stammered, intentionally, his eyes darting like a rat in a bright room.

She looked at him quizzically. "What is it? You have orders, and I will not begrudge you for carrying them out," she said, gently. Octavia's voice had a low tone; she sounded like an effeminate man when she spoke softly.

He took a long breath. "From that wretched Egyptian Queen, Your Excellency."

Octavia took a sharp breath. *Quintillus* wondered if Octavia had ever seen Her Majesty. And he also knew what was in that message.

Greetings to Her Excellency, Octavia, sister of Caesar Octavian. I commend you for your assistance in my husband's campaign, a duty that I have fulfilled as well, at this moment, by his side in Sidon, where he has expressed a desire to accompany me to Alexandria, where he shall rest until the time is right. Should he have departed Sidon with me, before your arrival, it is His Majesty Ptolemy Caesar's and my pleasure to invite you with honors to Alexandria.

And so we declare,

Cleopatra Philopator Philopatris, Wife of Mark Antony, Goddess Isis, Queen of Egypt, Coele-Syria, Cyrene, Cilicia, lower Judaea, and the Coasts of the East

Octavia's face lost its healthy pink complexion and turned pale. She stood immobile, her hands trembling. Her nostrils fluttered and she blinked rapidly, and her noble attempt to prevent a tear from escaping failed.

Quintillus felt sad for her, for he wished no harm upon a woman whose intentions were noble.

Octavia wiped the tear with the back of her hand and sniffled. "Was he still there when you left?"

The impostor Quintillus cleared his throat. "I am perhaps stepping out of my authority, Your Excellency, for I am only a messenger."

"You are also a person, Quintillus, and you can answer my questions," she said. Her voice had a calm softness to it, even if it cracked in sorrow.

"If I were to infer his preparations, Your Excellency," he said, wringing his hands and making a show of discomfort, "it appeared General Antony was preparing to leave for Alexandria."

Octavia was quiet. And then she asked again. "Do you think he has genuine affections for her?"

He clenched his fist and jaws and snorted. "If I may, overstepping my boundaries, Your Excellency."

"Go on."

"The officers are dismayed by the public display of affection unbecoming of a great general. It is everyone's opinion that the Egyptian harlot has poisoned his mind through her Eastern sorcery. To my death I am loyal to the General, Your Excellency, but we too are filled with anguish," he said, and nodded at the other man who hung his head and made noises of sadness.

"Would it be wise for me to go to Alexandria to meet Cleopatra? I have seen, but never interacted with her when she was here in Rome."

"You place me in uncomfortable quarters, Your Excellency. I would tell no high-born Roman woman to go to Alexandria. You have surely heard of the Ptolemies' appetite for intrigue and murder! Not to mention the indecent debauchery."

Octavia nodded, almost imperceptibly. She breathed in hard and looked to her side, while slowly squeezing the letter in her hand. And then, without a word, she signaled a maid who got her a parchment and seal wax. She sat on a table and penned a message. Surprisingly, she let the impostor Quintillus read it.

My dear husband, Lord M. Antony,

Perhaps the gods intend that I return to Rome, to your house, and care for the children, while you conquer the world. Your supplies are on the way.

Your loyal and obedient Octavia

"Convey these sentiments to him, should you lose the message somehow. When will you be returning?"

He had to make sure he did not misstep. "The plan was for me to return to Italy, Your Excellency, but it is my honor and duty to relay this to the General."

"And for that I am grateful," she said, with grace that he could only imagine. He knelt before her, causing her to flinch in surprise, and he chastised himself for the gesture, which was uncommon among Roman circles.

"Even you seem to be imbibing Egyptian ways," she said, drily, but said nothing more. She sealed the message, handed it to him, and removed a ring from her finger. "This you shall present to him as proof from my person."

"Yes, Your Excellency."

She stayed where she was, as if hesitating to say something but unsure. Finally, she said softly. "It seems I have lost my husband to the Queen, Quintillus, but perhaps the gods will return him to me."

The impostor Quintillus was genuinely moved by this woman. "The gods will always smile upon a kind and noble soul as yourself, Your Excellency, and may they bless you and your loved every day."

She nodded. "Tell the Queen that I have received her regards. May Dionysus keep you safe," Octavia said, finally, and turned and walked away.

CHAPTER 59
SIDON

CLEOPATRA

The man, in a Centurion's garb but with an Egyptian flair wearing a blue-dye necklace with the eye of Horus, saluted Antony. He then knelt before Cleopatra.

"Rise," she said. *Have you completed your mission, Euaristos?*

"Who are you?" Antony asked.

"My name is Euaristos, General. I traveled with the messenger Quintillus as protection."

Antony squinted. "I see. A message from Octavia?"

"Yes, General. Quintillus said he would retire after the mission, so I brought the message back."

Antony nodded. "When is she coming?"

Euaristos said, "here is her message, sir."

Antony took the sealed parchment and the ring. Convinced that this was from Octavia, he broke the seal and read the parchment. His expression changed from puzzlement to irritation. "Well, it appears she does not want to see me," he said, shrugging.

Cleopatra turned to him. "I thought you said she longed to be by your side?"

"Apparently not," Antony said, handing over the message. Cleopatra read it with secret glee. She would get details from Euaristos later.

"Do you think I should ask her to reconsider? I gave her the option to arrive or stay, but I never thought she would choose to return!" he said, his voice still with an edge to it.

"And how long will we be here then, husband?" she asked sharply. "You cannot sit here another month or more, now that we have lost all the time waiting for her response."

He nodded. And then his chin fell to his chest and he sighed deeply. "You are right," he said.

Meantime, she would ensure Antony did not listen to any other missives. She knew he hated the silent treatments and "hunger strikes," and she would employ them as needed.

Antony was hers, and hers alone.

CHAPTER 60
EGYPT
CLEOPATRA

Antony and Cleopatra walked with their children towards the massive pyramids near Memphis. Antony, for all his exploits as a conqueror elsewhere, was not quite the man who liked to venture in the desert to see things for leisure. It took much coaxing to get him out of his luxurious living in the palace to go and admire ancient structures of the land. On the contrary, Cleopatra was fascinated and had deep love for the many monuments and temples build by her forefathers and the Pharaohs long gone. She had dragged him to see the Pyramids.

Antony squinted at the magnificent structure, looming in the front, one of the three built by Pharaoh Khufu. "Well, I must admit it is breathtaking," he finally said.

"I told you, Antony. You, and the children, must learn about the land you will rule," she said. "And there is much joy in history."

"I have never met a woman who reads so much," he mumbled. She swatted his hand and walked energetically as the servants holding umbrellas followed.

"Do you know this is two-thousand years old, son?" she said, turning to Ptolemy Caesar, now twelve years old. Her son had grown to be an intelligent, introverted boy who loved spending hours in the library, sparring with his tutors, learning the ropes of administration. Metjen personally spent a few hours every week, taking the boy along as he supervised courts and projects. The Prime

Minister called Ptolemy Caesar the most thoughtful young prince. The five-year-old twins, Alexander and Cleopatra, on the other hand, were rambunctious little terrors.

"I have read much, mother," Ptolemy Caesar said. "And I also know that the smaller ones were built by his descendants."

"Indeed," she said, proud of him. "And long ago, the surface was smooth with brilliant white limestone, though most of it chipped now."

Antony had his hands on his hips. "This is larger than anything I have ever seen!"

She smiled. He was finally in awe of something. It was worth the effort of getting him off his couch to see some of this glorious land before he left again. Antony was getting ready to return to Parthia, this time to finish the unfinished business.

Alexander and Selene were running around throwing sand at each other, with harried maids chasing behind them.

"Stop it, both of you," Cleopatra yelled, and the children paid no heed between their cackles and screams.

Ptolemy Caesar walked beside his mother as Antony trailed, looking around.

"I had my architects and accountants estimate the cost of plastering the surface. It was too expensive to try," she said. "And did you know that the tip of the pyramid once had a gold cap?"

Her son nodded. They had reached the base of the largest Pyramid and Ptolemy Caesar ran his fingers on the edge of the massive stone blocks, now exposed since almost all of the coating in the bottom had been scraped. "Have you been inside the big pyramid, mother?"

"No," she said. "See how much of the base is buried in sand. I have to order excavations to find entries. Perhaps, someday."

They rode camels to visit the various complexes—the three pyramids, several smaller structures, the beautiful Sphinx, multiple temples dedicated to the Pharaohs, a field of falcons and smaller sphinxes, and dilapidated structures that were perhaps once builders' quarters. She thrilled the groups with more stories of the complexes past, of supposed hidden chambers and tunnels filled with gold (no one had found them), of curses and strange sightings.

Antony, for a chance, enjoyed the trip. While he was no patron of arts or history, he was willing to recognize the magnificence and complexity of what he saw. He said he had found new appreciation for Egypt, which wasn't so barbaric after all. *Says the Roman, she retorted.*

"What of Rome?" her son asked. He had begun to get increasingly interested in the affairs of the states.

"Your uncle, Octavian, is winning some important battles in the West. And they still do not like us," she said, ruffling his muddy brown hair. The boy was lanky, his face long, and she knew the Romans called him Caesarion, *Little Caesar.*

"Will Lord Antony ever rule alone in Rome?"

"Only the great Ra know that," she said, outside Antony's earshot. "But Antony needs to shake his appetite for luxury and go fight some wars."

"Did you say something about me?" Antony yelled from nearby.

"Not everything is about you, Antony!" she responded. She winked at her son and grinned.

They rested after the tiring day. The next morning they visited the ruins of the Memphis royal palace where the founder of her dynasty, Ptolemy Soter, once ruled. The vast complex had been crumbling, with many of its walls and stone blocks already chipped or broken for other constructions. Cleopatra regaled them with stories of Ptolemy, their founding mother Berenice, and their exploits. She took them to a location on the Nile where a commemoration stood, declaring Ptolemy's victory over Perdiccas, another of Alexander's generals who had invaded Egypt in response to Ptolemy hijacking Alexander's body. Perdiccas had attempted a disastrous crossing of the Nile, following which Ptolemy had maneuvered his assassination and put an end to external incursion into Egypt.

Alexander had ended the Persian rule in Egypt, and his death had ushered the Ptolemaic era. And Cleopatra was confident she would continue her dynasty for eternity.

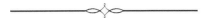

A month later Antony left for Parthia. This time he was sure he would subjugate the kingdom. And with him gone, Cleopatra returned to her governance, spending the next two years in relative quiet, watching the children grow and the kingdom's revenues increase.

Charmian had become the second most powerful woman in her kingdom, and the most powerful official next to Metjen. She and Kadmos welcomed a second child, a girl, and Cleopatra was pleased to see her dear attendant, now almost a friend, settle into a steady marriage. She enjoyed listening to Charmian's marital complaints and happy stories.

Metjen, the Prime Minister, had delegated many of his duties to Charmian, helping her rise. He had also privately requested Cleopatra to bless his retirement in a few years. *The limbs struggle in the morning and the mind is sometimes foggy, Your Majesty. Perhaps you are better served by Charmian.*

Cleopatra signed an edict to confer Metjen a great many benefits in advance of his retirement.

```
We have granted Metjen a personal exemption,
for life, from all taxes for an annual
exportation of five-hundred tons of wheat,
import of any liquid up to an annual twenty-
thousand gallons. To all his heirs combined we
exempt from all taxes annual exportation of
fifty-tons of wheat and five-thousand gallons
of wine. We have also granted Metjen five-
hundred talents of gold and permanent ownership
of the Prime Minister's quarters in the palace.
Let this be written and known to all those whom
it may concern.

Make it so!
```

She also allowed him to recede from rigorous work. He spent more time as her advisor, and even more time tending to his garden in his quarters near the palace.

In this time, Cleopatra sometimes reminisced on her younger days, including the joyful giggles with her feisty sister. They spent hours speaking of the quarrels, funny games, embarrassing incidents (*the time when Arsinoe was caught masturbating*), and when they annoyed the man trying to do a royal portrait. Why could Arsinoe not have settled quietly with her, Cleopatra wondered. On Charmian and Metjen's gentle prodding, Cleopatra allowed for a small shrine within the palace complex to commemorate Arsinoe. Following this action, she finally recognized Pothinus' and Achillas' service to Ptolemies, and ordered for stone carvings with their names. Their relatives were allowed to come out of the shadows, pay respects, and left to live freely without persecution.

Iras took over the full-time duties as her lady-in-waiting. Her garrulousness had subsided somewhat, though Cleopatra would not have anyone else in her place. When the days were boring, Iras brought life to it by talking about men (*the cavalry officer in Kadmos' legion is so attractive!*), the boys (*some of them keep staring at me, ugh*), the falcons (*still in love with them*), the dresses, the jewelry, and potential husbands now that she was nearly twenty (*find me a nobleman, Your Majesty! I am getting old!*). Cleopatra finally approved Iras' marriage to the son of an influential *Strategos*, administrator, of a revenue-rich subdivision near Memphis. But Iras would continue her role, and her husband moved to the palace to take up local duties. Cleopatra would often tell Iras how well she remembered when she first saw Iras as a toddler, licking the floor, banging a bronze vase on a pillar, and howling as she was taken away from a cat.

Charmian and Iras were almost family.

The news from Antony's Parthian incursion was better this time; even though he was nowhere near conquering Parthia, he had had considerable successes. At least he would return triumphant.

The seas were calm, the winds cool, and the harvests on time. And on this night, as she lay below blazing stars lighting up the Alexandrian sky, listening to Ramesses purr and claw at her, Cleopatra wondered what next.

ϱART III

Her Majesty Queen Cleopatra Philopater Philopatris, Pharaoh and Empress of Egypt and Lands surrounding, having graced the people for **thirty-five years** since her arrival from the heavens, has ruled her subjects for **eighteen years** after ascending the throne as Regent.

CHAPTER 61
ALEXANDRIA
CLEOPATRA

She dreaded this day.

The pain in her left lower molar had gotten worse in the last few weeks, and finally the pulsating agony of the tooth became too much to bear. She had a fever for a few days and lay in her bed, and while the fever had reduced yesterday, the pain still came and went.

Physicians had delivered her bad news. The prayers would have to be supplemented by surgical action. They would have to extract the tooth entirely or perform a cavity procedure in an attempt to heal the abscessed tooth.

After struggling with the options (*she hated having to lose a major tooth*), she had bravely agreed to the procedure. Problems with teeth were widespread in the population, and most simply suffered through it until the tooth rotted away, and in some cases, died from the poison of the rotting tooth seeping into the blood. Meaningful treatment was non-existent in the country, with only one exception–the palace.

Of all the wondrous medicines the ancients of this land had developed, the ones for the teeth were the least impactful.

The Alexandrian physicians were the best. They had access to a great many medicinal procedures, salves, ointments, fluids, and other concoctions, and books on healing from every corner of the world. The Royal Physician, who only went by the name of Eos, highly experienced having even treated her father decades ago, and her through all her illnesses and pains, prepared her for the treatment.

Her fever had reduced, and today was when they would proceed with the first of the many steps. Ramesses lingered nearby, having missed his Queen subject's attention for days. Charmian looked on with concern, and Metjen was nearby for any orders.

Eos explained what they would do. She had been through something similar six years ago, but then they had extracted a loose tooth. It was a miserable experience and she had cried like a little girl, and this time it seemed it would be worse.

Ear pain and tooth pain, the gods had imposed these on people to remind them of their mortality.

"Is Her Majesty ready to hear the procedure, before we begin?" Eos asked, his wrinkly cheeks and kind eyes looking at her with concern.

She nodded.

How I wish Antony was beside me. To place his palms on my temple. To tell me that the gods look upon me kindly and will heal me.

Almost as if he had heard her mind, Eos placed his gentle palm on her forehead. "You will recover, Your Majesty, Isis is in you."

She smiled weakly.

"Today, we will be pouring a sharp liquid in your abscess, once every few hours. This medicine comes from an Indian spice and an Ethiopian plant. Our library has guidance by Indian sages, Your Majesty. This liquid dulls the pain and reduces inflammation, and it wards the evil that has taken hold in the cavity."

I imagine a sharp-toothed little demon sitting in my tooth, gnawing at my gums.

Eos had also told her that traditional methods with dried mice liver extract, or earthworms boiled in oil and dripped into the ear, or using frogs tied to the jaw, all these remedies did little to actually heal the problem.

He continued. "We will continue that until tomorrow morning, by which you should be ready for the next stage."

May the gods of Egypt watch over me.

"We will insert medicinal pins into the cavity and clean the innards. You will be fed heady herbs to lull you to sleep, and to dull the pain. This cleaning will take an hour, Your Majesty, and is most important to remove the rot."

"How many times have you done this procedure, Eos? Do people do this in the countryside?"

He shook his head. "Very few have access to the skills and medicines Her Majesty's physicians have. I do this a few times a year to some of our senior administrators and priests, and that is all. It is safe, and in most cases, leads to healing."

"What happens if it does not work?" she asked, worried.

"Then we must wait to see if you develop new fevers, or we will dislodge the tooth."

Please, god Amun-Ra the all-powerful, not that.

"Let us begin."

"May the wings of Horus fly me to safety," she begged, under her breath.

As Eos poured the pungent liquid into the cavity, Cleopatra involuntarily extended her hand.

Charmian, recognizing the gesture, held her hand.

Cleopatra felt a strange sense of calm as the powerful liquid seeped and the pain swiftly turned from pulsing agony to a dull but pleasant sensation. Her tongue burned when it came in contact with the fluid.

They continued the procedure through the day, and she felt better. The next day, they did the procedure for which she was barely conscious. When it was all over, it took her a further five days to recover to normalcy. The fevers were gone, her tooth felt better, and the crude filling was doing its duties. Eos had said that over time the tooth would go brittle and break, and such was its nature. She accepted it reluctantly.

"I never want to go through that again," she said, having fully recovered, and lounging with her ladies.

"Sounded painful, Your Majesty."

"Did I look like a monkey with the swelling? Tell me the truth," she said.

"Like an almost-monkey, Your Majesty, the most royal monkey in the–"

"Idiot," she said, and pinched Charmian's shoulder. "It's miserable. With a baby it is over in hours. This thing lasts days," she said. "I do not want to even think about it anymore."

"Ramesses missed you," Charmian said.

Cleopatra picked him up and patted. He mewed but stayed with her. "Did you miss me?" she cooed. He looked at her with distaste and turned away. *All he wants is scratches and pets!*

"Where are my children?" She had not seen them in days, for it was considered improper to expose them to the evil that was within her. And now that it had been expunged, she wished to see them.

Iras ran to fetch her four children, who arrived obediently to be by her side. They all knelt before her, one by one, and then she hugged them.

"How are you all studying?" she asked, to no one in particular. The younger ones, Alexander, Cleopatra, and Ptolemy, all enthusiastically gave their reports. *Doing well, mother. Only a few kneel-downs. Guess what I learned?*

The thoughtful and gentle Ptolemy Caesar gave her a report of his administrative activities and military training. She beamed at the glowing commendation from Metjen. *His Highness Caesar shows all the skills and intelligence of his illustrious mother and his conquering father.* His only problem was with one of the tutors of Philosophy, the bristling old Areius, who, for whatever reason, had no great affection for her or her son. She tolerated his presence for his words were often wise, and his presence in Alexandria gave it a credence as a center of the universe on the subject.

She spent the day in their company. As family. Having lunch and dinner, going for a stroll in the cool beach and enjoying the sunset, and then settling down to play a game of Senet. The ancient game, played on a 20-square on an ivory box and ivory set-pieces, was an enjoyable way to pass time, regain the spirit, and indulge in playful competition. There was much shouting of *you are cheating* and *you are dumb* and *move the piece to the left, idiot!* and *did you not see that?* and *Selene, stop bothering your brother!* and *Ramesses don't step on the board!* and *Meow! Hiss!* She let the insults and hoots fly without formality. The utter misery of the last few weeks faded away.

Oh, only if Antony were here!

For all his follies, Antony was a continuous source of entertainment. If he was not busy annoying someone, he would perennially harass her with his silliness, she only mock protested his crude but hilarious remarks on Caesar Octavian (*the way he defeated Cassius was he got so afraid of the enemy force that he pissed a river, which caused a quicksand and the enemy got stuck in it.*), and his generally pleasing disposition towards his children. He was attentive when he was around, and the children loved being around their father who told them unending (and without question often fabricated) stories about his astonishing conquests. Ptolemy Caesar kept a respectful distance, but Antony was kind to him without treating him as a threat.

She missed her husband.

Metjen, The Prime Minister, she ordered to give a status of happenings around the kingdom. Everything was peaceful in the countryside. Farming output was normal. Shipbuilding and ship sales were robust. Tax collection was as good as it ever was. Apart from murmurs of frustration from Rome about export prices of grain, there was nothing that she had to immediately attend to.

And then there was one important happy news. Metjen informed her that Lord Mark Antony would be back in Alexandria in seven weeks.

CHAPTER 62
ALEXANDRIA
KADMOS

The vast colonnaded gymnasium, six-hundred feet long, was filled with Alexandrians on this celebratory day. In the front was an elevated hardwood stage on which was a smaller, silver platform. Long colorful flags hung from posts on either side of the stage. And on this day, the entire gymnasium was filled to the brim and the air buzzed with excitement.

Kadmos stood with four of his Royal Guard, behind two large and three small thrones on the platform, arrayed such that the two smaller thrones were on one side of a large one, and one on the other. Red-cloaked, crested-helmet centurions from Valentinus' force ringed either side of the platform, standing on the edge and looking down at the crowd. The two heavy gilded thrones had falcon-faces on the end of each armrest, with veins of lapis-lazuli and ruby studs on the borders of the headrest. Luxurious red-silk cushions lay on the seat. He watched as the assembly settled.

Trumpets, whistles, and occasional caning of the crowd helped everyone settle, until the guards blocked the entrance to the gymnasium. The quiet crowd waited in anticipation for the spectacle to begin. And not long after, a band of musicians and drummers entered the arena from behind the wooden platform. The loud rhythm of the drums was accompanied by a rousing performance of trumpets, cymbals, and bells. Servants ran around blowing fragrance into the air—rose, lavender, pomegranate, balsam, all to calm the smell of the unwashed.

And then it was time.

Two women wearing nothing but necklaces, bracelets, and gem-studded waistbands walked up from behind the platform, playing harps. And then, Egyptian priests appeared, blessed the crowd, and stood on either side of the thrones.

The audience barely breathed as they waited. Necks craned, people jumped up only to be shouted by those behind them. A few scuffles broke out and guards had to draw welts on some buttocks and backs. And finally, a loud chorus of trumpets brought the arena to a standstill.

Resplendent as the goddess Isis with her cow-horn and sun disk crown and the god Dionysus, Her Majesty Queen Cleopatra and Lord Mark Antony appeared on the platform. The Queen held Cleopatra Selene's hand. Antony held Alexander Helios' hand. A dignified Ptolemy Caesar walked beside Cleopatra Selene holding her other hand. The youngest, Ptolemy Philadelphos, was in Iras' hands. The crowd, packed along stone benches, all stood in respect, and those given to their customs fell to their knees. A huge chorus of cheers rose in the air, and as if on cue, a shower of bright pink fresh rose petals rained on the royals.

They stood and basked in adulation of the people as Kadmos quietly appraised the crowd for any mischief, but none seemed evident. On this day, named as the "Donations of Alexandria," Consul General Mark Antony had called for this forum to make important announcements. The Royals waited for the crowd to settle and go silent. Announcers were positioned in various corners to relay Antony's words in Greek and in Egyptian.

Cleopatra and the children took their thrones, while Antony remained standing.

Antony was bare-chested. On his head, he wore an ivy wreath. In his hand, he held a golden fennel stalk with blue silk ribbons tied to the top end. Around his waist, he wore a bright white linen skirt tied with silver threads. He wore kohl around his eyes and had dyed parts of his hair with streaks of red, matching his with that of Her Majesty.

Her Majesty wore a bright, pleated gold, vulture chiton that dropped down to her ankles. On her head rested the red-and-blue crown of Upper and Lower Egypt. She held in her hands the standard gold-and-blue crook-and-flail. It was a magnificent combination of Pharaonic visuals blending with the Greek imagery, captivating not just the audience, but even Kadmos, who had witnessed much by way of ceremonies. Her face exuded radiance, and her eyes sparkled and reflected the glowing torches, at this time of the evening. The children were obedient and quiet.

Kadmos stole a glance at his wife, Charmian, and she smiled at him, her face too filled with pride and awe.

Once the arena went silent, Mark Antony began. He first made many declarations of love and affection to his wife, Cleopatra, his children, including Ptolemy Caesar son of Gaius Julius Caesar, and for Egypt and Rome. After all the perfunctory messages and salutations, Antony finally arrived at what he had called this audience for.

"On this day blessed by the gods, I, Mark Antony, Consul of Rome, Lord of all East, wish to confer upon my wife and children what is rightfully theirs!" he said, drawing his arms in an arc at his family.

"And it is in my power, as attested by the gods and men that fight by my side, to bequeath upon them what belongs to them!"

A cheer rose in the audience, no doubt some planted, which caused the rest to rise and add to the chorus.

Antony continued. "As Lord of the East and a power vested by Rome, I first declare my dear wife, Her Majesty Cleopatra, Goddess, Father-Loving and Fatherland-Loving, being the Empress of Egypt and lands around, as Queen of Kings, and her consort and son by Gaius Julius Caesar, as King of Kings!"

Thunderous applause reverberated in the air. Kadmos noticed Valentinus' grave face–the Roman, even after a decade in Egypt, struggled with the idea that there could be *Queens of Kings* or *Kings of Kings*. Someone let go of a band of pigeons that fluttered and flew, to the *oohs* and *aahs* of the audience.

With a flourish, Antony lifted the fennel in his right hand, and extended his left to a waiting attendant to hand him a scroll wrapped in a bright red-dyed silk ribbon. He opened it and began to read.

"Furthermore, I donate the following to my children," he said, loudly, his deep and husky voice breaking as he strained. Antony turned to his first son by Cleopatra, Alexander Helios. The boy timidly stepped down from his little throne and walked to his father who held his hand. Alexander wore a bright tunic and a peacock-feather cap.

As the audience listened with rapt attention, Antony bequeathed the title of King of Kings to Alexander and authority over Armenia, Media, and the still not quite conquered Parthia. To his younger, two-year-old son Ptolemy Philadelphos, he gave Phoenicia, Cilicia, Syria, and portions of land west of the Euphrates river and plots in Samaria and Nabataea. To Cleopatra Selene he gave portions of Libya. The children, themselves dressed like little Cleopatra and Alexander the Great, enthralled the audience with their own virtuoso performance–kneeling before their parents, kissing their hands, raising little scepters, and greeting the people.

Kadmos marveled at how far Her Majesty had come since he met her in that smelly tent fourteen years ago in Syria. He had tried to flirt with her, he smiled inwardly, the future Queen of Kings and empress! He hoped she had forgotten all about that, which was unlikely, for she still sometimes teased Kadmos. *Do you still get stiff thinking about me, Kadmos?* she had once mortified him.

Charmian had told Kadmos that Her Majesty Cleopatra truly loved Antony and he, in turn, reciprocated that emotion. What had once seemed like an affair borne of expediency and ambition had evolved into that of mutual admiration, affection, and a common bond tied by their children. Antony was every bit the large-hearted, often profligate man, and his kindness to Ptolemy Caesar was evidence of his loyalty to Cleopatra. After all, Kadmos thought, no one would begrudge him for eliminating Ptolemy Caesar who might be a hindrance to his own children's ascension. That said, there was no question that with Gaius Julius Caesar Octavian becoming ever more powerful in Rome, Her Majesty desperately needed Antony by her side. And even if their desire for each other soured, they were still tied to each other for self-preservation; he for her influence and money, and she for his military prowess and control of Eastern satrapies.

Kadmos saw nothing that would break Antony and Cleopatra.

He returned to his senses as trumpets blared and the Royals descended from the podium, signaling the end of ceremony. No doubt that hasty messages would now be dispatched to Rome, where Caesar Octavian would throw a Republic-sized fit.

CHAPTER 63
ROME

OCTAVIAN

Caesar Octavian erupted in a fury at his soft-spoken sister. Not given to such emotions, he was now at his wits' end, struggling to balance the well-being of his loving sister and the stupid fuckery of the bastard cavorting with his whore mistress.

"He has no love for you anymore, my dear sister, have you not seen what he has done? How many times have I told you of the messages from Egypt and Greece?"

Octavia sniffled from the corner. She had been stubborn, refusing to divorce Antony, something that Octavian now wanted much for his own reasons. He adjusted the loose toga on his thin frame and walked to his sister. Kneeling by her side and holding her frail palms, Octavian implored her. "What dignity will you carry, my dear sister, when he cares for none of it? Do you even know what he has been doing? I have always refrained telling you the harshest truths for they cut you so deeply, but I must do so now!"

She shook her disheveled head. "You know Antony, brother. He is a man of loose passions, and perhaps Cleopatra has fooled him with eastern magic! I have heard of no egregious conduct except that he tends to his official affairs from Alexandria and is now in Athens for business."

How deluded and innocent is my sister?

Octavian resolved to be harsh, for the kindness had led him to no path towards resolution.

"Your husband, like a lovesick man, leaves his visiting Senators waiting as he follows his mistress's litter, like a slave," he said, his raspy voice accentuating the *slave*, a grave title to apply to a consul of Rome.

"How can you–"

"Quiet! Be quiet!" he shouted at her. Octavia shrunk in fear. "Listen to me, sister. It is time!"

Octavian placed his palms firmly on his thighs and leaned towards her. "My messengers tell me he loses foolish bets in the Alexandrian court and massages her feet," he said, making a spitting gesture.

Octavia watched with wide eyes. "Imagine! A Consul. A Roman commander. Massaging the foot of an Eastern maid who is on her throne because of *us!*"

He worked himself to a fine theatrical fury as he stood and paced around.

His sister listened without making a sound.

"What has it been? Just a year since he declared his sons Kings of Kings, and Cleopatra the Queen of Kings?" he said, accentuating the Queen's name as if it was a cockroach in his mouth.

He continued. "On whose authority? Did he listen to the Senate to come to Rome and make his case? He sees himself as a king now. He says he assigned no territory to himself, but only a stupid goat would not realize the ploy. All this is Cleopatra's doing!" he said, jabbing his finger at his sister. "That Egyptian trollop has ruined him, and through him she will destroy Rome!"

Octavia's eyes teared up and she examined her painted nails.

He continued to harangue her. "What respect has he shown to his loving, faithful, beautiful wife? None! Do you know what he has called me in his various letters?"

Octavia looked up surprised. She nodded her head.

"He said I was from a family with diluted blood. He said my grandfather was African. Not just that, did you know," he said, pausing for effect, gasping and taking great breaths, as if utterly disgusted and horrified at the allegations, "did you know, did you know, that he said I let my uncle bugger me, and that I blackmailed him into putting my name as his adoptee?"

Octavia's palm shot up to her mouth. She began to cry. His thin body shook pitifully.

He waited for her to calm down. "He has disrespected Rome. He has disrespected you. He is now just a drunk merrymaking eastern despot, with their barbaric ways and their love for monarchies. And his murdering bitch mistress is leading him by his cock," he said, making an obscene gesture cupping his hand before his crotch and thrusting his hips.

He was not done. "And you just watch. She will soon have him declare war on me, and if he wins, Rome will become a vassal state of Egypt and we will all be prostrating before her. Disgusting! Imagine that!"

Octavian took a few deep breaths and sat next to her. His sister placed her palm on his head affectionately. "Maybe he is changing, brother. Why is he in Athens?"

"He is there to shore up his defenses so he can fight me. Do you not see it? And he is there with Cleopatra, sister! I heard she is getting your statues torn down and installing her own. She is bribing the snow-beards of the city to worship her. She wishes to erase Athens' fondness for you.

Do you not see the inevitability of this? Declare your divorce before he does it to you!"

"I do not want to be the reason for the two most powerful men in Rome to fight, brother!" Octavia cried out.

"It is not because of you, oh my innocent and yet profoundly stupid sister!" Octavian threw his hands up and stomped his feet in frustration. "It is because of that fucking temptress!"

But Octavia would not relent. In her custom-driven religious mind, she would be by her husband's side, looking after his interests, until he left her. He had exaggerated Cleopatra's influence on Antony and even made up a few salacious stories, hoping to keep the blame on Octavia's husband to a minimum by painting all his behavior as *Cleopatra's* fault, but it had not worked. And so far, even after years, Antony had never said he would be divorcing Octavia. They argued some more, but it led to no resolution.

He would come home, she kept saying, and it was only a matter of time.

to the (dis)honorable M. Antonius,

The tears of my sister move me to grief, for you have shown no decency because of your shameless cavorting with a mistress who sleeps with you only to swallow all of Rome, and your drunk mind is too addled to see all of this. Rome is ashamed of your conduct, you kohl-wearing fool succumbing to backward Egyptian mores, and should you not reform your conduct, the people of Rome, and I after having tolerated your nonsense so long, will be pressed to seek your removal from all authority. We are aware of your failures in Parthia.

Imperator G. J. Caes. Octavianus

---

to the coward Octavianus

Do you think your weak propaganda moves anyone that matters, you fool, for all this invective is your own doing, creating distrust between my wife and me, as your sister is ashamed of a weakling for brother, who sat crying and wetting his thighs in Philippi too afraid to fight, and you call yourself an imperator! Yes, I enjoy sleeping with a queen, because no queen worth her dignity would come anywhere near a sniveling thin cock weakling like you. Rome loved Caesar and not his blackmailing uncle-fucking nephew, and they love me, so you care for your west and leave the rest to me. Speak no more of this matter or of Cleopatra who has stood by Rome's side, or consequences will be severe.

Lord of the East, Imperator, Consul M. Antonius

---

to Honorable Imperator Ju. Caes. Octavianus,

Greetings and may this find you well. I shall speak nothing of the matters between you and Lord Marcus Antonius, for I wish sense prevails. I hope you are satisfied by the timely grain and date deliveries at a discount, and that Rome and Egypt shall continue this collaboration.

Queen Cleopatra Philopator Philopatris

---

to Her Majesty Queen Cleopatra

The Senate thanks you for your timely deliveries that are to our satisfaction, though if Her Majesty may consider lowering the import duties for Rome's exports to Egypt. A fifth of all import is too high in these trying times, some of which, unfortunately, are the doing of a man who is fixated with you, for Rome desires a strong relationship with Egypt, which may be possible only under the promise of Egypt's neutrality and distancing from any ambition over Rome's territories or Rome itself.

The people of Rome send their kindness to your children,

Consul. Imp. Gaius. Jul. Caes. Octavianus

---

to Honorable Imperator Ju. Caes. Octavianus,

In accordance to your wishes I have decreed that import duties be reduced to a sixth, reducing the burden. To the question of Lord M. Antony, surely the Consul Imperator sees that he does not answer to me, and I have always sought to maintain cooperation with Rome, may that be noted.

As you know, Lord M. Antony is now in Athens, managing the affairs of the East, and I will be traveling to be with him soon, and will endeavor to smoothen relations.

The people of Egypt, and His Majesty Ptolemy Caesar, send their greetings,

Queen Cleopatra Philopator Philopatris

CHAPTER 64
ATHENS

CLEOPATRA

The dinner was meant to be a somber affair. Cleopatra, Antony, Quintus Dellius, Charmian, and Antony's friend Geminius who had arrived from Rome bringing news of Octavian' machinations and the actions of Antony's wife Octavia. Cleopatra did not trust the man, for who knew how his heart had turned when in Rome? But Antony commanded a loyal following due to his generosity to the men that followed him. Caesar Octavian was not such a man—Cleopatra knew him to be a devious, conniving, gossiper. Octavian was becoming increasingly powerful, yet Antony was still not taking him seriously. She was willing him to give him the benefit of the doubt, but she was more worried by how Antony would react.

They sat around a comfortably large table, with a sumptuous fare laid before them. Fowl, fruit, wine, goat, various kinds of hard and soft bread fresh from the ovens, toppings of date, figs, and even exotic and expensive spices from India that sometimes burned her mouth and caused her stomach to rebel. Ramesses sat near the chairs and had to be restrained from jumping on the table for some juicy bites. He hissed at everyone until Iras took him away. In the last two days, when Geminius was at the dinner table, both Cleopatra and Antony had made certain jokes at his expense (*Geminius is such a friend that he cups Antony's coins in one hand and Octavian's balls in the other, unsure which one is more valuable*), all in good spirit, but Geminius had not taken it kindly, complaining to Antony's general Canidius that he was being slighted. Cleopatra had no desire to frustrate the man, for she knew that an influential friend of Antony could return to Rome with impressions that might provide leverage to Octavian.

"You seem preoccupied, Geminius. I hope you did not take our ribbing too seriously," Cleopatra said, in a reconciliatory tone.

Geminius bowed politely. "A few pinches on the heart can be overcome, Your Majesty," he said.

"Geminius, who said you have a heart–" Antony began, when Cleopatra put an end to it.

"Pay no attention to your friend, Geminius. He seems to not know when to stop belittling his friends and start listening to them instead. You have news from Rome?"

Geminius, somewhat mollified, decided to address Cleopatra directly, nodded and began. "Antony is sorely wanted in Rome, Your Majesty. Caesar plots against him every day. He is levying taxes to raise more troops. He speaks ill of Antony and," he paused, and then proceeded, "you."

"What do they say of her?" Antony stepped in sharply.

She placed a palm on Antony's forearm.

"I know of all the things they say about me, Geminius. Every expletive and every insinuation that Lord Antony is but a clay putty in my hands. I have heard it all, for what better gossip for lesser men than to pontificate on the lack of virtues of an Egyptian barbarian and her husband? But what is it about Antony?"

Geminius, somewhat encouraged, nodded. "Then I shall not speak of the vileness of the gossip, Your Majesty. But Antony, I beg you to listen to what I have to say."

Antony nodded. She worried that he would soon be inebriated and no longer in the state of mind to listen to reason. Wine was a vice, and there was some truth to the matter that Antony's lack of discipline, his wayward ways and drunken stupidity had returned.

"May I speak my mind, Your Majesty, for this also involves your role."

"No doubt," she said.

Geminius took a small piece of spiced goat and chewed on it. His eyes rolled up and he racked up a cough. He drank copious amounts of water and apologized. The red specks of pepper had gotten to him.

"It is not so much that Antony conducts his affairs in the east without consulting the Senate or engaging in a bipartite discussion with Caesar, but Rome worries about his increasing propensity to adapt eastern sensibilities."

Antony scoffed but said nothing. Geminius looked to Cleopatra for affirmation. Encouraged by her nod, he continued. "You are well aware that while the people of Rome have affection for you, Your Majesty, Caesar has been calling on the Senate to censure Antony for his negligence and the time he spends in Alexandria."

"It is none of their business," Antony growled.

"But it is, Antony," Geminius said. "While you focus on the east, Caesar accuses you of a great many things, including imperial ambitions. He is unhappy about his sister's—"

"It is none of his business how I am with my wife!" Antony yelled.

Cleopatra flashed a warning to Geminius who held his tongue about the matter, but he was not done. "Caesar and the Senate, and many people in Rome, whether rightly or wrongly, see Her Highness' influence as dangerous. And that she must leave for Egypt and you must come to Rome."

"And why is it that I am the focus of this danger, Geminius? Do they not see that I have maintained cooperation with Rome?" she asked. There was an angle that Octavian was pursuing that she guessed, but needed to hear from Geminius. "Speak plainly about his ambition."

Geminius took a deep breath. "The strategy is simple, Your Majesty. Antony has many followers in Rome. Octavian's only way to gain supremacy in Rome is to undermine Antony, and the only way to do that is by painting you as the greatest threat, and how Antony has lost his mind *due to you*. Octavian is diabolic, and he seeks conflict. This is his way of creating one."

Antony gripped the table and his jaws clenched tightly. He fumed where he sat, breathing heavily, swaying gently.

She began to worry. None of this was surprising to Cleopatra. She had borne the brunt of vilification in the last few years as Caesar Octavian and Antony quarreled. Her bigger worry was Antony losing leverage and his power, which would expose her and her children to Octavian's anger. She had to cool–

Antony exploded with rage. He leaped from his table, flinging a plate against the wall. He wobbled where he stood and pointed at Geminius. "Fuck you and Caesar, that uncle-fucking disgraceful bastard! I will do what I want. I am the Lord of the East, and Caesar should shut his mouth and not comment on my affairs."

Cleopatra jumped up, trying to control the situation. "Lord Antony, calm down!"

"No, you be quiet! This is time for me to talk. Geminius, tell Caesar I care none for his words or his sister!"

She tried to balance him as Dellius tried to get him back on his chair. Antony swatted his friend and pushed Cleopatra back. His bloodshot eyes were wide open, and he pointed a finger to the sky.

"I hereby declare my divorce from Octavia. Take that message!"

Antony stumbled and landed on his back with a thud.

The audience was stunned. Antony picked himself up and stood holding his chair.

Cleopatra tried to calm him, but Antony kept shouting until Geminius fled from the dinner table. Cleopatra called after Geminius to wait, but he would not listen. "You have caused my friend to lose his manhood!" Geminius said, as his parting shot.

Charmian was frozen in her seat, and Kadmos, who stepped in worrying for Cleopatra's safety, grabbed her shoulders and pulled her away from Antony. Canidius came running, and he, along with Dellius, restrained Antony before he issued any more rash orders.

A shaken Cleopatra waited for them to take Antony away. Her heart thundered and her face was hot.

While on the surface Antony's defense of her and his divorce from Octavia was a welcome one demonstrating his commitment to her, Cleopatra was overcome with a strange foreboding, for the divorce was not what she wanted.

to Honorable Imperator Ju. Caes. Octavianus,

May it be known that the marital relations between Lord M. Antony and H. E. Octavia are no matter of concern to myself, and neither have I wished for discord, for Egypt does not view a

man's many relations as Rome does. It is also
with some disgust I view the immature behavior
of a distinguished person as yourself and also
M. Antony, and may it prevail that you
reconcile for the good of many lands.

Greetings from the people of Egypt, and His
Majesty Ptolemy Caesar

Queen Cleopatra Philopater Philopatris

Caesar Octavianus did not respond.

CHAPTER 65

OCTAVIAN

ROME

Octavian walked with purpose towards the drab, blocky building with its single big bronze door and sloped top. The Curia Julia, built by his uncle Julius Caesar, right by Caesar's forum, was the meeting place for the conduct of the Senate. The construction was incomplete. The plaster was exposed, the windows not finished, and portions of the back wall were in progress. He could hear the excited buzz inside. Two hundred and eighty influential Senators had been threatened, coerced, or summoned to be present for this announcement.

Knowing what had happened after Caesar's death and Octavian and Antony's proscriptions, no Senator was brave enough to stay back.

The Senators sat quietly on the wooden chairs. Octavian made an energetic entrance, his purple toga fitting well on his frail frame and his face tight with concentration.

Agrippa, his faithful commander, and admiral of the Navy, walked by him, casting a threatening look at every seated man. Octavian walked to the front to stand on a small raised marble platform. An announcer brought the senate to order. Octavian, true to his character, had several heavily armed guards outside the entrance, preventing commoners from entering, as they were customarily allowed to do.

"Today we talk of Antony," he said, addressing them all. There were some groans and eye rolls, but he ignored it all.

He would teach dissenters a lesson once this sordid affair was over.

Agrippa took a few paces and stood with his arms akimbo and legs spread.

"Who here thought Antony a friend and a statesman after he sought to right the wrongs of those cowards who murdered my father," he said, pointing to the marble statue of deified Caesar.

Many Senators nodded and some raised their hands.

"And how distant those memories! How fleeting that greatness! And what has become of that man who rode with my father?"

There were many murmurs of agreement, and a few of Antony's men yelled from somewhere. "Don't bore us! What do you want to say?"

Octavian had decided to ignore the taunts and challenges, for he had important things to summarize today. He would bring to an end all these grievances and grouses.

"Well, let me tell you what has become of Mark Antony," he said. "There he is, drunk in Athens one day and cavorting like a dandy in Alexandria the other, slave to a land-grabbing murderess whose every move had made less of a man of him!"

"Hear, hear! Shame!"

"Shame on you, Octavian, leveling charges like a coward without Antony's presence!"

"You be quiet, dandy's toe-licker!"

Octavian waited for silence.

"Who among here was not outraged when he simply gave away the timber rich portions of Cilicia to Cleopatra, as if it belonged to his mother?"

"Outrageous!"

"His mother is dead, you fool!"

Octavian knew his audience. The bribes and his recent military victories had made him strong, so he was confident of taking on Antony. He just needed to stir enough outrage, especially when the charismatic Antony was not here to defend himself.

"And Herod? We, the Senate, conferred upon him Judaea. And yet, on Cleopatra's insistence he bullies Herod to part with the richest provinces!"

"Shame!"

"And Parthia! So many of our brave men killed because of his abject stupidity. Perhaps his ball-master should have gone to fight. She may have done a better job!" Octavian said, doing a little dance like a woman.

There was much laughter at that, including fake ones. And a few outraged tones.

"Have you no shame, Octavian! When have you fought on such hostile terrain?"

"Octavian is good for fighting sheep and shepherds!"

"And Antony probably can't even do that when he's busy shagging that harlot!"

Octavian raised his hand and waited for calm again. "How many here are not outraged by news of a Roman consul massaging an eastern despot's feet?"

"Disgusting!"

"Horrible!"

"Lies! Just lies! This is Octavian's propaganda!"

"You shut up and sit down!"

"No, you be quiet, look at Octavian, he looks like a rat!"

Octavian waited. This was usual business. "And have you heard this, noble men of the Senate, that when Antony's friend Geminius went to implore him, not only did Cleopatra insult the man, she made him lick food from the floor during dinner, threatened him with torture, and she instigated Antony to announce his divorce from my sister!"

"Disgraceful!"

"Shame!"

"These Easterners have no decency!"

Much commotion filled the air, and the few shouts of *lies!* went unnoticed. Octavian was feeling more confident. But he was not done yet.

"What is Rome? It is that power that bends no knee to barbarians! And do you know what Cleopatra has been whispering in that drunk besotted fool's ears?" Octavian said dramatically, narrowing his eyes, facing the sky, and arcing his back.

"We are all ears, Octavian!"

"How much worse can this get?"

"More lies!"

Octavian took a deep breath. "Well, may you weep in despair, for she is hatching a plot to make Rome a province of Egypt, with Alexandria as capital!"

Of course, Octavian had heard of no such plot, but it had a powerful allure to it.

Great roars of anger drenched the chamber. Whatever dissent drowned in the deluge.

Octavian swooped like a bird, extending his arms like wings and pretending to scoop everything in its path.

When the audience finally settled, one loud voice rang out. "He is just making things up, it is all lies! Why are you listening to this drivel?"

Octavian stopped and eyed the Senator who said it was made up. "And why, dear Marcellus, do you think it is all made up?"

The gray-haired Patrician stood and crossed his arms. "How long have we known Queen Cleopatra to be ruling, Octavian? Nineteen years now? Or is it twenty? I do not remember."

"Nineteen since her regency," someone said helpfully.

"Nineteen. In that period, she has been with Caesar, she has visited Rome, and she has been with Antony. And throughout, she has supported our campaigns, including yours, Octavian. She has supplied us with grain and men, and kept Valentinus' army stationed without asking him to leave. She has also never sent her armies to provinces close to her, like Samaria and Judaea. Does that make you think that she is about to wage war on Rome?"

There were murmurs of agreement. And a few whispered warnings to Marcellus, *shut up and sit down, you old fool!*

Octavian waited again, not speaking, letting his supporters shout at Marcellus some more, though the old man looked on defiantly and kept shaking his head at the theories. "Well, our old friend Marcellus is aging like fine wine, except that he grows more distasteful," he said, causing ripples of laughter. Marcellus grinned as well.

"Dumb despots wage war and cause conflict when they are not ready, Marcellus, but we all know Cleopatra to be exceedingly clever. Have you paid no attention or is your addled memory not remembering the donations of

Alexandria where Antony bequeathed everything in the east to her?"

"And those were by Antony. None disputed Roman territory, Octavian, and the divisions were by agreement," Marcellus countered.

"And with her controlling all east, and with her hands firmly around Antony's shriveled member, where do you think she will turn next? Nubia which she already controls? The empty deserts of the West? It will be Rome!"

"Hear, hear!"

"She has expanded slowly and steadily, and she will not stop!"

"Looks like Marcellus went stiff in his toga when Cleopatra flirted with him!"

"Look at Marcellus, who really believes he has a cock?"

"You give too much credit to the woman," Marcellus said, but his voice had lost its defiant energy.

"Do I?" said Octavian. "She has survived all the plots against her. She trapped Caesar. She trapped Antony. Her brothers are all dead because of her. She had her sister beheaded on the steps of a temple!"

"How horrifying!"

"Has the woman no respect for the gods?"

"She comes from a family of murderers and conspirators!"

Octavian continued. "Her empire is larger than any of her ancestor's. Her compliance to Roman demands is a ruse, and if we sit like fools, ignoring the slights and insults, it will be you, Marcellus, massaging her one foot, and you Quintus, massaging the other!"

"Marcellus would not mind at all!"

"His toga might rise two inches as a result!"

Octavian smiled inwardly at the outrage and howls of laughter from the stands. Marcellus said nothing else.

Feeling invigorated by the reception, Octavian plowed on. "The reality is Antony has spent more time in Alexandria and in her company, than he should be conducting his official work. The reality is that he dons eastern garbs and struts like a king, appalling to any true Roman. And it seems some of you are still unconvinced, for I have something else!"

The Senators were hushed to silence by a yelling Agrippa, who had the voice of a loud and cantankerous bull.

Octavian pulled out a parchment from the folds of his toga. "I have learned, and for this I have asked the gods' blessing as it had to be done, that Antony wishes to be buried in Alexandria and not in Rome!"

A great shout arose at this, for a man's will told his truest intentions, and this was a sign of Antony's desire to detach himself from Rome. Any objections that Octavian opening Antony's will before his death was against law and egregious, was shouted down. Octavian had snatched it from the temple of the Vestal Virgins, and he would make the best use of it. Octavian read some more of the will, where Antony had left much to Cleopatra and his children by her, causing even more outrage. Octavian wiped a few fake tears at how this will had grievously wounded his pious sister.

"It is clear to all, except maybe a few fools and men no longer of the sound mind, that Antony and Cleopatra pose a danger to Rome like no one since Hannibal, and the treasonous scum Cassius and Brutus. And this time we shall not be caught unawares!" Octavian shouted, aware his face was red, and he was breathing hard.

The stands broke into a pandemonium of accusations and counter-accusations. Marcellus and a few others were driven out. Octavian cast a baleful glance at them as they left.

"Marcellus flees like a coward, but I wanted him to hear more. I seek no conflict with Antony! Was my own sister not married to the man? Have I not wept silently when he declared his divorce from a most wonderful woman of Roman virtues? Have I declared war when he neglected his children by Fulvia and celebrated his by Cleopatra? How much can a man ignore?"

"Hear! Hear!"

With only his loyalists now in the chamber and none to challenge his falsehoods or exaggerations, Octavian made the final remarks. "It is wise that we separate the drunk fool from the clever woman who seeks to destroy us through him. We are past forgiving Antony for his transgressions. But if we must bring any sense into his head, it must be through his separation from the queen!"

Someone in the stand raised a hand, and Octavian gestured for him to speak. "Do you propose we summon her to answer our charges? After all, she is the ruler of a client-state!"

Octavian sighed and shook his head while looking at the floor. "Should we summon her to answer our charges, he says," he said, mocking the tone. "Should we invite a hungry hyena to ask if it wishes to eat the goat? Would we ask Hannibal if he wishes to—"

"Are you saying Rome is a goat?" someone quipped, causing laughter.

Octavian grinned, and then returned to the shouting. "When all evidence is in front of us, and all signs point to a dangerous trend, no man of the Republic will waste time seeking attendance. And I have decided," he said, standing ramrod straight, sternly eyeing the Senators.

And then, when he had all their undivided attention, he raised his hand and pointed in the direction of Egypt. "It is time we take action. In due time I will move to set things right, and you shall stand behind me as I ward off the evil that threatens us!"

---

to Antony,

Rome has heard enough of you, my god-loving sister has heard enough of you. You have no more dignity than a beggar eating from trash, and you are a laughingstock of every dignified family, and instead of being consul you should become a dancer in the queen's court. You are nothing but a slave to that woman. She thinks she is Isis and Selene, but she is nothing such, but you drunk fool with no shred of dignity, you treat her like your ruler. I will be moving to strip you of your titles and remove you as consul, because Rome needs men of principles, honesty, integrity, none of which you even know the meaning.

Imperator G. J. Caes. Octavianus

Octavian,

Your hands shake like a harp player when they see the enemy, so stop lecturing me, we all know the lies you spread about me, but in secret, everyone laughs at the effeminate thin hoarse-voiced rat who diddles old men because no one desires him. Everyone knows that it was

Agrippa that won the wars for you while you hid
between his legs and got fever at the thought
of facing the enemy legions. Go build your
army, boy, because you know nothing about war,
or learn to respect those who have braved
battles and maybe you will have a future.
Cleopatra is more man than you will ever be.

Consul, Imperator, Dionysus M. Antony, Lord of
the East, master of Egypt

CHAPTER 66
GREECE
CLEOPATRA

"Oh by the fires of the great Ra, how stupid and bull-headed can you be, Antony! Do you not see what you are doing?" she screamed, pushing him on his chest. She had never felt such rage in a long time, and this man brought out the worst in her sometimes, making her lose control.

"I know what I am doing! I don't need a lecture from a woman who has never led a war in her entire life!" Antony yelled. He was disheveled, and while not drunk, thankfully, he was belligerent. It had only been two weeks since Geminius ran out, so no one knew what had happened in Rome.

"This *woman* is who financed you for all our wars, this *woman* got you the clothes, food, and coin, when you demanded, and this *woman* brought you back to discipline after your struggles in Parthia!" she said, pointing to herself. Somehow, arguments always landed with her being a woman, what did that have to do with anything?

"It doesn't change the fact that it was I who held the sword and my men who died!"

"And I never asked you to invade Parthia! So do not hold me responsible for what I did not do. Your *friend* Octavian does plenty of that," she mocked.

"Not everything is about you!"

"And not you, either," she said, yelling herself, "and I have a kingdom with millions to feed, and much to lose as well."

They both took a pause from the shouting. This daily occurrence of stress and recriminations had to stop.

Antony began again. "What are you so worried about, Cleopatra? I have my legions. You have your domains. We can crush Octavian!"

"By the wings of Horus, you don't have the support of the Senate, Antony," she said, exasperated. "You are either in Alexandria or Athens, or you are running around in the East. You should be in Rome building a coalition!"

Antony made a show of spitting on the side. His chest was slick with sweat and he wiped himself. "And what difference would that make?" he said, calming down. He tried holding her, but she swatted his hands in irritation. But Antony did not give up. "Listen to me, my love. Listen."

She turned away, refusing. Antony gripped her shoulders with surprising strength and turned her to him. "Listen! Just listen!"

Unable to get out of his hold, she relented. She exhaled and looked at him.

Antony pulled her to the couch. "You think that my anger is all about Octavian's disrespect to you and me. Know that he is a slimy bastard, and it won't matter what you do. You can go to Egypt. You can declare your divorce from me. You can pretend to declare war on me. It won't matter," he said, calmly, controlling his breath. It sounded like he was growling.

She pinched the bridge of her nose. "Why? What does he want?"

"What do you think? There can be no two kings, and you know that better than anyone else. He does not see a future with him and I carving the Roman territories. He wants it all."

A strange calm descended on her, and her heart fluttered as it released the stress. Antony was right. Nothing she did would dissuade Octavian from finding ways to demonize her and Antony.

"Should you not even try rapprochement?" she asked.

He did not answer. Instead, Antony held her hand and they spoke about their children, harvest, and how annoying the bugs here were.

CHAPTER 67
CLEOPATRA
GREECE

Cleopatra simmered and paced in her villa. She and Antony had moved further west from Athens, and she had not been home in months. Antony was making everything worse with his temper and frustrations. There was a time when she could argue and fight with him, or go on silent strikes to force him to listen to her, but those were not working. Even her tears moved him little, for Antony was a man whose mind was mired in confusion and conspiracies.

Stuck by Antony's side, she had summoned Metjen, asking him to nominate one of her loyal deputies as the Prime Minister in his absence. Metjen had made a risky but hasty journey across the seas to arrive before her. Octavian had not responded to her message, sent without Antony's knowledge, a sure sign of imminent breakdown of all relations.

Apart from Charmian, Metjen was the only other person allowed to speak with unbridled freedom before her, a privilege he did not abuse, and a privilege not conferred upon even Kadmos or Valentinus.

She was pleased to see the diminutive Egyptian walk through the door. Metjen looked tired, but his eyes sparkled with energy. His bright white shendyt and bronzed body were a contrast to the ochre floor and gray walls of her room. Metjen wore two prominent golden bracelets on his biceps and several silver rings.

"Your Majesty, I am honored to be before you again!" he said, as he knelt before her.

She bade him to rise, and uncharacteristically held his shoulders with affection. "I am overjoyed that Horus has brought you before me this quickly, Metjen. I need your counsel now."

"Charmian here says that without her wise uncle she feels lost," Cleopatra said, as Charmian walked forward and embraced Metjen. His tutelage had been invaluable for Charmian to deliver on her increasingly complex tasks of governance.

"And the halls of the palace are empty without Her Majesty's luminous presence, and Charmian and Iras' incessant chatter," he said, his smiling wrinkles lighting up his lean face.

"Reports say that with Her Majesty not there to keep an eye over you, Metjen, that you have been sleeping with every maid and getting them pregnant," Kadmos boomed from nearby.

Metjen laughed. "You are very right, Kadmos, and when you return you shall see the palace overrun by little Metjen's!"

"With all your jewelry, Metjen, I am surprised Antony's desperate men did not rob you on the way," Cleopatra said, laughing.

They proceeded to the dining area and had lunch together. Kadmos hovered nearby. And after lunch, she dismissed them all for taking a nap when the air was cool, with an order to reconvene in the evening.

After she woke up, refreshed, the four of them, Cleopatra, Charmian, Metjen, and Kadmos, retired to a small, well-appointed room in the far corner of the villa.

Ramesses followed in the hopes of attacking some treats, or maybe passing time swatting Kadmos' feet.

She got straight to the issues at hand. "Antony does not listen. Not to me. Not to his men. He puts me in a precarious position, Metjen. His relationship with Octavian has deteriorated to such an extent that they are abusing each other like schoolboys, in their letters, on a weekly basis."

"Is the relationship salvable, Your Majesty? Can you leave him and travel to Rome to talk directly to Octavian?"

She thought for a while. "Will I be safe? Would that be a sensible thing to do?"

Charmian spoke. "Your Majesty, all the reports we receive from Rome show that he is behind painting you as a terrible danger, apart from all the disgusting rumors that denigrate your person. Why would he listen to you? I beg you not to go to Rome without Lord Antony's knowledge."

Cleopatra nodded. "To alienate the man I am with, and to go to my enemy, would be dangerous. I cannot go to Rome without Antony's backing and his support for my mediation."

Metjen sighed. "An option that would not work, Your Majesty, and you know that."

Cleopatra placed her chin on her palm. She scratched Ramesses' ears as he purred with his eyes half-closed. "It would not. It will only add credence to the theory that Antony is in a woman's control, and Octavian will further use that as proof that he does my bidding and that I am the greatest danger."

"Are you?" Metjen asked, suddenly, his eyes penetrating into hers.

Cleopatra took a sharp breath. *Did she one day desire to subjugate Rome and bring it beneath her feet? It was no secret to Antony that if he lorded over the Roman realm, she would be Empress beside him. But her alone?*

"No, Metjen. I have no desire to separate myself from Antony and take on the Romans all by myself. It would be foolish, and we are far from prepared for such an action. Octavian's theory is that I seek to dominate them *through* Antony."

"And your only option is to send a message to Octavian that you seek no hostility between the two men, and that you have nothing to do with it," Metjen said.

"A letter of rapprochement? By Horus, Antony would be livid," Cleopatra said. "Kadmos, stop kicking Ramesses!"

"He needs you, Your Majesty. Without your money and materials Lord Antony has no chance in success. It would be easier to calm him after a couple's fight than to risk a war he might lose due to his errant behavior," Charmian said, having seen Antony much closer in the recent months.

Cleopatra stood and paced the floor. "I could send a letter. But I have no illusions as to whether it will help. Every exchange between Antony and Octavian has been hostile, with the divorce no doubt causing irreparable damage."

"Why did he do that?" Metjen asked. "After all, Roman law does not recognize the marriage of a Roman citizen to a foreigner, so he had no incentive to divorce his wife."

Cleopatra clucked and gave him a knowing nod. "And I cared little for having that title ratified by the Senate. My people care that we are together. I had no issue with the fact that he is married to that woman, for he barely spends time with her, and she has no interest in governance. But Antony's judgment is clouded. He *assumes* things about what I desire, without asking me first!"

"His passion for you overrides his sense for the politics, Your Majesty," Charmian said. "And nothing you say will change it."

Metjen straightened his back, and slapped his knee gently with his palms. "Unless, Your Majesty, you decide to tell him that you will leave him. If you strongly disassociate yourself from the man and leave for Egypt, proclaiming that Antony's battle with Rome is his alone, then you may receive the benefit of neutrality."

Cleopatra did not react. That was a factor she considered. Was Antony worth her losing everything? Her people, her kingdom, her children? She rubbed her cheeks and pinched her temple. "By the will of Isis, I cannot walk away from him, Metjen. Do you not see? We are irrevocably intertwined. If Antony loses my support, he will certainly lose the war, and we will be dangerously exposed to whatever Octavian decides. Additionally, Antony may even ask Valentinus' legions to turn on us. I cannot have both Romans against me!"

They sat quietly until Charmian's fidgeting caused Cleopatra to ask her. "You have something in your mind, Charmian. Go on."

Charmian smoothed her hair over her shoulder and mustered the courage. "Is there a case for you to seek marriage with the Parthians, Your Majesty? Our army combined with their may prove a deterrent to any Roman adventure. We can then tell Rome that we wish to stay out of conflict and be cooperative trade partners. Your fame and beauty are spread far and wide, surely the Eastern Kings will be falling all over themselves."

Cleopatra had not quite considered that option. Perhaps the Parthians would welcome the alliance given their own frustrations dealing with Rome. But would she have the time to forge such an alliance? Could she count on Parthian cooperation especially considering Antony had already claimed Parthia without conquering it?

"We have no time, Charmian. It would be too risky. Besides, there is the factor that while it may seem sentimental, I do have affection for Antony."

Charmian nodded. Cleopatra realized that this conversation was needed for her to determine if she would be so bold as to leave Antony, and the answer was a resolute no. Neither strategy nor the love for the man created an acceptable choice.

She sat and leaned back, resting her weight on her palms flat on the couch. "By the wings of Horus, I cannot leave Antony," she said, with finality in her voice.

CHAPTER 68
ROME

OCTAVIAN

Wearing a general's attire—a crested helmet with purple plumes, scarlet cloak, a gold-etched bronze armor, rich leather pteruges and high boots—Octavian marched towards the brown patch of land on the southern edge of the temple of Bellona. Agrippa and a few of his lieutenants tagged along, even as nearly two-hundred Senators waited.

It was a warm afternoon, with the sun shining in a cloudless sky, perfect for this theater. Octavian held a spear in his hand. The Senators parted as he made his way through the crowd, followed by Agrippa and several guards. Once in the center, he raised his face to the sky to soak the heat. He shook the spear with gusto and grunted, as if preparing for a momentous occasion.

Octavian closed his eyes and absorbed the sensations of smell, air, and sound.

Finally, hearing nothing but the soft whisper of the wind and a few birds, and knowing that he had the waiting men's rapt attention, Octavian nodded solemnly to a man nearby.

Two men dragged a loudly squealing pig to the patch. And then, one man pulled out his gladius, and with two others holding the fighting beast, slit its throat with one swift motion. Another man collected the gushing blood in a small bronze bucket until it filled and spilled over to the ground.

Octavian stood with his legs on both sides of the bucket, and slowly dipped the tip of the spear in the blood, drenching it and letting it glisten like a velvet coat. He lifted the spear high above his head, like a victorious man swinging his sword, and announced loudly. "On this day, on this sacred site, before this temple, before the distinguished men, before the gods that bless Rome, before the men that toil for it, before the men that fight for it, with tears in my eyes for a lost friend, and rage in the heart for a conniving, dangerous enemy with no virtues of a woman, I, Gaius Julius Caesar Octavianus, hereby declare war on Cleopatra of Egypt!"

A great roar rose from the crowd, now suddenly excited at the prospect of subjugating a woman who had humiliated them, and bringing down a man who had brought shame on himself and Rome. Many of Antony's men had already fled the city, and others scrambled to decide which way to lean.

Octavian raised the spear, arched his back like a gladiator and pointed it to the sky towards the direction of Egypt. He then flung it with force. The weapon arced through the air, a mesmerizing sight to the viewers as it flew gracefully and stuck a wooden plank placed strategically at a distance, carved with the Egyptian hieroglyphics of Queen Cleopatra.

"We march against Antony and Cleopatra!" he shouted to the cheers of the men around him.

PART IV

Her Majesty Queen Cleopatra Philopater Philopatris, Goddess Isis, Pharaoh and Empress of Egypt and Lands surrounding, Queen of Kings, Mother of King of Kings, Wife of Lord Marcus Antonius Dionysus, Master of the East, having graced the people for **thirty-seven years** since her arrival from the heavens, has ruled her subjects for **twenty years** after ascending the throne as Regent.

CHAPTER 69
GREECE
CLEOPATRA

"I cannot leave Antony," she said, sighing loudly. Ramesses looked at her with concern. She picked the cat and scratched his head.

Metjen bowed to her. "Then we must prepare for how Rome might react."

Cleopatra made herself comfortable on the couch and a maid began fanning her. Iras brought a cup of wine which she sipped. "There are a few things we must do, Metjen."

"Yes, Your Majesty. But Charmian's question on the Parthia still opens an opportunity. Instead of sending a missive that appears to be from you, we can send a message from someone who postures as a well-wisher, going without your knowledge, and seeking interest in an alliance. Would you approve of such an endeavor?"

Cleopatra smiled. "That may be a compelling option. Of course. We can then avoid conflict with Antony and find the willingness of the Parthians. If they are so inclined, then we may decide our move based on our circumstance."

Metjen was pleased. "I shall arrange for that, Your Majesty."

"How secure are our gold and silver holdings? How much is in the hidden vaults and how much in known treasury chambers?" she asked. Ramesses began to get restless in the crook of her arm. She let him jump off, and he went to explore the villa.

Metjen frowned, trying to remember. "Very secure, Your Majesty, but obviously most of the precious metals and gems are under guard in palace treasury, and only a fraction in hidden vaults."

She thought for a while. She would clearly need coin and grain to supply Antony if need be, but to what extent, she was unsure. She had not heard from Rome so far, and no one knew if Octavian would draw Antony to a conflict. Would there be skirmishes? Or more? Would there be demands on her? Everything was murky.

"Very well. Move five-thousand talents out of the palace treasuries into the vaults. A fifth in the vault east of Taposiris, a fifth to the vault in Memphis, a fifth in Thebes, a fifth in the underground chamber of the Serapeum in Alexandria, and another fifth where I will soon ask you to."

Metjen was surprised at the value and the decision. "That is quite a significant sum, Your Majesty. But perhaps it is for your safety that we preserve these reserves."

"Also order defensive fortifications near the palace, and have the architects dig a tunnel beneath my quarters to emerge somewhere safe beyond the Canopic."

Charmian and Metjen looked at each other, but did not question the orders.

Feeling restless, Cleopatra rose from her couch and stretched her back. "Send word to the Indian king of the western coast of India to expect my son Ptolemy Caesar and treat him with the greatest respect. Do not send my son away, Metjen, let us just send a message."

"Your Majesty."

"Do you really think we will be in serious danger, Your Majesty?" Charmian asked, her eyes now fearful.

Cleopatra nodded. "Nothing in my rule has confronted a situation so precarious, Charmian. This is no longer a quarrel between two little nobles. They are the two most powerful men of Rome, they control vast legions and resources, and they taunt each other like children. And we, unfortunately, are in the middle of it all."

"When do you wish for me to leave, Your Majesty?" Metjen asked.

Cleopatra walked up to him. "Rest for two days, Prime Minister. But in that time, there is one more thing."

They all looked at her.

"Prepare a mausoleum for me. It–"

"Your Majesty!" Charmian interrupted.

"Be quiet, Charmian. Let me speak," she scolded her confidante. Charmian, already tearing up, sulked.

"Build one quickly, make sure it has enough space inside to hold my most precious treasures. Let it be near my section of the palace, by the temple of Isis. Let there be two levels, with the place for my rest on the top. Let it look out to the sea. I pray to the gods that a day for me to use it may never come for many more years, but I cannot be unprepared."

Metjen did not challenge or argue with her. His eyes had softened, and they radiated a kind understanding.

"But why now, Your Majesty?" Charmian asked.

Cleopatra sighed. "Because war is coming, my dear Charmian. It is only a matter of time."

Notes

Thank you for reading the second book of the series! I would be immensely grateful if you took a few minutes to either rate the book or leave a review if you enjoyed it. This makes a huge difference to an author like me. You can also go to https://jaypenner.com/reviews for easy links.

Wondering about the history behind the major events in the book? Or the juvenile exchange of insults between Octavian and Antony? Or Cleopatra's encounter with Herod?

I offer notes on these events and more at the end of Book III (final book) in order to present a coherent narrative on the entire story.

War is here. Grab the final book of the trilogy, *Empress, The Last Pharaoh Book III* next! Journey to the mosquito-infested, humid battleground of Actium in Greece where Mark Antony and Cleopatra face their greatest threat– Caesar Octavian.

Want to virtually visit the locations mentioned in this book through a cool Google Earth flyby? There's something really exciting about going to the locations and imagining what it might have been two thousand years ago. Go to https://jaypenner.com/the-last-pharaoh/maps and ONLY visit the Book I or II maps (because the callouts may have spoilers). I hope you find it informative and fun.

Thank you, and until the next book,

Jay (https://jaypenner.com)

REFERENCES

The following works provided helpful historical references and commentary on the life of Cleopatra.

1. Cleopatra, a Life, by Stacy Schiff–Little, Brown and Company

2. The Parallel Lives by Plutarch, Loeb Classical Library edition–Life of Caesar, Pompey, and Antony (writing eighty to a hundred years after the events of this book)

3. Civil Wars by Julius Caesar, Loeb Classical Library–Book III (contemporary)

4. Alexandrian Wars, possibly in the name of Julius Caesar, Loeb Classical Library–contemporary

5. Showtime–The Hunt for Cleopatra's tomb

6. Cassius Dio, Roman History, Loeb Classical Library (writing about two hundred years after the events in this book)

7. Cicero's Letters to Atticus, Project Gutenburg, Translated by E. O. Winstedt

Made in the USA
Las Vegas, NV
22 August 2022